Women in Scientific and Engineering Professions

D1322247

Women in Scientific and Engineering Professions

Edited by Violet B. Haas and Carolyn C. Perrucci

with the assistance of Jean E. Brenchley,
Martha O. Chiscon, Lois N. Magner,
Geraldine M. Vest

Ann Arbor
The University of Michigan Press

To our children:
Richard, Elizabeth, and David Haas
Alissa and Martin Perrucci

1987   1986   1985   1984   4   3   2   1

Library of Congress Cataloging in Publication Data
Main entry under title:

Women in scientific and engineering professions.

Papers originally presented as part of a national
Conference on Women in the Professions: Science, Social
Science, Engineering, which was held at Purdue University,
Mar. 20–21, 1981.
Includes bibliographies and index.
1. Women in science—Congresses.   2. Women in engi-
neering—Congresses.   3. Women scientists—Congresses.
4. Women engineers—Congresses.   I. Haas, Violet, B.,
1921–   II. Perrucci, Carolyn Cummings.
Q130.W66 1984   305.4   83-23575
ISBN 0-472-10049-1
ISBN 0-472-08042-3 (pbk.)

Camera-ready copy for this volume has been provided by the editors.

Preface

The chapters collected in this volume were part of a national Conference on Women in the Professions: Science, Social Science, Engineering which was held at Purdue University on March 20-21, 1981. Conference objectives were both academic and action-oriented: to examine career opportunities and status of women professionals in science, social science and engineering; to present women's views of scientific views of women; and to draw on historical and contemporary experiences of women for ideas of ways to increase the participation, visibility, influence, and general success of women in the scientific community. Toward this end, a number of women professionals who shared these goals, all nationally renowned for their own achievements in relevant fields, were invited to give public lectures and/or lead workshop sessions during the two-day event. Each lecturer and two workshop leaders were later invited to revise their remarks for publication. It was one of our enjoyable tasks as co-chairs of the Conference Organizing Committee to work with the authors on their revisions.

For the conference itself, and hence this publication, we gratefully acknowledge generous support from the following sponsors at Purdue University: Committee on Women's Studies; Dean Allan H. Clark, School of Science; Dean Norma H. Compton, School of Consumer and Family Sciences; Dean John C. Hancock, Schools of Engineering; Dean Bernard J. Liska, School of Agriculture; and Dean Robert L. Ringel, School of Humanities, Social Science and Education. Additionally, we express deep appreciation for financial support from Cummins Engine Foundation; Lever Brothers Company Foundation; Motorola, Incorporated; PPG Industries Foundation; Union Carbide Corporation and United Technologies.

As usual in an undertaking of this scope, the assistance of many individuals was extremely valuable and we take this opportunity to acknowledge our indebtedness to at least some of them. Working invaluably with us as members of the Conference Organizing Committee were Professors Jean E. Brenchley and Martha O. Chiscon,

Biological Sciences; Lois N. Magner, History, and Geraldine M. Vest, Metalurgical Engineering. From the beginning, Ms. Cary A. Bowdich served as our liaison with the Purdue University Division of Conferences; by the end of the process we all had learned immensely from experiences at each step of the way. Professor William K. LeBold gave generously of his time and expertise at several points and obtained and analyzed attendees' evaluations of the Conference, evaluations which were enthusiastically positive, on the whole. Professors Dena B. Targ and Robert Perrucci provided most insightful comments and suggestions for the Introduction. For transcriptions of tapes of lectures and the typing of various drafts of papers, we thank Lisa Courtenay, Carol Edmundson, Pat Loomis, Mary A. Perigo, Kay Stanford Solomon and Melda Warner. We are particularly indebted to Pat Loomis for her patience in putting all material onto the word processor. Finally, we are grateful for the support of the School of Electrical Engineering and the Department of Sociology and Anthropology throughout this endeavor.

Violet B. Haas
Carolyn C. Perrucci

Contents

III. Alternative Science-Based Careers

IV. Women's Views of Scientific Views of Women

Epilogue

Central Issues Facing Women in the Science-Based Professions

Carolyn C. Perrucci

The study of women in the professions has covered a wide variety of topics for a variety of occupational fields. Nevertheless, important questions remain about the extent of women's recent gains in science-based professions; structural versus individual bases of this achievement; and the "nature" of women's contributions to science and engineering. One or more of these central issues is addressed in the chapters which comprise the four main sections of this volume.

All chapters focus on women's participation in science-based professions in the primary sector of the American labor market; that is, in that part of the market in which the jobs are characterized by their relative stability, mobility chains, opportunities for advancement, high salaries, good working conditions, and equitable administration of work rules (Piore 1975). A scientific basis is conceived broadly so that chapters focus variously on social scientists (e.g., patent attorneys, university psychologists) and engineers (including engineering managers) as well as natural and physical scientists.

The authors generally follow a status attainment or human capital theoretical approach, investigating the extent to which women's entry, advancement and contributions in science-based professions depend on supply-side or individual characteristics, especially quantity (Ph.D.s) and quality of graduate education. Frequently noting the significant but only partial explanation which such an approach provides, many of the authors also consider demand-side or employer-related characteristics, including sex discrimination and governmental attempts to promote equal employment opportunity. A final author takes a Marxist-feminist approach to explain the sex segregation of both market and unpaid home work and most women's subordinate status therein, by the dynamic relationship between patriarchy and capitalism in the modern-day United States. It is to an overview of each section of the book that we now turn.

Women in Science-Based Professions: A Time of Transition

In section one, cross-cultural and historical data on women and work provide important background for the assessment of contemporary American women in science-based professions. Data on effects of biological differences between men and women, ideology or beliefs about the character and motivation of men and women, and sex differences in economic opportunities outside the home are particularly informative.

First, as the chapter in this volume by Nanci Gonzalez notes, anthropological research on the roles of men and women indicates that sex is universally a basis for the division of labor in society. At the very least, biological differences between males and females underlie their specialized roles in reproduction. Beyond reproduction, however, the extent to which sex has been and is currently a basis for role allocation (sex differentiation) varies widely from society to society. In addition to bearing children and to providing nurturance to their families, women also have participated substantially in the subsistence (economic) activities of the societies in which they have lived (Aronoff and Crano 1975; Crano and Aronoff 1978). In a capitalistic industrial economy, however, women and men generally compete for jobs in different segments of the labor market (Blau and Jusenius 1976), leaving women underrepresented in the most prestigious and highly remunerated of occupations (i.e., the primary sector), including the science-based professions (Nielsen 1978; Rossiter 1982: Zuckerman and Cole 1975). Moreover, since most employed women are homemakers too, successful participation in the professions has often been achieved at the expense of lower-class women who have tended the elites' homes and children (Harris 1978).

Significantly, technological developments leading to more effective birth control techniques, infant formula and greater longevity have reduced substantially any necessity for parenthood to be most women's main role for large portions of their lives (Huber 1976). By reducing the relevance of physical strength, moreover, technological developments have also increased opportunities for women's participation in both the civilian labor force and the military (Gagnon 1971). Most of women's jobs are in the secondary sector, however, and automation here leads to unemployment (Hacker 1978). In general, comparable social participation to that of men appears to be a step toward general sex equality; that is, the less the sex differentiation beyond that in reproduction, the less likely are men, in comparison to women, to monopolize the valued scarce resources which their society has to offer (Holter 1970).

Secondly, the extent to which people *believe* that there are characteristics unique to men or women and *believe* that women should not work outside the home in intellectual or decision-making occupations varies somewhat across time and place. An ideology of women's inferiority is a long-standing characteristic of American culture and remains something of a barrier to women's participation in professional work, as the chapter in this volume by McAfee suggests. Interestingly, whether women's alleged differences from men are viewed as inferior characteristics (as is usually the case) or as superior characteristics (as is the case in the Hubbard chapter in this volume), the net result historically appears to be inferior rewards for women (Harris 1978).

Finally, in both developed and developing countries, the demand for women's market labor appears to be the most important determinant of its level. This is to say, when the economy or women's sector thereof is expanding and/or men are engaged in other activities, such as warfare, women are encouraged to work outside the home, even in the more highly rewarded fields that are considered to be men's fields. The Hornig chapter in this volume notes this to be the case in the U.S. during the recent Vietnam era, for example. However, when women must compete with men for jobs, women are encouraged or forced to leave the labor force or return to the lower-paying fields sex-typed as women's fields. This loss of jobs may result from employer discrimination, as the McAfee chapter in this volume notes was the case in the U.S. following World War II. Loss of jobs may also result from self-selection by women who believe that men have a prior claim on jobs, as the Gonzalez chapter contends was the case in the U.S. during the Great Depression.

Unfortunately, just as American women's higher educational attainments are reaching the former high level of the 1920s, as indicated by percent of doctorates earned, the demand for highly educated workers in many fields is not keeping pace (Vetter chapter in this volume; Carter and Carter 1981). For Gonzalez, then, the present political and economic climate represents a challenge of which American women professionals must be aware and must meet with fortitude. This, she believes, such women can best do by working with men within mainstream organizations, rather than within women's organizations. Given women's apparent dependence on aggregate market demand, moreover, it would appear fruitful for feminists to focus more political energies on influencing economic planning which would create and maintain high levels of demand and on full employment legislation (Sexton 1977).

The extent to which there have been positive versus negative changes from the early 1960's to 1980 in the education and employment of American women in science-based professions specifically is discussed in the chapter by Lilli Hornig. Without doubt, one significant positive change that has occurred is in the nature of scholarship on women. In the early 1960's, the dominant viewpoint in the social and natural sciences was one which attributed male/female inequality in science mainly to characteristics of women themselves--alleged differences from men in ability and motivation which indicated women's inferiority and which presumably could not be overcome. As Hornig relates, such an orientation generally characterized the writings of males and females alike, as exemplified importantly by most of the presentations at the landmark Symposium on American Women in Science and Engineering held at M.I.T. in 1964 (Mattfeld and Van Aken 1965).

During the mid- to late-1960's, however, there began a resurgence of the Women's Movement in America, including the growth of feminist scholarship on women which took the form of Women's Studies programs on many campuses across the country (Howe 1977; Howe and Ahlum 1973).. In theoretical considerations of gender inequality, explanations began to focus increasingly on systemic, rather than individual, characteristics. That is, scholars began to devote more attention to determining the nature and extent of structural constraints--limits to professional educational training and employment opportunities--as explanations for male/female inequality in science and engineering. Sokoloff (1980), for example, insightfully compares dual labor market and status attainment theories in economics and sociology.

Moreover, as the definition of the problem shifted from individual to systemic imperfections, so did intervention strategies. As both the Hornig and Rosenfeld chapters in this volume note, during the 1970's, many colleges and universities, along with other large-scale organizations, became subject to a variety of federal laws and regulations which were designed, in part, to overcome sex discrimination in education and employment (United States Equal Employment Opportunity Commission 1974). There was increasing recognition that sex (and race) discrimination could be unintentional as well as intentional, and institutional as well as acts of lone individuals (Alvarez, Lutterman, and Associates 1979; Feagin and Eckberg 1980; Feagin and Feagin 1978). The anti-discrimination regulations and efforts to enforce them remain surrounded in controversy; moreover, there is a paucity of research evidence regarding their effectiveness (Bayer and Astin 1975; Koch and Chizmar 1976; Lester 1974; Silvestri and Kane 1975; Sowell 1976; WEAL 1981). Nevertheless, some gains for women can be documented, particularly in access to scientific and technical training (Vance 1981).

Data presented in the Hornig and Vetter chapters in this volume make it clear that beginning in the 1960's and continuing through the 1970's, women responded to increased opportunities by increasingly pursuing degrees at all levels of education, including doctorates in science and engineering. By 1975 women's share of science and engineering doctorates reached the previous "record" set in the 1920's, with highest concentrations now being in the biological, behavioral and social sciences.

Despite gains in education attainment, aggregate data on science doctorates for the 1970's shows a continuation of significant sex discrepancies in employment prospects (unemployment rates) and, among those who attain employment, considerable sex segregation in employment sector, work function, rank and salary. It also indicates that some change is occurring, however, such that the educational and employment patterns of men and women are converging in terms of numbers of people, curricular choices, career choices, timing of schooling and work activities, and ultimate achievements therein.

Betty Vetter concludes that women doctorates' employment opportunities can be improved even more rapidly by providing women information about Bureau of Labor forecasts and encouraging them to move in these directions. She reports that for the next few years, projections are for greater opportunities generally in industry (than in academia or government). Moreover, projections through 1985 are that the supply and demand for engineers and physical and environmental scientists will be closer in balance than for life scientists, behavioral and social scientists. Because of oversupply in these latter areas, more and more doctorates are expected to be employed in jobs that do not or have not in the past required Ph.D. degrees.

Additional strategies for increasing the numbers and percentages of women in science-based professions are outlined in the chapter by Jewel Plummer Cobb. Some of these strategies have the long-range aim of changing the sex role socialization process by eliminating sexism on the part of parents and school teachers at all levels of formal education (Safilios-Rothschild 1979). The focus here and also the chapter in this volume by Campbell and Geller is on increasing girls' interest and performance in both mathematics and science. Other strategies include the provision of special fellowships, awards, courses, and appointments for women who are now at many different stages of scientific career development; they range from special math courses for junior high school girls to re-entry programs for middle-aged women (Women's Re-entry Project 1980). As Cobb notes, the effectiveness of many such strategies can be documented (Humphreys 1982). The challenge at this time is to obtain and maintain resources for their implementation (American Association of University Professors 1981).

Women Scientists and Engineers in Academe

Although doctorate women scientists and engineers are somewhat less likely than before to work in academic settings, academe continues to be their single largest employer. Rachel Rosenfeld's chapter in this volume reviews the sociology of science literature, including her own research on academic psychologists, to compare women with men doctorates at three stages of the academic career in order to shed light on the question of why women are less likely than men to attain the goal of being a widely recognized, tenured professor at a high prestige research university. This analysis aims to increase women's awareness of the consequences of the work-related decisions that they make as well as possible points of intervention in women's roles and in the organization of higher education. It is also important because sex differences in academic rank are important determinants of sex differences in salary (i.e., lower salaries for women), as noted in the Vetter chapter in this volume.

Rosenfeld concludes that at the first stage to be considered, graduate school, comparable proportions of women and men go to the various types (prestige level) of schools. The relatively sparse empirical evidence leaves it less clear whether the *quality* of selected graduate school experiences is also comparable for women (e.g., strength of faculty sponsorship, existence of few social ties with fellow graduate students which could result in a smaller and weaker collegial network for women later, etc.). There is some evidence that women faculty (and administrators) see it in their interest to actively build networks (Welch 1980) among themselves, with men, and with students, as the chapter in this volume by Dresselhaus indicates.

Despite comparability between men and women in prestige of the graduate schools in which they receive training, women appear to be less able than men to build on advantages that result from attending the most prestigious graduate schools. Thus, at the second stage, that of first job, men and women's career paths diverge significantly. Rosenfeld and others (Perrucci 1970; National Academy of Sciences 1979) document not only the greater tendency of women than men to be employed initially in academic (versus industrial or governmental) institutions but also the tendency within higher education for women to be employed in lower quality institutions and in marginal non-tenure track positions and the lowest tenure-track academic ranks. For women, but not men, employment in high prestige schools decreases chances of being on tenure track and the level of rank held, if on tenure track.

For the third stage, the initial eight years of the post-Ph.D. career, moreover, the paths of men and women tend to diverge more and more. Women are less likely to be employed in "distinguished" or "strong" departments. Non-tenure track positions are more difficult to leave for women than men. Additionally, as aggregate data presented in the Hornig chapter also show, for those women on tenure track, higher rank is less likely to have been achieved, especially in high prestige departments. For women, in contrast to men, probability of holding a high rank position eight years after the Ph.D. is improved less by beginning their careers in academia, less from older age, less from scholarly publications, and not at all by high prestige of the graduate schools in which they received their training.

Rosenfeld presents some evidence that women's career patterns are affected adversely by geographical and family constraints. That women are less geographically mobile than men is indicated by data that over half of women but over two-thirds of men make geographic moves from graduate school to first position. Unlike men, women are unable to gain occupational mobility (i.e., hold a tenure track position) from geographical mobility. Also, a negative relation between size of urbanized area in which doctorates hold their first position and their academic rank is stronger for women than men.

Additionally, family situation affects the extent to which some women are periodically unemployed or part-time employed, both of which hamper chances for further career advancement. Women's drop-out rates are relatively low, however, and wide variations by field or discipline could lead one to attribute the cause primarily to employers rather than women themselves.

As Rosenfeld notes, an important direction for future research would be to follow careers of doctorate cohorts through the decade of the 1970's to discern effects, if any, of changes in demand in the academic labor market, as well as from equal opportunity/affirmative action regulations promulgated then (Bach and Perrucci 1982). More research attention to effects of organizational policies and practices, in contrast to individual actions, is also needed (Szafran 1982).

In addition to achieving excellence in the traditional faculty responsibilities of research, teaching and service, participation in extra-curricular activities by "established" women is also vital for the continued progress of women scientists and engineers in academia, according to the chapter in this volume by Mildred Dresselhaus. A noted engineering professor herself, Dresselhaus first discusses the impact that successful women faculty can have locally on students--as role models, as counselors, as advocates--and provides examples of effective extra-curricular activities from her experiences at the Massachusetts Institute of Technology. Moreover, senior women faculty can facilitate the success of junior women faculty and professionals by serving as mentors and advocates. Nationally, the participation of women faculty in professional societies, advisory committees, and the like all serve to advance the position of women in the science-based professions. Hence, Dresselhaus contends that these as well as the activities at the local level, are important *extra*-curricular activities which successful women faculty can and must share, at least until such time as there is no further need for affirmative action on the nation's campuses.

Alternative Science-Based Careers

One alternative to the ideal-typical career (Lantz 1980; Women's Reentry Project 1980) which is analyzed in the chapter in this volume by Rosenfeld, is exemplified in the autobiographical chapter by Esther Hopkins. She describes alternative careers, including her own, as differing from the "male model" by lacking "consecutive, progressive achievement" in a scientific profession. Rather, because of discrimination (sexual and racial), family-related endeavors, and/or a "certain restlessness" with conventional career progression, some individuals, such as herself, embark on careers in which science is applied in various ways that are of benefit to society. Hopkins' own career to date combines training and experience as a chemist with that of law--as a patent attorney. Her determination in the face of blocked opportunities and her success in creating an alternative career will inspire other women scientists to do likewise.

Next, the autobiographical account of Anne Briscoe's scientific career, and the aggregate data on chemists which she reports, illustrate many of the institutional barriers, including overt sex discrimination, to women's pursuit of the conventional academic career depicted in this volume by Rosenfeld. Briscoe's advanced training in biochemistry occurred in a highly prestigious graduate program, and it led to a prestigious post-doctoral appointment. However, completion of post-doctoral training did not translate into a regular, academic appointment, the type of position she desired. Once employed, moreover, an inordinate length of time passed before a promotion occurred, and that to a rank not commensurate with her vast experience and professional performance.

Briscoe proposes to aid young women scientists by forewarning them of possible career pitfalls--stressing institutional sexism, rather than individual inadequacies. In addition, she and others (Fact-File 1980) offer assistance, her own focus being the Association for Women in Science. Through participation in such professional advocacy groups, and in the political arena more generally, she contends that women can empower themselves and increase their options in the professions and in society generally.

The third chapter in this section, by Naomi McAfee, begins by documenting the uniqueness of engineering as a field in which beginning salaries of women not only equal, but frequently surpass those of men, at least among B.S. degree recipients. However, her data also show that three years after college graduation, women engineers' salaries drop below those of men and this sex discrepancy continues to increase over the course of the career. Moreover, there is a form of stratification within engineering whereby women are underrepresented in engineering management.

Although a number of factors have been suggested as possible explanations for the low representation of women in management positions, the dominant theoretical paradigm to date is person-centered; that is, it focuses on personal skills or dispositions of individual women (Riger and Galligan 1980). Similarly, in the work-a-day world, perceptions of women's versus men's attributes can pose significant barriers to women's employment and success in management (Ferber, Huber, and Spitze 1979; Kanter 1977). McAfee alerts readers to the sexism underlying commonly held stereotypes about women and to evidence of an anti-feminist backlash in our country now.

Women's Views of Scientific Views of Women

Along with completion of advanced education have come increased opportunities to construct (or reconstruct) reality about the nature of women and their contributions to society on the part of feminist mathematicians, historians, social scientists and biologists. In the Campbell and Geller chapter in this volume, a math educator and mathematician address the question of why women apparently experience mathematics anxiety more frequently than men and perform less well on some specific measures of mathematics achievement (Fox 1980). Rather than presume that such sex differences have genetic causes, which are immutable, the authors review the considerable research evidence that extant sex differences in attitudes and performance result from early and continuing socialization, which is modifiable. They also discuss selected on-going school programs which are aimed at reducing and eliminating high school girls' mathematics anxiety and math avoidance in order to facilitate more college women's entry into scientific and technical fields of study and employment.

Among social scientists and humanists who are contributing to the new scholarship on women, historians are conducting careful searches for written materials in libraries and archives regarding the past participation of women in science and technology. Martha Trescott's analysis of such documents, together with data from questionnaires, surveys and interviews with engineers of various ages, reveal that women have been making notable contributions to engineering for quite some time. This has occurred despite the facts that the number of women trained as engineers has not been large, and that their professional achievements generally have been underrewarded and have not been publicly recognized. Little known materials housed in the Gilbreth Collection at Purdue University, for example, provide an important basis for Trescott's delineation of Lillian Gilbreth's approach, which is characterized as a holistic or systems approach, and some of her significant contributions to industrial engineering and its precursors. Without doubt, the creation and dissemination of such feminist scholarship informs engineers and the discipline of history in a manner benefiting both men and women alike.

Taking a different approach, the Hubbard and Haraway chapters in this volume maintain that many women have something special or unique to offer in the development of science and engineering. Unlike Gilbreth, who was more concerned with efficiency of the worker on the line, such women are more concerned with worker's job control or job satisfaction. Thus, Ruth Hubbard indicates that to work within "mainstream" organizations and professions may be difficult for many women whose nature and socialization is rather incompatible with a work structure which, to date, has been defined primarily by men (e.g., requirements for the primacy of employment over other facets of life; hierarchical rather than egalitarian work structures; special problems that derive from the numerical rarity of women in most scientific work groups, and so on).

Moreover, both the Hubbard and Haraway chapters contend that it is not only the structure of the scientific professions but also their methodology and content, which are largely male defined, and, therefore, different from the views of nature and practice of the scientific enterprise by at least some women scientists. Women, Hubbard posits, tend more than men to have a more intuitive style of scientific work, to be more inclined to cooperate with, rather than exercise control over nature, and to think more in terms of relationships and multiple interactions, rather than in terms of hierarchies and unidirectional causal paths. Hubbard and Haraway urge that rather than changing themselves, therefore, women scientists should take pride in whatever "alternative" skills and abilities they may have and try to modify the present practice and content of science accordingly.

Bringing the reader full circle to the discussion of women and work cross-culturally with which this introduction began, Donna Haraway underscores the social class and race ghettoization of women as workers (Davis 1982) and urges more women scientists to use their talents to eliminate all three bases of domination around the world.

In summary, the chapters which comprise this volume discuss trends and possibilities of greater equity for women within the scientific and technical professions. In their visions of both goals and means to their attainment, the authors exemplify generally shared themes as well as some diversity in their theoretical orientations and activities in the ongoing Women's Liberation Movement. The authors share a belief in the importance of women's training and employment in science-based professions as a necessary if not sufficient condition for general sex equality in a technological society such as our own. They also recognize the necessity of sexual and reproductive freedom, egalitarian family relationships, and nonsexist socialization throughout the life cycle (Perrucci and Targ 1974). A minority, moreover, look to socialism, in contrast to capitalism, as a precondition for equality between the sexes (Sokoloff 1980).

In discussions of scientific training and employment, it is sometimes women's own abilities and motivations that are highlighted. The authors clearly vary in their relative emphasis on similarities versus differences in male/female attributes and on the implications that they derive for women and for the scientific enterprise, nationally and internationally. Usually, discussions of scientific training and employment focus primarily on structural factors that impede or facilitate women's access and performance. As Lilli Hornig aptly concludes, "Equality in education and work has turned out to be a moving target, but women have learned to take much better aim." If this volume further improves the aim, it will have served its purpose.

References

Alvarez, R., K. G. Lutterman, and Associates. 1979. *Discrimination in organizations.* San Francisco: Jossey-Bass Publishers.

American Association of University Professors. 1981. The impact of the 1982 federal budget on women in higher education. *Academe* 67: 202-05.

Aronoff, J., and W. D. Crano. 1975. A re-examination of the cross-cultural principles of task segregation and sex role differentiation in the family. *American Sociological Review* 40: 12-20.

Bach, R. L. and C. C. Perrucci. 1982. Organizational influences on the sex composition of faculty: A comparison of colleges and universities. Paper presented at seventy-seventh annual meeting of the American Sociological Association, San Francisco, California.

Bayer, A. E., and H. S. Astin. 1975. Sex differentials in the academic reward system. *Science* 188: 796-802.

Blau, F. D., and C. L. Jusenius. 1976. Economists approaches to sex segregation in the labor market: An appraisal. *Signs* 3:181-200.

Carter, M. J., and S. B. Carter. 1981. Women's recent progress in the professions or, women get a ticket to ride after the gravy train has left the station. *Feminist Studies* 7:475-504.

Crano, W. D., and J. Aronoff. 1978. A cross-cultural study of expressive and instrumental role complementarity in the family. *American Sociological Review* 43:463-71.

Davis, A. 1982. *Women, race and class.* New York: Random House, Inc.

Fact-File. 1980. Women's units in 69 organizations. *Chronicle of Higher Education* 2:9-10.

Feagin, J. R., and D. L. Eckberg. 1980. Discrimination: Motivation, action, effects and context. *Annual Review of Sociology* 6:1-20.

Feagin, J. R., and C. B. Feagin. 1978. *Discrimination American style: Institutional sexism and racism.* Englewood Cliffs, N.J.: Prentice-Hall.

Ferber, M. J., J. Huber, and G. Spitze. 1979. Preference for men as bosses and professionals. *Social Forces* 58:466-76.

Fox, L. H. 1980. *The problem of women and mathematics.* New York: The Ford Foundation.

Gagnon, J. H. 1971. Physical strength, once of significance. *Impact of Science on Society* 21:31-42.

Hacker, S. 1978. Sex stratification, technology, and organizational change: A longitudinal analysis of AT&T. Paper presented at the annual meeting of the American Sociological Association, San Francisco, California.

Harris, B. J. 1978. *Beyond her sphere: Women and the professions in American history.* Westport, Conn.: Greenwood Press.

Holter, H. 1970. *Sex roles and social structure.* Oslo, Norway: Universitetsforlaget.

Howe, F. 1977. *Seven years later: Women's studies programs in 1976.* A Report of the National Advisory Council on Women's Educational Programs. Washington, D.C.: The Council.

Howe, F. and C. Ahlum. 1973. Women's studies and social change. In *Academic women on the move,* ed. A. S. Rossi and A. Calderwood, 393-423. New York: Russell-Sage.

Huber, J. 1976. Toward a sociotechnological theory of the women's movement. *Social Problems* 23: 371-88.

Humphreys, S. M. 1982. *Women and minorities in science: Strategies for increasing participation.* Boulder, Colo.: Westview Press Books.

Kanter, R. M. 1977. *Men and women of the corporation.* New York: Basic Books.

Koch, J. V., and J. F. Chizmer, Jr. 1976. *The economics of affirmative action.* Lexington, Mass.: D. C. Heath and Company.

Lantz, A. E. 1980. *Reentry programs for female scientists.* New York: Praeger Publishers.

Lester, R. A. 1974. *Antibias regulations of universities: Faculty problems and their solutions.* New York: McGraw-Hill.

Mattfeld, J. A., and C. G. Van Aken, eds. 1965. *Women and the scientific professions.* Cambridge: MIT Press.

National Academy of Sciences. 1979. *Climbing the academic ladder: Doctoral women scientists in academe.* Washington, D.C.: Report of the Committee on the Education and Employment of Women in Science and Engineering, Commission on Human Resources.

Nielsen, J. M. 1978. *Sex in society: Perspectives on stratification.* Belmont, Calif.: Wadsworth.

Perrucci, C. C. 1970. Minority status and the pursuit of professional careers: women in science and engineering. *Social Forces* 49:245-59.

Perrucci, C. C., and D. B. Targ. 1974. *Marriage and the family: A critical analysis and proposals for change.* New York: David McKay Company.

Piore, M. 1975. Notes for a theory of labor market segmentation. In *Labor market segmentation,* ed. R. C. Edwards, M. Reich, and D. M. Gordon, 125-50. Lexington, Mass.: D.C. Heath.

Riger, S. and P. Galligan. 1980. Women in management: An exploration of competing paradigms. *American Psychologist* 35:902-10.

Rossiter, M. W. 1982. *Women scientists in America.* Baltimore, Md.: Johns Hopkins Univ. Press.

Safilios-Rothschild, C. 1979. *Sex role socialization and sex discrimination: A synthesis and critique of the literature.* Washington, D.C.: National Institute of Education.

Sexton, P. C. 1977. *Women and work.* R&D Monograph 46, Employment and Training Administration, U.S. Department of Labor. Washington, D.C.: U.S. Government Printing Office

Silvestri, M. J., and P. L. Kane. 1975. How affirmative is the action for administrative positions in higher education? *Journal of Higher Education* 46:445-50.

Sokoloff, N.J. 1980. *Between money and love.* New York: Praeger Publishers.

Sowell, T. 1976. Affirmative action reconsidered. *The Public Interest* 42:47-65.

Szafran, R. F. 1982. What kinds of firms hire and promote women and blacks? A review of the literature. *The Sociological Quarterly* 23:171-90.

United States Equal Employment Opportunity Commission. 1974. *Affirmative action and equal employment: A guidebook for employers, Volume 1.* Washington, D.C.: U.S. Government Printing Office.

Vance, S. M. 1981. *Title IX: The half full, half empty glass.* Washington, D.C.: National Advisory Council on Women's Educational Programs.

WEAL Washington Report. 1981. Hiring goals need enforcement, not burial. *WEAL Washington Report* 10:4.

Welch, M. S. 1980. *Networking: The great new way for women to get ahead.* New York: Harcourt Brace Jovanovich.

Women's Re-entry Project. 1980a. *Student support services: Re-entry women need them too.* Washington, D.C.: Project on the Status and Education of Women, Association of American Colleges.

——————. 1980b. *Confidence and competence: Basic skills programs and refresher courses for re-entry women.* Washington, D.C.: Project on the Status and Education of Women, Association of American Colleges.

——————. 1980c. *Re-entry women: Part-time enrollment, full-time commitment.* Washington, D.C.: Project on the Status and Education of Women, Association of American Colleges.

——————. 1980d. *Re-entry women and graduate school.* Washington, D.C.: Project on the Status and Education of Women, Association of American Colleges.

Zuckerman, H., and J. R. Cole. 1975. Women in American science. *Minerva* 13:82-102.

Women in Science-Based Professions:
A Time of Transition

Professional Women in Developing Nations: The United States and the Third World Compared

Nancie L. Gonzalez

"Women in Development" issues have lately focused on the impact of policies designed to increase agricultural and industrial productivity in third world nations on the role of women in the poorer sectors, and especially in the countryside. Concern has been expressed not only about how development, most often designed and implemented by men, may adversely affect the status of large numbers of women, but also how failure to mobilize these women's talents may work contrary to the aim of increasing economic growth.[1]

Although this newer thrust is important, we must not lose sight of the fact that it is the more educated upper strata--especially the growing middle class, which will provide the leadership within each country for the continuing struggle for women's rights and freedoms. Furthermore, the middle class itself is both a product and an instrument of economic development. In this paper I intend to deal with the concepts of professionalism and professional women, especially as these relate to economic development and modernization. I will draw upon examples from present-day developing countries as well as from historical and anthropological sources in presenting my argument, which is based upon an evolutionary view of sociocultural phenomena.

By "development" I refer to the processes by which a society moves toward greater self-determination and independence *vis-a-vis* others in its efforts to improve life for a larger proportion of its own people. Advances in medical knowledge and the delivery of health care have caused populations everywhere to expand beyond the capacities of primitive technologies to provide for their needs. It is difficult to imagine isolated development in today's world, for the fuel and information revolutions have produced a superior technology which is in demand everywhere. The fact that this technology is based on the combination of scientific know-how (including navigation) and fossil fuels first developed in western Europe, made that continent the source and primary agent of change until well into this century.[2] Following World War II the United States, itself a product of earlier "development," became the world leader in such efforts, which were frequently sponsored or monitored by international bodies. Both the earlier colonial and neocolonial periods, however, may be thought of as having stimulated development on a world-wide scale, even though the benefits to the technologically less advantaged nations were slower, not always demonstrable, and some would say, nonexistent.

Women as a class have only occasionally been the target or focus of development efforts over the years. Sometimes they have been approached as mothers and homemakers with the goal of improving nutrition and child care generally to combat high infant mortality. In other cases they have been sought as factory workers because they were thought to exceed men in "manual dexterity." Education beyond basic literacy has sometimes been urged upon them so they might raise their children, especially boys, to be more aware of the world outside their home community, and thus better citizens of a modernizing nation-state. It has only been in the past generation, however, that education has been offered to both girls and boys in much of the third world's rural sectors. This has tended to emphasize basic skills, including the three R's, but with some concentration on practical matters for which modern science and technology are necessary or useful.

However, even modest technological changes have social and cultural concomitants, and there are similar occupational structures in all nations today regardless of political persuasion or cultural heritage. As the world struggles, through development, to influence the balance between population and production, two major changes affecting women's roles have occurred: (1) it is no longer the case that most females must devote their primary energies and attention to bearing and raising children in order to perpetuate the species and, (2) greater socio-economic complexity has created a demand for diverse skills and talents, many of which seem better supplied by women. I shall develop each of these points in turn.

The Evolution of Professionalism Among Women

One of Margaret Mead's (1963) major contributions was (and remains, regardless of recent criticisms)[3] to show that roles are differentiated by gender in all societies, but that the specific behaviors mandated are not predetermined by biology except insofar as the actual reproductive process is concerned. Thus, motherhood and fatherhood entail different limitations and possibilities in relation to social roles. In all societies some provision must be made to ensure that enough babies are conceived, born, and raised to replace each generation.[4] If this requires the participation of all or most of the women, there will inevitably be customs and beliefs which glorify the maternal role while at the same time discouraging women from diverting their attention elsewhere. In symmetrical fashion, men may be excluded from the whole realm of birthing (Paul 1974), with emphasis placed on their importance in protecting children and their mothers, as well as in helping provide food and other necessities. For hundreds of thousands of years this division of labor served our ancestors well, and the evidence suggests that both males and females were respected to the extent they excelled in their socially assigned roles. Specialization allowed each sector to concentrate on perfecting the behavior patterns most likely to bring success.

As new tasks developed in the course of social and cultural evolution, they became identified in different societies sometimes with men and sometimes with women, as in pottery-making, weaving, and trading. I will here reserve the term "profession" for those specialized skills which only some people acquire, whether or not they devote full time to practicing them. In early Neolithic, as well as in many ethnographically known societies, the above mentioned rarely became true professions, since all or most adults of the relevant sex engaged in them in addition to their other productive activities.

One of the characteristics of economic development, whether we are dealing with the present day or the historical record, is increasing specialization of labor. As food production becomes more efficient, fewer hands are needed in the effort, and alternative occupations appear, some of which emerge as full-time efforts from amongst those previously done part-time by nearly everyone as part of his or her gender-related adult assignment. Others, such as priest, metal-worker, carpenter, and scribe, reflect a more complex sociocultural order, and are true specializations, though they may still be gender-linked. Through history, as the associated tasks became more complex, longer training periods were required, and gradually a hierarchy of specializations developed, so that in the complex modern industrial world the "professions" have come to mean those occupations requiring in-depth knowledge and skills, and usually, post-secondary formal training. In addition, a profession is characterized by a setting apart of its practitioners, who become known by special dress, insignia or behavior patterns, and who are themselves united by a special *esprit de corps,* often enhanced by membership in formal organizations such as secret societies, guilds, professional associations, or unions. Until recently the professions have been gender-linked in most, if not all, societies.

Contrary to the old cliché, prostitution is at best the second oldest profession, even if only women's occupations are considered. Probably the physician--as curer of disease, psychiatrist and obstetrician--was first, and in many early societies this health specialist was as likely or more likely to be female. Even where males predominated in curing, often calling on the supernatural for assistance, women attended childbirth, and became highly respected as specialists in a matter which until this century was the leading cause of death among females of child-bearing age. Women were also involved in religious matters in various ways, ranging from invoking the supernatural for help in curing, to the priesthood itself. Prostitution was more likely a much later development, probably appearing concomitantly with town life and commercialism, and was sometimes linked with religion--perhaps in connection with fertility rites and beliefs. Significantly, both of these professions are related to aspects of women's biological nature, and thus belong to what I would call a primary or primitive stage in the development of professionalism among them.

Today we often divide women's work into that which is done inside versus that done outside the home, even though increasingly that distinction has seemed less useful.[5] Analytically, we can separate the two, so long as we recognize the historical background which has given us this way of thinking. We should remember too that both men and women once worked within "the home," if by that we mean the entire domestic establishment and not just the house itself. With the development of larger political entities, however, men were likely to be called away, either to fight or labor on behalf of a king, deity, or government. In their absence, women continued to farm, care for livestock, manufacture needed implements, and trade. In later times and places, including the United States during and the Soviet Union after World War II, women engaged in nearly every necessary occupation at all levels, from the most menial to the most highly professional. Women sometimes became trained hurriedly to undertake professional slots temporarily vacated by men.[6]

However, it is significant that when men are again in good supply, women tend to drop out of the most coveted and prestigious positions.[7] This is one of the major social facts in both developed and developing industrial countries today. Although upward mobility is constrained by other factors as well,[8] it remains true everywhere that women as a class tend to be relegated permanently to the lower echelons, where they frequently work harder and under worse conditions for less pay. This is true even when they have demonstrated their abilities during the crises which brought them out of their homes in the first place. There is a vicious circle here, for the absence of prominent role models in permanent positions leads both women and men to believe that women are less capable or worthy, and to discount "success" stories as being unusual, overstated or evidences of heroic or sacrificial behavior, inappropriate for "normal" women in "normal" times.

In addition to instances in which women have left the home to replace men during crises, there have been times in history when large numbers of them have been forced out of marriage and family participation altogether. This may also be one of the characteristics of economic development. Perry (1978) has shown how women in what she calls "early modern" (16th century) Spain entered prostitution or religious orders in larger numbers than previously in response to overpopulation, agricultural depression, and massive emigration of men to the New World. Usually such phenomena are treated in the literature in terms of their negative societal impacts. Prostitution, however, may be a springboard to considerable affluence, prestige and political power, as Dirasse (1978) has shown. There have been too few ethnographic studies of the role of prostitution in developing societies. These might enlighten us on the impact of the occupation on the women themselves, as well as on the society at large.

Similarly, other female choices which replace or interfere with marriage have been largely viewed by both the public and some scholars as unfortunate, though without the opprobrium of prostitution. Thus, in pre-Civil War New England, when overpopulation had forced the outmigration of thousands of men, more women than ever joined the ranks of the "spinsters" or "old maids." Teaching, one of the most prevalent female professions in developing countries today, became a respectable alternative to marriage, as had the convent for centuries earlier throughout Europe. Also, during that time nursing became more in demand than it had been previously. Thus, by the third quarter of the 19th century many elements in Western society had recognized that women might also be able to use some of their domestic skills outside the home, and thus be useful in a variety of ways, starting with the education of children and the care of the sick. These may be thought of as merely extensions of woman's maternal role, but even so, they lie outside the strictly biological realm, and I think it fair to speak of having reached the second stage in the evolution of female professionalism. In this, professions are gender-linked, even though they do not depend upon or derive from the sexuality of the individuals practicing them.

The third stage, which we are only now approaching, dissociates profession entirely from both gender and sex, but can only be achieved after significant rearrangement or development of our domestic institutions, as I shall describe below. First, I must lay the historical groundwork for my argument.

Indices of Female Professionalism

In order to compare previous patterns of female professionalism with what we find in the world today, it is necessary to use indices which are both sociologically relevant and for which reasonably accurate statistics exist. In what follows, I will use employment, education and political participation as the general areas of concern, believing that women's professional status is intimately bound up with all three, which are themselves causally interrelated.

Let us start with 1870, since that is the first year for which U.S. census records containing the kind of information we need may be found. It was also only a few years after the close of the Civil War, which may be seen as a major turning point in the economic and social history of this nation. In that year women constituted fifteen percent of the total work force in the United States, and of those, four and nine-tenths percent were listed as being in "professional and technical" occupations. Only two and six-tenths percent of the total work force was professional, yet women made up twenty-seven and one-half percent of all professionals (Bernard 1971, 123; Blitz 1975, 500). We were still a predominantly agricultural society at the time, and the fact that a higher percentage of women who worked were professional than was the case for men is, therefore, not really remarkable, since most men were still farmers. The figures also reflect the ravages of the recent war, which left many women without husbands or pools of men from which to find them. This problem was exacerbated by the general chaos and depression following the war in both the north and the south. Many of the remaining eastern men sought their fortunes on the frontier, either in Central America or the Great Plains and California. Some women followed them, but many remained behind as seamstresses, factory workers, nurses, and most of all, as schoolteachers. In New England especially, basic literacy for everyone had long been an ideal, and as early as the mid 18th century it was not unusual for both boys and girls of even humble rural homes to be able to read. Thus, there was a supply of educated and educable women, as well as a large demand for their services in both the rural and urban sectors.

Between 1870 and 1930 American women continued to move steadily into teaching and other professions as opportunities for them to secure higher education expanded through the rapid development of women's colleges and what we might call "affirmative action" by the administrators of many institutions formerly limited to men. By 1920, the year women won the vote in the United States, they constituted forty-seven percent of the country's undergraduate enrollment--a proportion that proved to be an all-time high until 1977 (McDonald 1979, 10). In 1930 women comprised nearly half of the professional work force, though of course not half of each profession. They were still most prominently represented in teaching and nursing, and least often in architecture and law.

During this same period a number of international women's organizations were formed, indicating that similar things were happening elsewhere in the world. Many of the earliest groups were religious or politically based, but between 1916 and 1930 the largest number of newly formed women's organizations were professionally oriented.

Following the International Council of Nurses, organized before the turn of the century, came alliances of midwives, lawyers, architects, engineers, scientists, and medical doctors, as well as more generalized business and professional or executive women's clubs. Most of the members of these came from the United States and the more highly developed European nations. As Elise Boulding has pointed out, these organizations paralleled those dominated by or limited to men and reflect not only the fact that more women were entering the professions, but that increasingly they formed an "elite of the powerless" (Boulding 1977, 196). The phrase is apt, because even though women were members, they had little opportunity to give expression to their public and professional concerns or to direct the activities of the societies--thus not differing from their less well trained sisters at home. It has only been over the past decade or so that women in the United States have been elected to office in numbers more appropriate to their representation in such groups. The American Association for the Advancement of Science, for example, has elected four women presidents in the past fourteen years, after well over a century of exclusively male prexies.

Let us now consider the status of professional women in some countries whose development has been slower than ours. In Latin America, which I know best, the earliest women to have achieved something we might call professional stature were writers--some, like Sor Juana Inez de la Cruz, who lived in Mexico in the 17th century, found a haven within the convent. Indeed, although the American consular wife, Fanny Calderon de la Barca (1966), was personally horrified by the idea of a young woman in 19th century Mexico abandoning "the world" for the cloister, her own account suggests, if one reads between the lines, that this was still the only place a woman then might achieve the life of the mind or of public service in that country. Many nuns became teachers or did what we might today term charity or social work. Some rose to "executive" or managerial ranks and wielded considerable influence even outside the order.

However, not all the intellectuals were in the convents. In Argentina and Peru some extraordinary women found outlets for both their literary and political interests in the regular salons or *tertulias*, where they were admitted on an equal basis with men of similar mind (Chaney 1979, 52). Yet it was not until the end of the 19th century and the beginning of the 20th that the *work* of Latin American women writers generally came to be widely recognized (Hollander 1973).

Education is a necessary prerequisite for professional status as I am defining it, but not all those who become trained actually seek employment. Higher education, especially among the upper strata, is often considered to have intrinsic value, and it also serves as a class marker. Sons of wealthy land owners in 19th and early 20th century Latin America, for example, frequently took degrees in medicine or law, but never practiced. Their feminine counterparts have sometimes done the same, though they were more likely to study literature or the classics. Even today, the middle and upper classes in nations as diverse as Japan, Kuwait and Brazil are sending their women to college in large numbers, even though most of them will never be employed outside their homes. Ironically, in many developing nations those women who do manage to move into active professional lives can do so only because they are able to employ other, less educated, women to care for their children, cook, clean house and do all the other domestic chores for which their sex is universally still held responsible. Furthermore, such professionals frequently exploit and mistreat the women who work for them, often at wages far below those of male workers (Smith 1973, 204).

By the 1880's, perhaps influenced by similar movements in the United States, upper class women in many Latin American countries, including Chile, Cuba, the Dominican Republic, Guatemala, Argentina, and Uruguay were able to become fairly well educated. The University of Chile was the first in Latin America to open its doors to women, in 1877, following only seven years behind the University of Michigan. Within a decade women were earning doctorates--especially in medicine (Schiefelbein and Farrell 1982, 229). By 1970 women constituted forty-six percent of the student body at the University of Chile and only thirty-eight percent at Michigan (McDonald 1979). Similar statistics from other developing nations today demonstrate that modern women are becoming better educated everywhere. Not only is female illiteracy declining, but women's proportion of total university degrees continues to climb--much like figures for the United States before 1930. In Japan, the number of female college students multiplied by twenty-six between 1950 and 1975, and they now constitute one third of all students--the same as in Western Europe and Latin America (Newland

1979, 35). In the Philippines, they form fifty-five percent of the total student body and twenty-two percent in India (up from eleven percent in 1951).

The Realities of the Labor Force

Can we conclude from all this that things have "turned around" for professional women, both here and abroad--that their intellectual and artistic talents are being recognized, nurtured and put to use for the benefit of society? I think not. In fact, there are many worrisome problems which do not appear on the surface, but which bother both social scientists and concerned citizens, female and male alike. Many of these are reminiscent of what happened in our country following our early period of development, i.e., between 1870-1930, when women seemed to be moving into the professions in large numbers. Let me try to put the situation into both historical and sociocultural perspective.

First of all, after the impressive gains before 1930, the percentage of those receiving advanced degrees who were female declined in the United States, and has not yet returned to the 1930 level of fifteen and four-tenths (Bernard 1971, 122; Vetter 1980). Furthermore, of those who do receive such degrees, a smaller percentage of women than of men actually finds employment at appropriate, that is professional, levels. The evidence is that highly trained women, presumably capable of independent work or managerial functions, are working in clerical and/or technical, rather than professional positions in ever increasing numbers. This appears to be true for many or most developing countries as well (Tinker and Bramsen 1976, 30). In Egypt, for example, where large numbers of women have been trained in medicine, law and agriculture, most are unable to find jobs outside of government clerical offices upon graduation (Howard-Merriam 1981). I have heard the same story in China and India.[11]

It has long been known that level of education correlates positively with political participation for both sexes, but it is also true that working women are more likely than non-working women to vote (Baxter and Lansing 1980, 153). Since 1895, when New Zealand became the first country to give women the franchise, over 100 countries have followed suit. But as happened when women were admitted to professional organizations, having the vote has not necessarily led to power in the form of representation in elected and appointed offices. In 1977, although twenty percent of the Finnish Parliament was female, women constituted only three and four-tenths percent of the United States Congress, and that percentage decreased considerably after the 1982 elections. As is often the case in developing societies, the lower organizational levels show somewhat higher percentages of women. Thus, at the state level in the U.S., the average was nine and two-tenths percent, though the range was from twenty-eight percent in New Hampshire to six percent in Indiana. In 1975 women held thirty-five percent of the seats in the Supreme Soviet, though only two percent of those on the Central Committee, and they were absent altogether from the Politburo (Baxter and Lansing 1980).

Chaney's excellent book (1979) on women politicians in Latin America shows that the number and percentage of women who have been active in elected and appointed governmental roles in the past seems to be declining in this decade. She attributes this to what she believes to be a universal phenomenon. "Women," Chaney (1979, 23) says,..."tend to become active only in times of extreme challenge." There is other evidence to support her view. Some comes from a recent restudy of one of the New Guinean societies made famous by Margaret Mead (Gewertz 1981). Gewertz (1981, 97) suggests that Mead's 1933 description of Tchambuli sex roles and personality characteristics was based on observations of a peculiar situation obtaining at that time. She points out that although Tchambuli women have always controlled the means of production, as Mead reported, they do not control the products of their labor and have had little access to the political arena in which their products are used to enhance the status and power of their husbands and fathers. Gewertz suggests that at the time of Mead's work the Tchambuli had just returned from a forced exile of nearly a generation, and that it was largely through the aggressive bartering behavior of their women that they were able to reestablish their former status among their neighbors. Once achieved, the behavior patterns of both sexes apparently changed drastically, with women taking a considerably less aggressive and visible role than Mead had observed.

Political activity among women takes many forms, as the above indicates. In the U.S., the League of Women Voters has moved into a leadership role in relation to the whole society and not only in respect to so-called "women's issues," as illustrated by their sponsorship of the Presidential debates. However, as indicated above, women themselves continue to be under-represented in the top party circles, as well as in higher level, more prestigious positions. The judiciary, for example, is still woefully bereft of female talent, in spite of the recent appointment of a woman to the Supreme Court, where she is likely to remain a token--an answer to criticisms and women's pressures. Still, eleven percent of the Supreme Court is far better than the one and eight-tenths percent characterizing the state judiciary level in 1977 (U.S. Congress, 1978). This situation might be expected to change in the future as more women enter the legal profession. It is possible that more of them may be appointed to the juvenile courts, and also to hear divorce cases, since both of these are "growth" areas in our society and are most often considered to be domestic, or "women's" issues.

Other areas, however, are less clear. Though women comprised eleven and six-tenths percent of all degree recipients in engineering in 1982, only five and seven-tenths percent of all working engineers were women in 1983. Unemployment rates for women scientists and engineers have been more than twice as high as for men (Vetter 1980, 21), and even when women do manage to secure positions commensurate with their training, salary differentials persist. It is not difficult to muster evidence supporting a generally gloomy picture. Are these the fruits of development and of women's emancipation? What went wrong? How has this state of affairs come to pass? Has affirmative action gained us nothing? Why was women's position apparently better a century ago than today?

It is well that we should ask, for although we continue to push for "women's rights" in our development efforts, some might wonder whether we have any right to claim special knowledge on the subject. Indeed, it is frequently suggested that professional women are better off in the developing nations than in the United States today, and as Blitz (1974) has shown, apparent evidence for this can be found. But if so, should they anticipate similar backsliding in the years ahead? Is there any lesson to be learned from our experience which might be put to good use as we go forth with our "Women in Development" banners?

Protection of Women

The early 1930s brought not only the zenith in percentages of women trained for professional positions in the United States, but the period also saw the beginning of modern scientific and humanistic interest in what we have come to call "sex roles." Then it came under the general heading, "status of women." Doctoral dissertations were written on the subject (mostly by men), and the International Labor Organization sponsored several studies to look into the conditions of women's work (ILO 1932). Most of these concentrated on skilled and unskilled labor, but others documented conditions relevant to salaried professionals as well.

In many countries laws were passed limiting the number of hours women might work and in other ways regulating the work place, by requiring rest periods, sick leave, and lounge space. Betty Friedan (1963, 118) has said, "Protectiveness has often muffled the sound of doors closing against women; it has often cloaked a very real prejudice, even when it is offered in the name of science." Until recently in most, and still in some colleges and universities, women faculty members have been excused from committee work, the supervision of graduate students, and even from faculty meetings "in exchange" for teaching an extra course. The rationale was to "lighten the burden" so the women could count on regular hours and be able to spend more time in their households and with their families. Of course in so doing these women usually failed to achieve tenure, or if they did, it was without promotion, extra pay or stature in their disciplines. They hardly heard the doors closing in their faces, and sadly enough, many went willingly to a professional demise. Most often they did so in the name of family harmony and their husbands' success.

This is now changing--and as it does, it will be momentarily harder for women. They will not be able to manage two jobs (or even two half-time jobs) at once. However, why do the problems persist? Why should not men also be concerned about family harmony and their wives' success? Many are, of course, but even well-meaning men may not have been socialized to be sensitive to such issues.

It has become commonplace to note that boys and girls are reared differently everywhere, and that this creates differences in their behavior patterns which are later thought of as being innate or natural to each sex (Mead 1949). However, in the United States, Europe, and among the "modern sectors" in developing countries girls are presumably receiving the same education as boys. A more refined analysis, of course, shows that their experiences in the classroom and in related educational activities are not really the same as for boys.[12] This is only partly related to content, i.e., whether they take home "ec" or "shop," or whether their curricular materials are overtly or covertly biased. It has often been suggested that girls are reared both at home and in school in a manner which tends to suppress rather than stimulate their highest talents (Bernard 1964, 126). Radloff (1980, 107) points out that from childhood, females are less well or often rewarded for competence than are males, and even when they do receive recognition of success it may be muted by a simultaneous punishment in the form of social rejection. At the very least a girl may be made to feel that she is "less feminine" if she persists in doing things well. In the final analysis, our society still teaches that marriage and a family are the most important means to feminine success. Therefore, many women professors happily accept jobs which seem to allow them the best of both possible worlds, even when they may have a sneaking suspicion that their professional interests are not being served so well as are those of their male colleagues. But what price do they pay?

Women seem to have lower expectations of success in many endeavors, according to Radloff. They often attribute their accomplishments to luck, while blaming themselves fully for failures.[13] This in turn makes them prey to the ravages of depression, which has been repeatedly demonstrated to occur more frequently among women. It seems reasonable to hypothesize that women's upbringing has given them inadequate means for coping with stress. This subject has been given a good deal of attention in recent years, and we have learned quite a bit about the kinds of events and situations which trigger stress in modern society, as well as something about the effects of stress upon behavior and well-being.

A recent study of stress among faculty members found that married females experience more stress and less satisfaction in their jobs than either unmarried females or married males (Vetter 1980, 26). It seems clear that this is another indictment of the society which demands that working women shoulder two jobs. Looking at still another aspect of stress, Haynes (1980) discovered that working women as a group have no greater incidence of heart disease than women not working outside the home, but female clerical and sales workers have twice the coronary disease rate of other women. Iglehart (1979) found a good bit of expressed job dissatisfaction among women who were employed at levels lower than their educational levels would suggest, especially among clerical and sales workers.

The problem, then, is not only that women cannot cope with success or be comfortable in leadership roles, or find it difficult to manage two fulltime jobs at once, but that they are still not being given sufficient opportunities to use their talents. This is a surefire way to trigger frustration, dissatisfaction, and stress. The underuse of women can be seen in politics and government, in management, in academia, and even in the labor movement itself (Foner 1981). However, the formation of women's caucuses within many institutional settings today does seem to offer hope for the future, at the same time that it signals change already underway. The presence of larger numbers of women in each of the professions has had an effect--more in some than in others, of course. As women are appointed to committees, whether through affirmative action or simply because they offer talent and needed knowledge, they will become better known and their voices more powerful.

A case can be made, I believe, that women lost ground between 1930 and 1970 in this country because we allowed ourselves to be "protected," because we continued to align ourselves with women's associations rather than making ourselves felt in the mainstream, and because we were faint-hearted--(in keeping, I suppose, with our stereotyped image). This seems to be the way professional women in the developing world today are reacting to similar pressures.

Now, in a sense this might sound a bit like the game of blaming the victim, but it's up to us to avoid being victimized and to assist women in the developing world to recognize and defend themselves from a similar fate. Women cannot maintain full participation in the professions while they also juggle a traditional family life which demands a strict separation of sex roles and puts the major burden of housework upon females. Family structure is changing rapidly, as is evidenced by divorce statistics, new types of marital and domestic arrangements (including single-parent households, communal households, the compounding of in-law and grandparental roles, etc.), lower birth rates, and a new male viewpoint which does not necessarily denigrate or eschew childcare and housekeeping functions.

Furthermore, we have to recognize and teach women that self-fulfillment can be obtained through contributing to society at large and not merely through service to their own families. This, in my opinion, is the key to achieving the next stage in the evolution of female professionalism. It must be understood and accepted that some women may be better senators or prime ministers than mothers--just as some men are better judges than fathers. However, the parenting role should no longer be placed in *contrast* to the professional for women, just as it rarely is for men. This will require a shift in the conviction that women are naturally more nurturant and caring than men, and the concomitant view that "no one loves you like your mother does." We need to widen our kinship, neighborhood and friendship networks to provide a warm and protective support system for both children and hard-working adults of both sexes. There is evidence that changes in this direction are underway in the United States and parts of Europe today. Consider, for example, the many cooperative baby-sitting and nursery school groups, the "marriage encounter" movement, the resurgence of religious communities, and even the increasing importance of condominium and neighborhood development in large cities. Although the concept of "house-husband" remains a poor joke, so increasingly is the type of man characterized by Dagwood Bumstead. This trend has probably progressed furthest among the more highly educated professionals, whose life styles today depend upon affluence without great wealth, and where both partners see their work as a necessary part of their lives.

The Changing Position of Women in Developing Nations

The developing nations are also changing in this regard, but more at the lower levels than among those with university degrees. So long as extremes in income persist, professional women will not be truly liberated because they will merely pass on their domestic chores to the women they hire, although they themselves will continue to be held responsible. Men will not by themselves change this order of things-- but the economic system may be giving women a helping hand.

Domestic help will become more expensive as young women from the lower classes become better educated and aspire to more exciting and prestigious, as well as less demanding and well-paid positions. Although traditions, particularly when supported by religious dogma, die hard, there is some evidence that women in the lower economic brackets in some countries are already becoming liberated from complete domination by men. For example, many women now migrate to cities, both in their native countries and abroad, where they become economically independent and learn new values. The number of female-headed households is increasing in both rural and urban zones. This does not necessarily presage a decline in quality of life, as is so often assumed, although it may signal greater poverty for some women and children if ways are not found to keep resources flowing into the household--either through the woman's own work or through contributions by "significant males."[14] As incomes and educational levels rise in this group, we might also predict a lowering of the birthrate, which in turn will improve the well-being of the entire household.

Most agencies concerned with international development have taken strong stands on the matter of improving or at least not diminishing the status of women. UNESCO stimulated much discussion in the early 1960s (Chaton 1968) and eventually sponsored the International Year of the Woman in 1975. The World Bank, USAID, the U.S. Department of Labor, and even the Rand Corporation (Haber 1958) have sponsored studies, symposia and various publications. Although I admit, as this paper intimates, that progress has been slow and sporadic, and that the gap between men and women has seemed to widen (Tinker 1974); I suggest we are now on the threshold of a real revolution. This is not to say there may not still be temporary setbacks as opinion-makers with different views come into political power and social prominence. However, I do believe we have the ball in our court.[15]

The current interest in women in development is both a product of and a stimulant to the advancement of women in countries such as our own. The topic has formed a rallying point from which we have influenced both theory and policy. It is an undeniable fact that women in the developing world--especially in agricultural sectors, but increasingly in the cities as well--are crucial to the success of many projects and to improved production generally. They also will ultimately decide whether to limit their births, and as that becomes a matter of concern for the whole world, planners will find bold new ways to work with them.

At the same time, increased attention to the international scene has multiplied the ideas formerly available to the women of any one country or region. The number of journals publishing special issues on women skyrocketed during 1975, and the pace seems to have been maintained since then (Boulding 1977, 190). What is particularly significant, in my opinion, is the fact that many or most of the institutions sponsoring women's efforts today are not themselves exclusively devoted to women. Although women's organizations definitely had a role to play in the past, and although many women will still find psychological support in belonging to them, I believe we are further ahead by working from within.[16] Not only are we thus enabled to prove our competence first hand, but we may be able to effect changes in the organization which will have a lasting impact on the status of women and on the nature of society.

A Look to the Future

In an earlier publication (Gonzalez 1973) I suggested that women were really not interested in moving into the public domain on issues unrelated to domesticity. I argued then that women's more humanistic socialization made them uncomfortable or impatient with both the issues and the styles found in top level national and international political spheres. Clearly times have changed, and today I have modified my stance in two respects. First, our "ideal types" for both sexes have become modified with role models such as Margaret Thatcher and Jerry Brown. Although it might be argued (as I previously did) that these are exceptions, I now believe that individual personality is increasingly less attributable to gender than formerly. At the same time, it now appears to me that all issues are in some way related to how people survive in the most basic social units, and that women must be, and I believe are, enormously interested in working toward a more peaceful and productive world and thus, toward happier personal lives for all. This work will be done in the home, in the fields, in the marketplace, in the courts, in academia, in city hall or any other domain where professionals carry on their specialized tasks. Thus, the newest stage of professionalism among women finds us increasingly free of both sex and gender limitations, thanks to a whole new social order which has redefined the meaning and patterning of both production and reproduction.

Yet, I must end with a query and a warning in relation to the developing countries. Must women there go through the same evolutionary sequence I have outlined for the United States? As women leave the rural zones, become educated and seek fulfillment in increasingly less gender-related roles, will the larger social organization keep up with them? Perhaps our "Women in Development" efforts need to continue to think about ways in which we can be influential at this level as well.

Notes

1. I will here not review what has become a massive literature on that subject, but refer interested persons to the bibliographies prepared by Saulniers and Rakowski on Africa and Latin America (1977) and by Nelson (1979) on South East Asia.

2. It is important and interesting to note that science was really born and nurtured in the Middle East by the Greeks and later, the Arabs. It was the coal of northwestern Europe and America, however, that provided the fuel in the early days, and which gave those areas hegemony over the circum-Mediterranean even after oil became the world's most important fossil fuel. Recently Macfarlane (1979) has suggested that the early development of the nuclear family in England may have been a contributing factor in the industrial revolution. What woman's role may have been in this has not been spelled out.

3. Derek Freeman's recent book (1983) is a useful addition to the anthropological literature updating our knowledge of particular peoples and cultures. In no way does it negate the important conclusions drawn by Mead and hundreds of other researchers in relation to how sex roles vary from society to society.

4. "Enough", of course, is a relative term, and its definition will be specific to each society, depending upon variables affecting mortality at different ages and productive capacity of the system as a whole. The value system will tend to support whatever turns out to be "enough"--whether this be "an only child," or whatever. Sometimes

values from a previous societal condition hang on for a while even when they work contrary to the best interests of the society. Either they change relatively quickly, or the society is doomed--unless, of course, some other variable changes as well.

5. Recently a good bit of feminist and social scientific attention has been paid to this issue. See Gutek, *et al.*, (1981), Reagan and Blaxall (1976), and Sacks (1979), for an introduction.

6. A recent article on Mao's China illustrates how female nurses were sometimes simply elevated to doctor when the latter were in short supply (Gordon 1983).

7. Note, however, that an alternative model has been for the profession itself to lose status if it continues to be dominated by women. This remains the case in the Soviet Union, and seems to be developing in Britain for physicians under socialized medicine.

8. In different times and places people have been discriminated against on the basis of factors such as race, religion, mode of dress, and other things. Nevertheless, it remains true that even within such categories women have usually been worse off than their menfolk when it comes to gaining access to the power structure.

9. One important scholar, Arturo Torres-Rioseco (1959), not only failed to give credit to most of the earlier talents, but his bow to some more recent women writers suggests they earned their positions by default. Torres-Rioseco (1959, 120) states, "One of the most interesting single events in this contemporary period is the emergence of women in the realm of Spanish American letters. Formerly relegated to a role of unimportance in intellectual life, women are today coming to the fore in journalism, lecturing, editing, teaching, writing, and more particularly in the field of poetry. Some of this change is due to the growing material prosperity of countries like Argentina, Brazil, and Chile, where men are too busy with practical tasks in the pampas, the mines, the rubber plantation, the factories, to pay much attention to poetry--which is thus permitted to become feminine art."

10. Of married women in Brazil who work, some five-tenths of a percent of the population, sixty-five and eight-tenths percent have completed university degrees, yet illiterate Brazilian married women, comprising thirty-nine and six-tenths percent of the total population, make up only six and three-tenths percent of the labor force (Newland 1979, 41). Presumably, the latter have no one whom they may employ,

even were they to find jobs.

11. The situation in China is not clear. Only about three percent of all persons who graduate from secondary school are permitted to go to college. The Chinese insist there is no discrimination on the basis of gender, *per se,* yet at the same time I was repeatedly told that women are less intelligent than men, on the average. Even a young woman rural school teacher in Guangdong province insisted that this was true, as evidenced, she said, by the higher dropout rate of girls at all school levels. The evidence from Chile is provocative, and may also explain the Chinese facts. See below.

It is also true that most professionals and persons in higher party ranks in China are men. Several Chinese suggested to me in 1981 that the heavier burdens borne by women in the household prevent them from doing as well as men in jobs outside the home, thus precluding advancement.

The Indian situation, poignantly described by Raj (1982), is complicated by the Prime Minister being female, even though it is clear that relatively few women in that country can aspire to top positions. Emigration of educated women, with or without husbands, is an important, though less well documented phenomenon (pers. com. with Dr. Angara Ramanamma 1982).

12. It might be argued that were they really the same, the results might be equally devastating to the mental health of women who later discover that the real world in no way resembles the one in which they were reared.

13. Not only do women tend to blame themselves for failure on the job. When a professional couple gets divorced, the burden of guilt for "failure" of the marriage is likely to be assumed by the woman, regardless of the circumstances.

14. Such males may be husbands, brothers, sons or lovers. In the consanguineal household, about which I have written extensively (Gonzalez 1969), two or more women (usually related) may combine forces by sharing both earnings and domestic chores to the benefit of their several children and other coresident kin. See, also, Stack (1974).

15. Use of a sports metaphor seems appropriate here, since sports have heretofore been largely a male monopoly. Women's tennis has only in this decade finally hit the monetary big-time, though we have yet to see a women's basketball game on national television.

16. It is significant that women politicians in Chile, Peru and the United States tend not to belong to women's organizations (Chaney 1979, U.S. Congress 1978).

References

Baxter, S. and M. Lansing. 1980. *Women and politics: The invisible majority.* Ann Arbor: Univ. of Michigan Press.

Bernard, J. 1964. *Academic Women.* University Park: Pennsylvania State Univ. Press.

——————. 1971. *Women and the public interest: An essay on policy and protest.* Chicago: Aldine.

Blitz, R. C. 1974. Women in the professions, 1870-1970. *Monthly Labor Review.* 97:34-39.

Boulding, E. 1977. *Women in the twentieth century world.* New York: John Wiley and Sons.

Calderon de la Barca, F. 1966. *Life in Mexico.* Garden City: Double-day.

Chaney, E. M. 1979. *Supermadre: Women in politics in Latin America.* Austin: Univ. of Texas Press for Institute of Latin American Studies.

Chaton, J. H. 1968. The UNESCO long-range program for the advancement of women. *Annals of the American Academy of Political and Social Science,* 375:145-53.

Dirasse, L. 1978. *The socioeconomic position of Women in Addis Ababa: The case of prostitution.* Ph.D. diss., Boston University.

Foner, P. S. 1981. *Women in the American labor movement: From World War I to the present.* New York: Free Press.

Freeman, D. 1983. *Margaret Mead and Samoa: The making and unmaking of an anothropoligcal myth.* Cambridge, Mass.: Harvard Univ. Press.

Friedan, B. 1963. *The Feminine mystique.* New York: Dell.

Gewertz, D. 1981. A historical reconsideration of female dominance among the Chambri of Papua New Guinea, *The American Ethnolologist,* 8:94-106.

Gonzalez, N. L. 1969. *Black Carib household structure.* Seattle: Univ. of Washington Press.

——————. 1973. Women and the jural domain: An evolutionary

perspective. In *A Sampler of Women's Studies,* ed. D. G. McGuigan. 47-58. Ann Arbor: Univ. of Michigan, Center for the Continuing Education for Women.

Gordon, B. B. 1983. Making rounds in the Peoples' Republic. *Science 83,* 4:56-63.

Gutek, B. A., C. Y. Nakamura, and V. F. Nieva. 1981. The interdependence of work and family roles. *Journal of Occupational Behavior* 2:1-16.

Haber, S. 1958. Female labor force participation and economic development. Paper No. P-1504. Santa Monica: Rand Corporation.

Haynes, S. 1980. *Women, work and coronary heart disease.* Bethesda, Maryland: National Institute of Health.

Hollander, N. C. 1973. Women: The forgotten half of Argentine history. In *Female and male in Latin America: Essays,* ed. A. Pescatello, 141-58, Pittsburgh: Univ. of Pittsburgh Press.

Howard-Merriam, K. 1981. The female rural development administrator in Egypt: A case of undercultivated potential? Paper presented at fifteenth annual meeting of Middle East Studies Association, Seattle, Washington.

Iglehart, A. P. 1979. *Married women and work.* Lexington, Mass.: D. C. Heath.

International Labor Organization. 1932. *Women's work under labor law: A survey of protective legislation.* Geneva: International Labor Organization.

Macfarlane, A. 1979. *The origins of English individualism.* New York: Cambridge Univ. Press.

McDonald, K. 1979. Women in higher education. *The College Board Review.* 111:10-13, 21.

Mead, M. 1963. *Sex and temperament in three primitive societies.* New York: Morrow.

————. 1949. *Male and female: A study of the sexes in a changing world.* New York: Morrow.

Nelson, N. 1979. *Why has development neglected rural women? A review of the South Asian literature.* Oxford: Pergamon.

Newland, K. 1979. *The sisterhood of man.* New York: W. W. Norton.

Paul, L. 1974. The mastery of work and the mystery of sex in a Guatemalan village. In *Woman, culture, and society.* ed. M. Z.

Rosaldo and L. Lamphere, 281-99. Stanford: Stanford Univ. Press.

Perry, M. E. 1978. Lost women in early modern Seville: The politics of prostitution. *Feminist Studies*, 4:195-214.

Radloff, L. S. 1980. *Risk factors for depression: What do we learn from them?* In *The mental health of women*, ed. M. Guttentag, S. Salasin, and D. Belle, 93-109. New York: Academic Press.

Raj, M. K. 1982. Women, work and science in India. In *Women's education in the third world: Comparative perspectives*, ed. G. P. Kelly and C. M. Elliott, 249-63. Albany: State Univ. of New York.

Reagan, B. and M. Blaxall, eds. 1976. Women and the workplace. *Signs* 1: 3.

Sacks, K. 1979. *Sisters and wives*. Westport, Conn.: Greenwood Press.

Saulniers, S. S., and C. A. Rakowski. 1977. *Women in the development process: A select bibliography on women in sub-Saharan Africa and Latin America*. Austin: Univ. of Texas, Institute of Latin American Studies.

Schiefelbein, E., and J. P. Farrell. 1982. Women, schooling, and work in Chile: Evidence from a longitudinal study. In *Women's education in the third world*, ed. G. P. Kelly and C. M. Elliott, 228-48. Albany: State Univ. of New York.

Smith, M. 1973. Domestic service as a channel of upward mobility for the lower-class woman: The Lima case. In *Female and Male in Latin America*, ed., A. Pescatello, 191-207. Pittsburgh: Univ. of Pittsburgh Press.

Stack, C. 1974. *All our kin*. New York: Harper, Colophon.

Tinker, I. 1974. The widening gap between men and women at almost every level of society. *International Development Review* 16: 40-42.

Tinker, I. and M. B. Bramsen, eds. 1976. *Women and world development*. Washington, D.C.: Overseas Development Council.

Torres-Rioseco, A. 1959. *The epic of Latin American literature*. Berkeley and Los Angeles: Univ. of California Press.

U.S. Congress. 1978. *Women in public office*, 2d ed. Washington, D.C.: U.S. Government Printing Office.

Vetter, B. M., ed. 1980. *Manpower Comments* 17:8. Washington: Scientific Manpower Commission.

Professional Women in Transition

Lilli S. Hornig

The modern feminist movement is less than two decades old, yet the transformations that have occurred in that short span in the aspirations and expectations of women are enormous, and they have already altered the fabric of our society in irreversible ways. Women have become publicly active participants in that society during these years; to prepare themselves for careers and professional roles they have flocked into colleges, universities, graduate, and professional schools in unprecedented and still growing numbers. In that process, not only has society changed its assumptions about women's place, but so have women themselves. Yet, because success in the professions requires many years of training and experience, many of the effects of this expansion of horizons are still in their early stages; professional women are moving toward equality but they have not attained it yet.

A convenient starting point for an assessment of the issues in this transition of women to full professional status is provided by two early reviews of the status of women in the professions published in 1964: an issue of *Daedalus* called *The Woman in America,* and the proceedings of a conference held at the Massachusetts Institute of Technology under the title *Women and the Scientific Professions.* Also in 1964, the Civil Rights Act outlawed sex-based discrimination in many areas of education and employment, an event that promised somewhat more than it delivered. It did not yet create a new social reality, but it did legitimate the effort to develop one. One of its immediate and important effects was to induce in women the perception that they *could* be equal, and hence that it was realistic to aspire to equality in their own planning for education and professional careers.

That such aspirations were a far cry from the reality which existed in 1964 is amply confirmed by a close reading of the *Daedalus* volume and the record of the MIT symposium. Both are pervaded by an oppressive preoccupation with the functional limitations that Freudian views imposed on women, and an equally oppressive acceptance of the idea that whatever steps toward equality might be possible were not a social responsibility but would have to be taken by women alone. Almost all the contributors believe in the propositions that marriage and family come first, that they must limit women's careers, that women prefer it that way, and that in any case, it is *their* problem. The two volumes are introduced, respectively, by essays by Erik Erikson and Bruno Bettelheim. With a naively benevolent charm, Erikson (1964) elaborates his concept that women's "inner space" must determine what they can and wish to do in life; women's physical structure must set boundaries for their minds and focus their concerns on limited objectives. The theory is based on observations of the play behavior of twelve-year-old children in Berkeley, California. His underlying assumption that anything twelve-year-olds do is shaped so exclusively by biological determinism and remains unaffected by social experience seems to have gone entirely unchallenged. Bettelheim (1965, 15) asserts, rather less innocently and without benefit of evidence, that "as much as women want to be good scientists or engineers, they want first and foremost to be womanly companions of men and to be mothers." Not by accident, these essays set the philosophical framework for the two volumes, in an accurate reflection of conditions in the early 1960's: no one yet questioned whether women's inadequate participation and subordinate roles in the professions might have arisen from some real imperfections in the system of access, training, and rewards; the imperfections were all to be found within women, and therefore could be ameliorated with such band-aids as flexible working hours or continuing education, but they could not be cured. The message, in short, was that women could do better, but they could never do as well as men. Even such a supposedly staunch supporter of women as Jessie Bernard (1965, 166-167) clearly entertained reservations about women's abilities; here is what she suggested for relieving the faculty shortages then existing in engineering: "Women constitute very good material for building a faculty; they tend to prefer teaching to research and writing. They would....be especially useful on engineering faculties where research and consulting take a big bite out of faculty resources. They tend to stay home and mind the store." To drive home the point that women's talents are of a lesser order than men's, Bernard continues:

"Women are most successful as teachers in areas where there is a standard, classic, authoritative body of traditional knowledge to be transmitted....that is increasing at a moderate rather than a rapid rate."

Among over two dozen participants in these two sets of discussions, only Alice Rossi (1964) suggested the possibility of institutional change toward equality, making what she termed "An Immodest Proposal" for improved childcare policies, for changing residential patterns to liberate women from suburban limitations, and for more equal education in the primary grades, with girls taking shop and boys taking cooking.

Several other authors do indeed discuss women in higher education and the scientific professions, pointing a somewhat accusing finger at their low participation and low status. In the context of the other papers, the message of these contributors is that somehow, no matter what advantages are offered, women remain inferior. Providing more of them with access to education and employment might help them to realize such potential as they have, but given the perceived necessities of family life and adaptation to even a cooperative husband's legitimate professional and personal demands, no one holds out much prospect of equal achievement.

The tragedy of that era lay in how many able women not only accepted this judgment without protest but actually came to believe that it might be fair. If even their best efforts led only to subordinate positions in mediocre or segregated institutions, perhaps it was true that they just weren't good enough for real universities. However, there was no way to ascertain that because they were never admitted to the real competition.

At any rate there were too few professionally educated women to have had much impact. In the 1950's and early 1960's the proportion of women Ph.D.s had dropped to a historic low of only ten percent, and the implication many people drew from that fact was that as scientific and scholarly fields had become increasingly sophisticated, women simply hadn't been able to keep up. No one seemed to recognize that the actual numbers of women in these fields had continued to grow substantially; they were just overshadowed by the huge numbers of men who attended college and graduate school on GI benefits and other new forms of support less available to women, including loans.

The idea that women would naturally fade out as modern science advances was simply too appealing to be readily displaced by any more rational explanation. Nonetheless it was soon to be tested.

One result of the 1964 Civil Rights Act and its associated Executive Orders was to generate a number of lawsuits concerning equal opportunity. The pursuit of these legal actions prompted the collection and assembly of massive amounts of statistical data and general information on the education and employment of women. In a parallel development, the infant field of women's studies was born and grew rapidly. These two trends together produced a multitude of insights into the lives of women in general and professional women in particular.

The new findings of research on women and the disaggregation by sex of educational data made explicit many of the barriers to women's educational and professional progress that had existed unchallenged for nearly a century. It became clear, for example, that access to college or graduate school was not equal if men had financial support but women did not. It also became clear that the low proportions of baccalaureates earned by women (thirty-five percent of the total in 1960) could not be blamed solely on women's low aspirations; institutions maintained quotas of various kinds for the admission of women students, often based on the availability of "female beds" (Conable 1977, 112) and such quotas obviously resulted in higher selectivity for women. Hence, women in colleges and graduate schools maintained higher grade point averages than men (Feldman 1974, 18) and women who earned Ph.D.s had better academic records than comparable men (Harmon 1965). Differential admissions were especially marked in professional schools and were generally rationalized with the argument that women were either unlikely to finish their training or, should they do so against all odds, unlikely to practice their professions. It took some time and a good deal of effort to demonstrate that this was a circular argument: if women could not get financial support to the same extent as men, they would *have* to drop out, and if they could not find employment in their professions they could not practice them. Barriers certainly existed, but the most damaging ones were imposed on women by institutional practices.

After nearly twenty years of advocacy for equal opportunity in education and of legal actions to enforce the laws we have, these and many other explicit barriers no longer exist, but they remain of more than historical interest because they have cast long shadows before them. Girls who have been tracked out of math in high school can't go to engineering school; women who graduate from college with degrees in education or "liberal studies" are not prepared to become scientists or physicians. The educational lead times required for entry to the professions are of the order of ten years, and that is already far longer than even an early version of equal opportunity has existed in higher education.

As the barriers fell, then, and - perhaps even more importantly - as young women began to believe that their opportunities would in fact be equal, they flocked into higher education in unprecedented numbers. Currently they are over half of all undergraduates, earn almost half of all bachelor's degrees (National Center for Education Statistics 1980) and about thirty percent of all doctorates (National Academy of Sciences 1981). At the doctorate and professional degree levels, women's growth rate outstrips that at the baccalaureate level, which means that increasing proportions of women who earn bachelor's degrees continue to advanced training (figure 1). Much of the increase in women's participation is occurring in the sciences. Overall, we are witnessing a marked convergence in the educational patterns of men and women with respect to factors such as field distribution, timing, level of achievement and persistence (figure 2).

Are these larger cohorts of women scientists equal in quality to the men? The answer is yes, to the extent that one can assess such an elusive characteristic: "quality" at receipt of the Ph.D. is estimated by a combination of proxy measures - such things as elapsed time since the BA, relative youth, graduating from a good or excellent department, and having had high grades and test scores. By all of these assessments, women Ph.D.s do just as well as men or better, particularly with respect to academic records. Their speedy completion of a doctorate is a phenomenon of the last decade, quite likely accelerated by the equalization of financial aid and financial credit. (National Academy of Sciences 1979, 38).

What accounts for such large-scale and fundamental shifts in educational and career aspirations? For men we are used to explaining such effects by relating them to the employment outlook, the amount of financial aid, the balance between predoctoral and postdoctoral

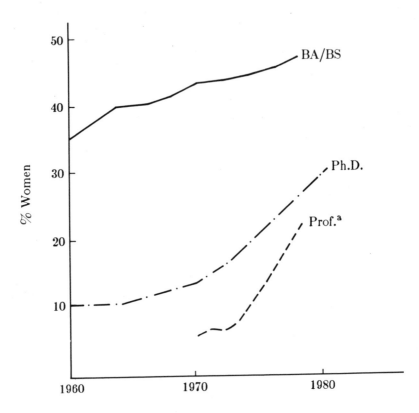

^aProfessional Degrees include MD, JD, DVM.

Figure 1. Percent Degrees to Women

Sources: Compiled from data from National Center for Education Statistics (1980); and National Academy of Sciences (1981).

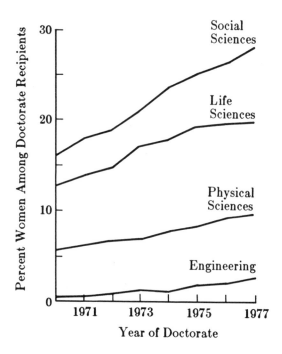

Figure 2. Percent of Doctoral Degrees in Science and Engineering Awarded to Women, 1970-1977

Source: National Academy of Sciences. 1980. *Women Scientists in Industry and Government.* Washington, D.C.: Commission on Human Resources, p. 8.

fellowship support, and the opportunity costs of staying in school versus the long-term benefits of human capital formation. With respect to women, these concepts are only beginning to be used; it is still more usual to discuss women's educational and employment choices in a more personal frame of reference, weighing the benefits of career preparation against the advantages of marriage. Ideas like cost-benefit comparisons and human capital formation may still seem out of place when applied to women. Choices involving marriage and family are commonly supposed to control women's behavior to a much greater extent than professional ones. When asked, women themselves will often respond that their personal decisions take precedence over career considerations - "my family comes first." Yet their behavior does not really bear this out.

Somewhere around 1970 a real discontinuity appeared in all of the educational and employment data involving women. Something quite fundamental seemed to have changed. Young women rather suddenly began making very long-term educational and career commitments in much larger numbers than ever before. Ascribing this simply to equal employment opportunity or affirmative action is a simplistic answer. The increases reflected a more fundamental social change. There is little question that they arose from women's new *perception* that their chances for equal employment were guaranteed by law and that their place in the world was changing. For one thing, divorce statistics made it clear that marriage no longer offered a secure future; at least one woman in three would have to be able to support herself independently and very likely her children too. Women were therefore forced to reassess their future with totally new alternatives - reasonable security grounded in their own careers as opposed to tenuous promises of permanence in depending on a husband. The expectation that high career aspirations could now actually be fulfilled and maintained led them very naturally into sustained education for those careers - not only in science but also in law, medicine, and business.

Through the recognition fostered by career education and support programs that career progress depends in large measure on career continuity, this expectation also led to a quite revolutionary new pattern of women's labor force participation which totally confounded the forecasters in the 1970's. The traditional pattern had been for women to work for a few years after completing their education, then drop out for a fairly lengthy period to raise families, and eventually return in relatively small numbers. This work pattern, or its minor variants, largely accounts for the typically unstructured nature of "women's occupations" which have few upward steps and few rewards for experience, seniority, or quality of performance on the assumption that work experience will be discontinuous and skills may only become rusty but not obsolete. During the 1970's the pattern changed radically to one of essentially uninterrupted labor force attachment; it was this that accounted for the much larger increases in women's labor force participation than had been predicted.

There can be little doubt that this massive shift into the labor market and into permanent work was based on women's expectations of the equal opportunity in education, hiring, promotion, and pay which the new laws seemed to guarantee. How realistic were these expectations for women in the scientific professions? Additionally, did affirmative action make a difference?

To answer these questions, we draw on several studies and comprehensive data sets from which we can determine in some detail the circumstances and conditions of employment for professional women in science fields (Ahern and Scott 1981; National Academy of Sciences, 1979, 1980). Certain generalizations about women scientists' employment as contrasted with men's emerge from these studies.

First, women scientists are far more likely than men to be either unemployed or underemployed (i.e., involuntary part-timers or working outside their field of training because jobs in the field are not available). Figure 3 shows the details of this situation by field; the excess unemployment and underemployment of women is most severe in fields such as physics where jobs are scarce, and least severe in high-demand fields like computer sciences.

Second, male and female scientists are distributed differently in the job market; a larger proportion of women, sixty-seven percent, than of men, fifty-five percent, are employed in academe, while men are much more likely to work in industry. This difference is due only partially to different field distributions (National Academy of Sciences 1979, 59).

Third, although women scientists are overrepresented in academe relative to men, they are distributed very differently both across ranks and among types of institutions. Across all institutional types, the

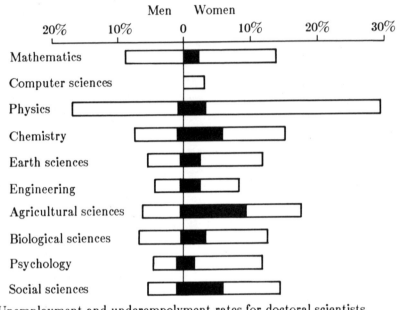

Unemployment and underempolyment rates for doctoral scientists and engineers, 1979

■ Unemployed and seeking   ☐ All underemployed categorie

Figure 3. Unemployment and Underemployment Rates for Doctoral Scientists and Engineers, 1979

Source: Compiled from data from National Academy of Sciences, *Survey of Doctorate Recipients*, 1979.

largest single group of women scientists (between thirty-one and thirty-eight percent) is at the assistant professor level, while the largest single group of men (between thirty-seven and forty-five percent) is at the full professor level (National Academy of Sciences 1979, 60). In the top fifty institutions, however, between thirty and forty percent of all women scientists are in off-ladder positions. Figure 4 details these skewed distributions by institutional rank.

Fourth, overall, women scientists are overrepresented in the least prestigious institutions, at the lower ranks, with correspondingly lower salaries, and underrepresented in industry, where pay is higher. The distributions by work activity (figure 5) and salaries (figure 6) of women in industry parallel those in academe, with women underrepresented at management levels.

Some advances for women were apparent in the mid-1970's, specifically in hiring rates in industry (National Academy of Sciences 1980, 11) and in high-ranking universities, where women accounted for almost half of new (predominantly junior) faculty hires (National Academy of Sciences 1979, 67). In no case, however, did the proportion of women approximate their representation in the Ph.D. pool. Thus, while equal opportunity programs did have some impact, it was limited largely to entry-level positions.

Do the remaining sex differences, then, confirm the old assumptions about the primacy of women's family commitments, lesser dedication to a career, and related factors such as reduced mobility? Two findings - first, that sex differences in career outcomes vary considerably by field and second, that they do not vary significantly by marital or parental status, suggest that the stereotypes cannot explain the results. To test that conclusion, a large sample of female and male academic scientists and humanists matched by field and year of Ph.D., quality of doctoral department, race, and length of professional experience was analyzed (Ahern and Scott 1981). The findings confirmed that objective factors cannot account for the large differences in rank, tenure, promotion rates, and salaries that remain. Some degree of employment discrimination based on sex alone clearly persists despite the laws that prohibit it.

Nevertheless, there are grounds for cautious optimism, because the pre-existing balance has been altered. Women are now about one-fifth of the youngest, more recently trained scientists who are at the cutting

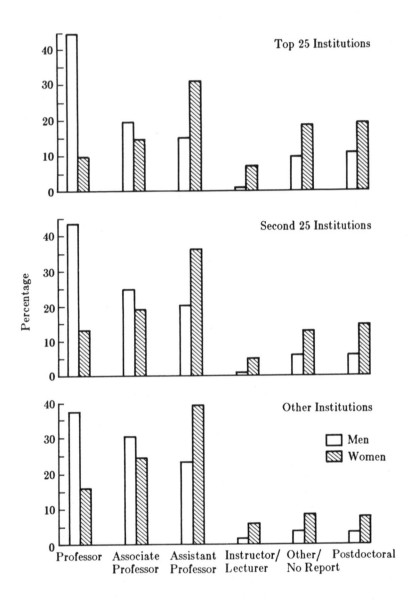

Figure 4. Faculty Rank Distribution of Doctoral Scientists and Engineers by R&D Expenditures of Institution and Sex, 1977

Source: National Academy of Sciences. 1979. *Climbing the Academic Ladder: Doctoral Women Scientists in Academe.* Washington, D.C.: Commission on Human Resources, p. 61.

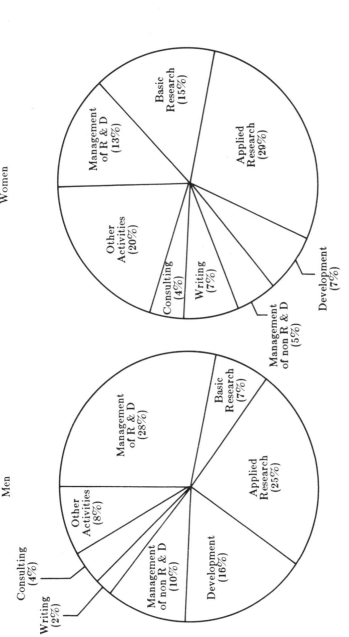

Women

Men

Figure 5. Primary Work Activities of Doctoral Scientists and Engineers in Industry, 1977

Source: National Academy of Sciences. 1980. *Women Scientists in Industry and Government.* Washington, D.C.: Commission on Human Resources, p. 12.

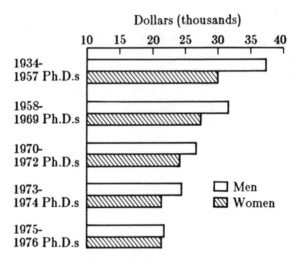

Figure 6. Median Salaries of Doctoral Scientists and Engineers in Industry by Cohort and Sex, 1977

Source: National Academy of Sciences. 1980. *Women Scientists in Industry and Government.* Washington, D.C.: Commission on Human Resources, p. 15.

edge of their disciplines, where in the past there were almost none; some women are achieving the positions of prominence commensurate with their ability and training. The sense of personal failure many women felt in the past has been transmuted into efforts to eradicate the institutional barriers that generated it in the first place. Equality in education and work has turned out to be a moving target, but women have learned to take much better aim.

References

Ahern, N. and E. Scott. 1981. *Career outcomes in a matched sample of men and women Ph.D.s.* Report of the Committee on the Education and Employment of Women in Science and Engineering. Washington, D.C.: Commission on Human Resources.

Bernard, J. 1965. The present situation in the academic world of women trained in engineering. In *Women and the scientific professions,* ed. J. A. Mattfeld and C. G. Van Aken, 163-82. Cambridge: MIT Press.

Bettelheim, B. 1965. The commitment required of a woman entering a scientific profession in present-day American society. In *Women and the scientific professions,* ed. J. A. Mattfeld and C. G. Van Aken, 3-19. Cambridge: MIT Press.

Conable, C. W. 1977. *Women at Cornell: The myth of equal education.* Ithaca, N.Y.: Cornell Univ. Press.

Erikson, E. H. 1964. Inner and outer space: Reflections on womanhood. *Daedalus* 93:582-606.

Feldman, S. D. 1974. *Escape from the doll's house.* New York: McGraw-Hill.

Harmon, L. R. 1965. *High school ability patterns: A backward look from the doctorate.* Scientific Manpower Report No. 6. Washington, D.C.: National Academy of Sciences.

National Academy of Sciences. 1979. *Climbing the academic ladder: Doctoral women scientists in academe.* Report of the Committee on the Education and Employment of Women in Science and Engineering. Washington, D.C.: Commission on Human Resources.

——————————. 1980. *Women scientists in industry and government.* Report of the Committee on the Education and

Employment of Women in Science and Engineering. Washington, D.C.: Commission on Human Resources.

—————————. 1981. *Summary report. 1980 Doctorate recipients from United States universities.* Washington, D.C.: National Research Council.

National Center for Education Statistics. *The condition of education 1980.* Washington, D.C.: National Center for Education Statistics.

Rossi, A. S. 1964. Equality between the sexes: An immodest proposal. *Daedalus* 93:607-52.

Changing Patterns of Recruitment
and Employment

Betty M. Vetter

Fifteen years ago, or even ten, we would not have gathered at a national conference to examine the status of women in the sciences. There were almost too few to call a meeting. The single most important change in the U.S. labor force that has occurred since the Industrial Revolution is the precipitous entry of women over the past decade. Although the majority of professional women are still employed in traditionally female occupations such as nursing and elementary school teaching, women also are changing the makeup of the technological labor force.

Once before, women made a significant dent in the sturdy armor of the male science community. During the decade of the 1920's, women earned twelve of every one hundred Ph.D.'s awarded in science and engineering, but this was a higher proportion than they ever would again until 1975. The depression of the 1930's, World War II in the 1940's and the G.I. bill for returning veterans led into the 1950's when women's share of the science and engineering doctorates dropped below seven percent. However, slowly in the 1960's and faster and faster in the 1970's, their proportions rose again (figure 1).

There weren't a lot of Ph.D.'s awarded before World War II - less than 8,000 in the 1920's, 16,000 in the 1930's and 20,000 in the 1940's. The physical and mathematical sciences were dominant, with the life science and social science degrees trailing behind.

In the fifties, the number of science and engineering Ph.D.'s jumped to 53,000, only 3,500 of them earned by women. One hundred five thousand were awarded in the 1960's and 187,000 in the 1970's. In this past decade, women earned fifteen of every one hundred Ph.D.'s awarded in these fields (figure 2).

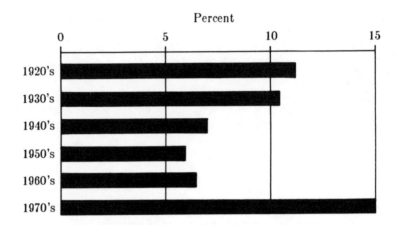

Figure 1. Percent of Science and Engineering Doctorates Earned by Women. 1920's - 1970's

Sources: Compiled from data from National Academy of Sciences. 1970-1979. *Doctorate Recipients from United States Universities, Summary Reports;* and *Doctorates Awarded 1920 to 1971 by Subfield of Doctorate, Sex and Decade,* March 1973. Washington, D. C.: National Research Council.

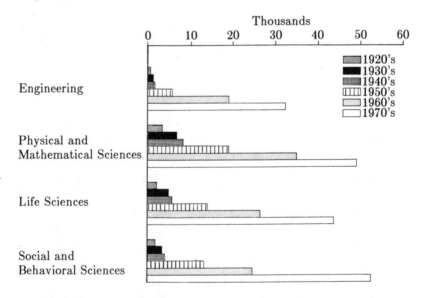

Figure 2. Doctorate Degrees Awarded, 1920's - 1970's

Sources: Compiled from data from National Academy of Sciences. 1970-1979. *Doctorate Recipients from United States Universities, Summary Reports;* and *Doctorates Awarded 1920 to 1971 by Subfield of Doctorate, Sex and Decade,* March 1973. Washington, D.C.: National Research Council.

The 1970's also saw the end of domination by the physical and mathematical sciences. Life science degrees pulled ahead by 1976 and the social and behavioral sciences shot above all of the natural science fields.

Since 1970, women have doubled their share of Ph.D.'s in science and engineering, rising from nine percent of the total in 1970 to twenty-one percent in 1979. Their proportions are highest, of course, in the fields where they tend to concentrate - psychology, biological sciences and social sciences (figure 3).

Further, these are the fields where the total number of graduates has held steady or continued to increase over the decade, while the number in the physical sciences and engineering has dropped. The decreases are at least in part a response to the recession of the early 1970's, when widespread unemployment also brought higher unemployment rates for scientists and engineers - rates which even at their worst, remained far below that of the general population. Men reacted by slowing their race to graduate school, but women came in increasing numbers.

The unemployment rate for all doctoral scientists and engineers in 1979 was only nine-tenths of a percent, slightly below the one and two-tenths percent rate of both 1973 and 1977.

However, these unemployment rates, as small as they are, are not proportionately distributed by sex. For every field except computer science and in every year, the proportion of women Ph.D.'s who were unemployed and seeking work was two to five times higher than for men. In 1979, although unemployment was low for all Ph.D. scientists and engineers, it was four times higher for women than for men. Only eleven of every one hundred doctoral scientists and engineers are women, but thirty-two of every one hundred who are unemployed and seeking work are women.

The unemployment rates differ by field, ranging from zero for both sexes in computer science to an astonishing nine percent for women in the agricultural sciences. For both sexes combined, the biological and social sciences have the highest unemployment rates (figure 4).

Women scientists not only have more difficulty finding employment than do men with comparable education and experience, they also find it more difficult to advance as we can see by examining their salaries. Annual salaries of scientists and engineers vary by degree

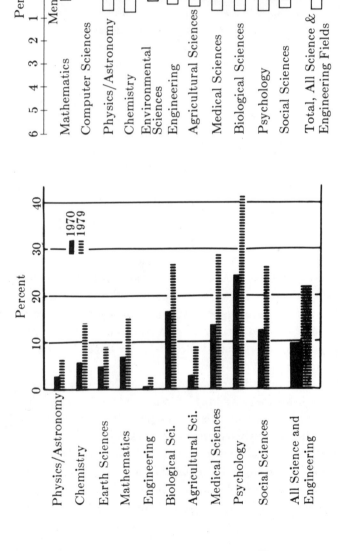

Figure 3. Proportion of Doctorates Earned by Women 1970 and 1979

Source: Compiled from data from National Academy of Sciences. 1970-1979. *Doctorate Recipients from United States Universities, Summary Reports.* Washington, D.C.: National Research Council.

Figure 4. Unemployment Rates of Doctoral Scientists & Engineers, 1970.

Source: Compiled from data from National Academy of Sciences. *Science, Engineering and Humanities Doctorates in the United States, 1977 Profile, 1978 Profile and 1979 Profile.* Washington, D.C.: National Research Council.

level, by field, by age, and by employment sector. They also vary by sex within each of these categories. In 1979, the salaries of women doctoral scientists and engineers were lower than those of men in all fields and at every level of experience. The salary difference widens with years of professional experience, indicating the slower promotions for women, but even at entry into the workforce immediately following a doctorate, women's salaries lagged $2,200 or eleven percent below men's. This difference was greater in 1979 than in 1973 (figure 5).

However, there is improvement in the entering salary gap among bachelor's graduates, at least for some fields. Offers by government, business and industry to new women baccalaurate graduates continue to be below offers to men in most fields, but average offers to women engineering graduates are about $250 a year higher than the offers to men. That's only seventy cents a day, but it is important because engineering is the only field where it occurs. Average offers to women in chemistry are only $250 less than to men. In the social sciences, men are starting out $1,500 ahead of women, and in the health professions, they are offered more than $3,000 per year above the offers to women with whom they graduate (figure 6).

Starting salaries are also an indicator of the job market. The more rare a needed commodity, the higher the price that is paid for it. Thus, graduates in the humanities get average salary offers that are almost $8,000 per year below the average offers to graduates in chemical engineering. Physical scientists and computer scientists average about $4,500 more than social scientists at the end of a bachelor's degree.

There is overwhelming evidence that men and women scientists are not yet equal in terms of their opportunities for employment and for advancement. Women do not get paid as much as similarly qualified men. These inequalities and the reasons for them have been the subject of numerous studies, articles, books and lectures. Some authors suggest that the difference lies in the greater number of publications by men. But even Jonathan Cole, whose book *Fair Science* (1979) attempts to prove that women scientists with Ph.D.'s are as likely as men to find good jobs in academe, found the women in his study holding significantly lower rank than the men [from the same Ph.D. class] twelve years after the Ph.D. He (1979, 77) found "no evidence ... that prolific women are systematically excluded from or

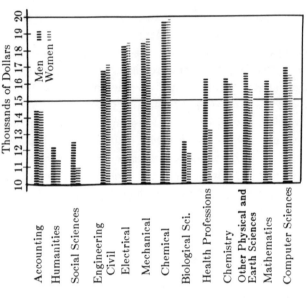

Figure 6. Beginning Offers to Bachelor's Graduates, 1979

Source: College Placement Council. 1979. *CPC Salary Survey, A Study of Beginning Offers, 1978-79, Final Report.* Bethlehem, Penn.: College Placement Council.

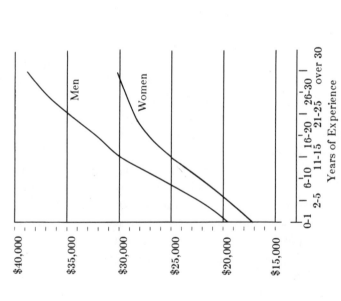

Figure 5. Salaries of Full Time Ph.D. Scientists and Engineers 1979

Source: National Academy of Sciences. 1980. *Science, Engineering and Humanities Doctorates in the United States, 1977 Profile, 1978 Profile* and *1979 Profile.* Washington, D.C.: National Research Council.

pushed out of good science departments," but he did find that these prolific women "are not nearly as likely to hold high-ranking positions ... as are their equally prolific male colleagues." So much for the theory that lower publishing rates are responsible for women's failure to advance as fast as their male cohorts.

Some attribute the difference to the fact that women's careers are interrupted for family and child care, but Helen Astin (1969) found that nine of ten women Ph.D.'s never left the labor force, and other studies since have corroborated this finding.

Marriage itself has been blamed for the average woman's inferior position in science - because she has a family to care for and cannot devote herself to her career; because of old nepotism rules (generally now abolished) that restrict her employment opportunities; because she is not mobile, and can't take advantage of opportunities; because she is too mobile, not staying in the same place long enough to achieve tenure; and most recently, even because married women are more likely to settle in large urban centers, thus somehow affecting their promotions by limiting "their freedom to make strategic job shifts to advance their careers." (Marwell, Rosenfeld, and Spilerman 1979, 1228). It makes one wonder how many great job offers at universities women scientists have rejected to stay in their community colleges!

If "marriage" is the key to women's lack of advancement, then surely single women must find jobs and advance as easily as men. However, several studies have found this not to be the case. Married women scientists publish more than single ones; and the advancement of single women scientists as a group is well behind that of men (married or single) in the same field from the same Ph.D. cohort (Centra 1974, Cole 1979).

Whatever the reasons that women have not advanced as fast or as far as men, the situation still continues even for women who graduated after discrimination became illegal; that is, for those who earned their doctorates after 1970.

One example of this can be seen in the academic rank in 1979 of men and women who earned Ph.D.'s in science and engineering between 1970 and 1974. Among the academically employed men, nine and four-tenths percent were full professors compared to only four percent of the women. Forty-two percent of the men, but only twenty-eight percent of the women had advanced to associate professor rank.

Importantly, less than one percent of the men were still instructors compared to four percent of the women. Similar if less dramatic results show up for the 1979 faculty who earned their doctorates between 1975 and 1978 (National Academy of Sciences 1980).

Despite the inequalities still existing between the sexes and whatever the reasons for them, most indicators show continuing improvement in the status of women in science, even if that improvement comes more slowly than some of us would like. What can be done to improve these opportunities more rapidly? First of all, we can try to see where the best opportunities exist, and where the forecasts indicate that they will exist a few years from now, and encourage more women to head in these directions, rather than into fields that already are oversupplied.

Where opportunities are and are expected to be is mostly in industry. Neither academic hiring nor government hiring can expand as both did in the 1960's; the first because of the demographics of the student age population and the second because of the increasing reluctance of taxpayers to support government in the manner to which it became accustomed in earlier years. Of course, basic research will continue to be performed in academe, and it will also continue in industry, along with applied research, development, testing, manufacturing and selling.

The mix of science specialists employed by industry is significantly different than that in academe; and the job outlook is better in some fields than in others. We can examine both the current status and some projections of supply and demand in science and engineering. The Department of Labor (1980) now projects 2,700,000 more college graduates by 1985 than the number of job openings which will require a college degree. This means that one graduate in every four will not find a job which previously required a college education (figure 7).

The good news in that statistic is that some fields will have much less surplus than others, and some fields such as computer science are even projecting shortages. Engineering and the physical and environmental science fields are much closer in balance than are the life sciences, the behavioral sciences, and the social sciences.

Looking in more detail at the science and engineering fields, we find that even today some look better than others. If we compare the proportion of all job offers by industry in broad fields with the

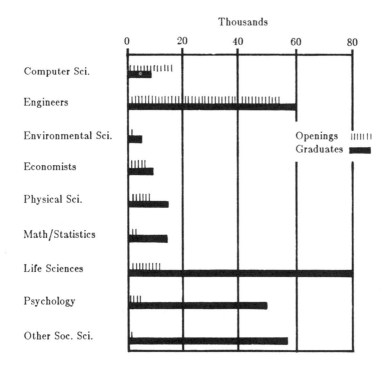

Figure 7. Average Annual Openings and Average Annual Bachelor's Graduates, 1976-1985

Source: Compiled from data from U.S. Department of Labor. 1979. *Occupational Projections and Training Data,* Bulletin 2020. Bureau of Labor Statistics. Washington, D.C.: U.S. Government Printing Office.

proportion of all job offers by industry in those same fields in 1979, we find that graduates in engineering, business and math or computer sciences received a higher proportion of offers than their proportion of earned degrees Graduates in the physical sciences are approximately in balance with job offers, while social science, life science and humanities graduates have a much lower share of job offers than their share of earned degrees (College Placement Council 1979; National Center for Education Statistics 1948-1978).

The professional entry level for engineering is the bachelor's degree, but approximately a third of the bachelor's graduates can be expected to earn a graduate degree, either in engineering or in some other field. Women earned ten percent of the bachelor's degrees granted in 1980, six percent of the master's and three percent of the Ph.D.'s.

The demand for engineers has been high over the past eight years. Both the number of offers made to engineering graduates and the beginning salary levels that we examined earlier indicate present strong demand, which is expected to remain generally strong over most of the present decade. Indeed, real shortages already exist and are projected to worsen for engineering faculty members. Far too few U.S. students are continuing their graduate education to the Ph.D., and a third of the engineering doctorates awarded last year were to non-citizens on temporary visas. Women who can and wish to prepare themselves to move into faculty slots in engineering should find ample opportunity for employment. Because faculty salaries are well below those paid by industry, earnings would not be as high as in industrial employment where opportunities at all degree levels also can be expected to be good. If you'd like to work in academe, however, engineering needs you.

Another field already experiencing acute faculty shortages, and for many of the same reasons of high salaries and lots of offers at the end of the bachelor's degree - is computer science. Comparing projections for the number of graduates to the number of anticipated openings, we find a huge surplus of jobs over available graduates in computer sciences at least through the middle of the decade. In mathematics, on the other hand, the number of job openings is far below the number of graduates anticipated. Many of these mathematics majors, provided they have acquired backgrounds in applied mathematics, will move to computer science jobs (U.S. Department of Labor 1979).

Chemistry graduates will be approximately in balance with openings, since many baccalaureate graduates move on into medicine or other fields. Geology and physics also are expected to be approximately in balance, since the majority of persons seeking a career in these fields will obtain an advanced degree. Physics has been oversupplied with graduates over the past several years, but the smaller number of graduates anticipated will bring the supply closer into balance with employment opportunities

Despite a steady increase in job growth in the life sciences over the past three decades, the number of persons trained in many of these fields has exceeded the number of job openings. Unemployment rates, particularly for women in agriculture and a lesser extent the biosciences, are significantly higher than among physical scientists or engineers. The high unemployment rate for women in the agricultural sciences appears in every data set at all degree levels. (National Academy of Sciences 1980; National Science Foundation 1980).

Salary levels also reflect a weaker marketplace for some life scientists than for other natural scientists. Starting salaries for men with bachelor's degrees in biology are only seventy-eight percent of those in chemistry and seventy-four percent of those in computer sciences, for example. Among women, the differences are even wider. Women graduates in biology get average starting offers more than $4,000 per year below the offers to women graduates in chemistry. Agriculture graduates average more than $5,000 per year below those in computer science (College Placement Council 1979).

The supply of life scientists is expected to stay well above the number of job openings over the next decade. The number of Ph.D. and master's graduates expected each year to 1985 exceeds the average number of job openings, so that biology and agriculture graduates with only a bachelor's degree may have little opportunity for employment in these fields (U.S. Department of Labor 1979).

Social and behavioral scientists are about twelve percent of all scientists and engineers in the United States, and almost twenty-eight percent of the doctoral population. In 1978, the National Science Foundation estimates that there were almost 337,000 social and behavioral scientists in the United States, of whom thirty percent were women. Psychologists had the largest representation, making up forty

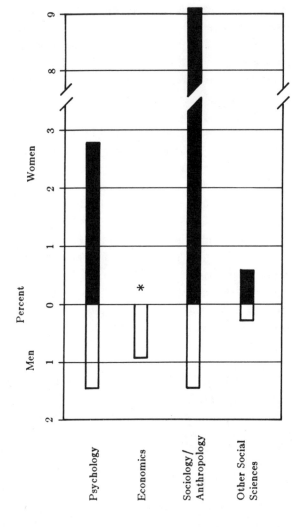

Figure 8. Unemployment Rates, 1978
Source: National Science Foundation. *U.S. Scientists and Engineers: 1978, Detailed Statistical Tables*, NSF 80-304. Washington, D.C.: National Science Foundation.

percent of the total. Although sociologists and anthropologists were the smallest group within this field, women were least represented among economists.

As is true in other fields, the unemployment rates for women are much higher than for men. Among women in sociology and anthropology, more than nine percent were reported as unemployed and seeking work in 1978 compared to one and one-half percent of men (figure 8).

Among doctorate psychologists in 1979, the unemployment rate was less than one percent for men but twice as high for women. In the social sciences, only seven-tenths percent of men but three and one-half percent of women were unemployed and seeking work (figure 9).

The Bureau of Labor Statistics anticipates about 5,600 openings per year for psychologists between 1976 and 1985 - less than half the number of master's and Ph.D.'s expected to be awarded. In sociology, anthropology and political science, the squeeze is even tighter, with fewer job openings anticipated than Ph.D.'s (figure 12). Persons with only a bachelor's degree in these fields will find few professional opportunities.

In economics on the other hand, the 6,400 annual job openings anticipated exceeds the number of master's and Ph.D.'s expected so that some opportunity will be available even at the bachelor's level. Except in economics, the number of qualified workers in the social and behavioral sciences is expected to be larger than the number of job openings at least to the middle of the decade. However, an education in the social sciences provides a background that should enable graduates to work effectively in the non-traditional areas where many will find employment.

At the doctorate level, forty-five percent of all persons awarded Ph.D.'s between 1970 and 1985 are expected to enter non-traditional employment; that is, take a job that does not or has not in the past required a doctorate degree. By 1976, some 80,000 Ph.D.'s were in such non-traditional jobs - some by choice and some because they could not find employment in a typical PhD. situation. (Braddock 1978).

We have already examined the projections in the science fields in some detail. In engineering, although some non-traditional employment exists, a shortage of doctoral engineers also exists and is expected to worsen. Note that the most severe surpluses anticipated by 1985 are

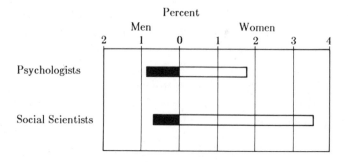

Figure 9. Unemployment Rates for Ph.D.'s, 1979

Source: National Academy of Sciences. *Science, Engineering and Humanities Doctorates in the United States, 1977 Profile, 1978 Profile* and *1979 Profile.* Washington, D.C.: National Research Council.

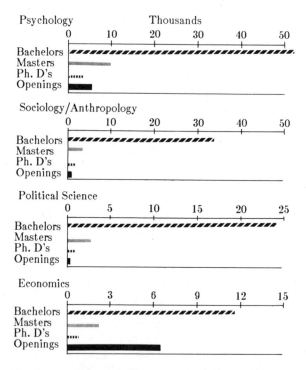

Figure 10. Average Annual Degrees and Employment Openings, 1976-1985

U.S. Department of Labor, 1979. *Occupational Projections and Training Data,* Bulletin 2020. 1979. Bureau of Labor Statistics. Washington, D.C.: U.S. Government Printing Office.

in the arts and humanities and education. This does not mean that these additional doctorates need waste their talents or their education. It does mean that many highly educated people will be entering employment that is different from the kind of employment found by Ph.D.'s in the past.

Many opportunities in science and engineering will depend upon the decisions of the federal government, including the amounts of money appropriated for activities utilizing large numbers of persons with technological training. Congressional decisions for funding energy programs, environmental activities, defense procurement, health care and a host of other national enterprises will affect the demand for scientists and engineers. We presently have a shortage of toxicologists, for example, because of new requirements in the Environmental Protection Act.

We cannot always forecast what these government decisions will be. Neither can we predict that unexpected discovery or happening that will change the forecasts, although we can be quite sure that something unexpected will occur. For example, the projections of supply and demand in the life sciences were made before the industrial potential of recombinant DNA was seriously considered. This may or may not change the number of opportunities for persons in the related doctoral specialties.

It is important to remember when examining projections of supply and demand that there is a difference between demand and need. The difference is money. No matter how many scientists and engineers may be needed to accomplish some national objective, none can be hired until money is available to pay for their services.

Over the next decade, the nation's needs for technologically trained experts will not have diminished. We will still be trying to produce adequate, clean energy; maintain a habitable environment; and provide affordable health care, while maintaining our national defense. The state of the economy and the reordering of priorities by different administrations will all affect the relative demand among the various areas of science and engineering.

Patterns of recruitment and employment are changing, and one of those changes is the recognition that women are in science and engineering to stay. Their numbers will continue to increase and their proportion of the total technological community will continue to grow.

Ultimately, I believe they will have equal opportunity with men to share in all aspects of the scientific enterprise. However, this will not happen by itself. We have come a long way, but we cannot stop to rest on our laurels. If we may paraphrase Robert Frost, we still have promises to keep and miles to go before we sleep.

References

Astin, H. 1969. *The woman doctorate in America.* New York: Russell Sage Foundation.

Braddock, D. 1978. The oversupply of Ph.D.'s to continue through 1985. *Monthly Labor Review* 101:48-50.

Centra, J. 1974. *Women, men and the doctorate.* Princeton, N.J.: Educational Testing Service.

Cole, J. R. 1979. *Fair science: Women in the scientific community.* New York: Free Press.

College Placement Council. 1979. *CPC Salary Survey, A Study of Beginning Offers, 1978-79, Final Report.* Bethlehem, Penn.: College Placement Council.

Marwell, G., R. A. Rosenfeld and S. Spilerman. 1979. Geographic constraints on women's careers in academia. *Science* 205: 1225-31.

National Academy of Sciences. 1980. *Science, engineering and humanities doctorates in the United States: 1979 Profile.* Washington, D.C.: Commission on Human Resources.

National Center for Education Statistics. *Earned Degrees Conferred,* Series of annual reports, 1947-48 through 1977-78. Washington, D.C.: National Center for Education Statistics.

National Science Foundation. 1980. *U.S. Scientists and engineers 1978, detailed statistical tables,* NSF 80-304. Washington, D.C.: National Science Foundation.

U.S. Department of Labor. 1979. *Occupation projections and training data.* Bulletin 2020. Bureau of Labor Statistics. Washington, D.C.: U.S. Government Printing Office.

——————————————. 1980. *Occupational projections and training data, 1980 edition.* Bulletin 2052. Bureau of Labor Statistics. Washington, D.C.: U.S. Government Printing Office.

Planning Strategies for Women in Scientific Professions

Jewel Plummer Cobb

Strategy is defined in the dictionary as "skillful management in getting the better of an adversary or attaining an end." For women in scientific professions, the adversary is society which says that sex differences mean impediments for women and superiority for men. In our Conference at Purdue it is science on which we focus our attention. We must share ideas to bring about change.

There are several important measures of successful change for women in scientific professions. These include (1) when the proportion of women in a field is no longer an issue; (2) when parents no longer perceive of their little girl's interest in math as unusual or odd; (3) when the salaries of women in science and technology are equal to the salaries of men; (4) when there are as many women as men working in science-based industries, in science branches in governments, or in science departments of public and private institutions with bachelor's, master's or doctoral degrees in such fields as industrial, mechanical, civil, chemical, or electrical engineering, geology, computer science, textile, plastics, ceramic engineering, mining, petroleum or electro-optics engineering; or (5) when women are moving easily around the country in management positions as metallurgists, geophysicists, environmental scientists, botanists, radiologists, hydrologists, organic chemists, physical chemists, accounting and marketing specialists, to name only a few.

Regarding existing sex differences, of those employed in research and development in 1974 only five percent of one-half million scientists and engineers were women. In 1977 less than six percent of a little more than one-half million were so employed and, of course, that's too low. Among scientists, women are a bit over thirteen percent of the total. In this small group, however, women below the doctorate level are working principally in research as laboratory assistant personnel. They are more likely to be working in basic research, less likely in applied research, much less likely to be in development and less than half as likely as men to be engaged in administration or management of research and development.

In the 1980's, women scientists and engineers are more likely than men to be employed in education where more than fifty percent of basic research occurs and demographers' projections of the job market for new engineering faculty at least, appear promising. Women are less likely to be in industry or government. One of the fastest growing areas is research and development in industry - precisely where few women are now found. Within academe, women scientists are less likely than men to be employed by the top fifty universities, but are more likely than men to be in two and four-year colleges. Women have doubled their share of bachelor's degrees and almost tripled their proportion of Ph.D.'s since 1960, according to Betty Vetter (see her chapter in this volume). The employment of women in engineering and women scientists with doctorates increased from seven and seven-tenths percent to nine and seven-tenths percent in 1977. This increase was at a faster rate than men. However, in 1978 there were still only 19,800 women versus 1,248,500 men. Although fast growth rates for computer scientists and engineers continue, women represent only a small fraction of doctorate-holders in this area. Growth rates were large in the social science fields, which had fourteen percent in 1977. Women are concentrated in psychology, life sciences and social sciences, while men are in engineering and physical sciences. The number of jobs projected for the areas women are currently concentrated in are far lower than the number of trained professionals; it is appropriate that we encourage women to enter the other fields in greater numbers.

Strategy Number One

Remind parents-to-be that girls' images of themselves are made in part by the adults who help to shape the mind-body concept of the child. The issues of biological and social causations of sexual differences involve a complex series of circumstances that span cultural and geographical boundaries. That sex differences do exist is obvious from a physical examination of the newborn baby. The problem arises when parents attach a series of "imperfections" and different social rewards to female children. The evidence in this decade for a linkage of spatial ability and cerebral lateralization with subsequent cognitive tasks is fragile and exaggerated. While sex differences in certain cognitive abilities are well known, such as higher verbal ability in women and greater spatial perception in men, on the average, the results of a review of all studies on the effects of prenatal sex hormones on general intelligence are fairly negative. Ehrhardt and Meyer-Bahlburg (1980, 1317) report that the "relatively well-controlled studies seem to indicate a lack of any positive effect of prenatal androgens, progestogens and estrogens on postnatal mental functioning. Effects of prenatal sex hormones on sex-dimorphic cognitive abilities have usually not been demonstrated in those few studies in which this issue has been investigated." There is no direct evidence that all girls have poorer spatial performance and that performance is linked by biologic virtue to general cognitive ability. A discussion of these sophisticated sexist conclusions now abroad in the literature was ably presented by Helen Lambert (1978), who comments that sex differences in brain lateralization might well be the popular version of "Biology is women's destiny."

Until I have proof that is unequivocal and stripped of socialization variables, I cannot accept sex differences in intellectual capacity in mathematics, for example, as valid. Neither can I accept the stereotypical response that girls are just "shy" or don't really like sports or simply can't do math. The scarcity of women in science and mathematics in college and beyond is not due to a sex-linked trait. When we begin to factor out all the variables, I will then look at the data. History shows us that in a conservative political era we are likely to find reversion to maximizing differences - defects among people as the cause of all problems - another way of blaming the victim. I would decry the day that parents really believe that girls are just not capable of the same mathematical achievement as boys. This gender related attitude smacks of the same unfortunate cloth that Jensen (1969) and Schockley (1971) portray in relation to Blacks and intelligence.

The main point here is that childhood sex-roles are established early, beginning literally in the crib. If parents can watch carefully their behavior in the home that signals to female children to desist, check or "don't do," they may avoid the stifling of free body behavior. We know that children learn behavior through contiguity and that sex behavior is shaped very early in the home. The female child learns at two, three and four years of age certain sex-linked behavior, and that passivity and dependency are generally acceptable. Stereotypes of feminine passivity for girls or masculine aggressiveness for boys are encouraged by parents, and their behavior is culture-bound.

A strategy for us as parents and prospective parents should include a campaign to develop spatial skills in our preschool daughters as we do in our sons. For a child this involves playing with toys that utilize shapes, physical links and structures that challenge them and capture their attention. Creative toys that maximize the use of moving parts or interconnecting construction toys now abound. If a girl is going to play dolls and use a doll house as her mother did, why can't we have her build the doll house as would her brother? A chemistry set for boys is really exactly the same as the chemistry involved in cooking, but we give girls only the cups and saucers to move around and none of the solutions, mixes and powders to make the "food"!

Strategy Number Two

If we're really to combat the ceaseless, pervading socialization that sets in early for girls, we as parents and teachers will have to carry out planned programming for girls to master numbers or mathematics and physics in grade school. Girls' exposure to the average elementary school teacher, who is most often a woman with whom she identifies, conveys at a most unconscious level anxiety about numbers and the physical sciences. In contrast, I witnessed recently a Saturday school in Atlanta where girls and boys were immersed in an exciting teaching mode called Discovery Learning. In that classroom of ten to fourteen-year-olds, I observed excitement and fun in solving a geometry problem by equal numbers of girls and boys. Yet, how often do we translate our negative expectations for girls in a class on physics and math? This has been documented very clearly in a study by John Ernest (1976) who questioned a sample of elementary school teachers about their attitudes on teaching math. Although all questioned said they enjoyed teaching math better than other subjects, forty-one percent felt that boys did better in math and none felt that girls did better. Hence, a strong program is needed to sensitize the teachers of sixth through eighth-graders in terms of subtle "put downs" that can be exercised unknowingly.

Strategy Number Three

Another strategy involves developing a school-wide program of motivational tactics for teenage girls. These can be science clubs or special groups after school. National institutions like the "Y's" should write new policy directives that include science literacy for youth, in this case for the millions of young women in their membership. I remember in high school I was part of a "Y" teen club called the Girl Reserves. Our motto went something like this: Gracious in Manner, Impartial in Judgement, Ready for Service, Loyal to Friends and so on for the remaining eight letters in our name. I suggest that one of the "S's" should have been Superior in Science. The YWCA, YWHA, Campfire Girls, Girl Scouts and related community-based programs for girls can include prizes for solving science puzzles, building new mechanical inventions, or math bees in place of spelling bees and knitting bees.

Despite equal scores in mathematics and science achievement tests for girls and boys at age nine, a study showed that at ages thirteen, seventeen and twenty-six to thirty-five, males perform increasingly better than females (National Assessment of Educational Progress 1978). It is distressing, but not surprising. As girls and boys proceed through school, they are subject to pressures to conform to societal expectations of sex-appropriate behavior and interests.

Strategy Number Four

Perhaps one of the most difficult challenges is to break down the barriers of mathematics understanding by adult women. Mini-courses can be designed and taught through the numerous advising centers now available as outreach functions of colleges and universities. We tried the following in Douglass College with some success. We decided that a group of twelve older women was the critical size. The leader was a woman skilled in teaching mathematics and she approached the problem by combining math skills with group dynamics. The women shared anxieties and talked to each other about how awful they were with numbers. Each meeting became a mixture of free "confessions," complaining and also learning how to be comfortable with the vocabulary and the operations necessary in pre-college math. As confidence grew by practice *and* understanding, the women in the group gained courage to use their information and to eventually take a college course in statistics or in calculus.

Strategy Number Five

The fifth strategy should include sensitization of male college science professors and college administrators to think about ways in which they can encourage women to major and progress in science. Spot the blossoming woman math scholar and take an extra moment to let her know that her performance on the last test or the recent lab experiment write-up was really very good. A study has shown us that girls are twice as likely as boys to conclude that a poor grade in math was due to a lack of ability rather than a lack of effort. Unfortunately, male science faculty predominate in most colleges and universities except for some women's colleges, and an implied, if not spoken, message gets across to students that science is for males. Poor self-image in math is common among women. Furthermore, women students are not encouraged by family and society to "stick it out" with math. Men are encouraged because certain careers they want will require a mathematics background. Therefore, this extra encouragement of women is needed. Creative new activities can be developed. As a woman scientist, maximize the opportunity to develop innovative programs for the women faculty and students in your department if you are in an educational institution, or assume the same leadership role in your industry group. One such program might be to plan a series of weekly or biweekly seminars where women doing research in your discipline are invited to speak. The invitee is a role model for those who are younger or less developed scientifically. She is a connecting link and entree for you to visit her lab because of shared research interests. It is also a chance for the visiting speaker to know about you as a woman scientist. She is a new scientific connection through whom a new job may develop or an invitation to give a paper at a prestigious national or international meeting in your field may develop.

Strategy Number Six

When I was Dean of Douglass College, I invited women faculty and students to my home to discuss some common concerns of new women faculty and graduate students at the University . Once a month we had a brown bag lunch and discussed ways to help each other. One month we talked about mentoring. It turned out that very few women faculty in our group had ever thought about a mentor! This means that as graduate students they never consciously looked around them to see who among those professors could advise them, not only in day-to-day affairs, but also with long range plans, and give them their aggressive support. The graduate students who were present suddenly had a revelation, and after that meeting I expected that they'd plan their strategies.

The sponsor of my research project was my mentor and he was a male. I knew in the 1940s in graduate school at NYU that I had to pick a scientist to work under for my research and I selected one of my three professors who, in an intuitive way, seemed genuinely interested in me; it was a wise choice. There was no woman professor for me to select as a mentor. I didn't have any women professors, except one who was not eligible to take on graduate students! My main point here is to select a mentor and she may have to be a male!

Strategy Number Seven

Join the women's caucus of your professional society and offer your help on committees associated with the group. Some caucuses are better organized than others; some are waiting for your leadership. These groups are invaluable in identifying policy issues, unfair employment practices and major goals for the national agenda. At a more personal level, you can meet women scientists at other institutions who may invite you to visit or who can alert you to a job opening you didn't know about. We must work at our version - in the positive sense - of the "old boy's network."

Strategy Number Eight

Try to bring to the attention of your various constituencies, whether they be associated directly or indirectly with an educational institution, the following suggested programs that can be instituted whether they are government sponsored or not.

ABD (all but the final degree) Two-year Non-tenured Woman Science Professorship. To facilitate research that will enhance a woman's opportunity for tenure either at her present institution or at some other, a two-year fellowship might allow her to work with a research team full-time or to complete the writing of a science book, for example. Such fellowships at the non-tenured level can be justified as "remedial" until women are as significant a portion of senior tenured faculty at major institutions as they are of the Ph.D. pool, small though this group is.

Dissertation Completion Award. This would be a variation of the ABD two-year non-tenured woman science professorship, in which support would be provided only for the completion of the dissertation.

One-half Time Ph.D. at Ranking Institutions. Women awardees would be provided partial support for a three-year period at top-rank institutions where they would be able to acquire the kind of background which would be of value in moving ahead rapidly in their professions. The other partial support should be provided by their own employing institutions as proof of commitment. Some preference should be given to institutions where the women grantees will have access to mentors who can be useful in support roles and in providing training of another crop of women professionals.

Junior Female Scholar. One-year rather than three-year fellowship-type awards would be made to women who received Honorable Mentions in the regular competition for three-year fellowships. Awardees would be called Junior Female Scholars rather than Fellows because the latter term has a legally defined meaning. Support might be limited to those Honorable Mentions who are planning to do graduate work in fields where women are most under-represented, e.g., engineering, physics, mathematics, economics. These women would doubtless receive some kind of assistance anyway, but these awards would enable them to attend the institutions of their choice.

Reentry Grants. These grants would encourage women who have dropped out to return to the campus to take courses for several semesters and then to apply for a research grant.

Short Courses. This would consist of a series of short or year-long refresher courses, research internships, and/or combinations of these for women scientists who want to re-enter their professional fields.

Female Second-Chance Math. This might be administered as a Student Science Training (SST) program in which the field would be mathematics and the participants would be female. Regular SST programs are normally held during the summer between the junior and senior high school years.

Female Visitation Science Program. Visits would be made to senior high schools and colleges by one prominent woman scientist together with a graduate student, male or female. The objective would be to stimulate and motivate women students through seminars, informal discussions, rap sessions, etc.

Science Career Workshops. A series of workshops would be held to advise women students who are about to begin a search for employment.

Strategy Number Nine

Continue to update your resume and keep it available at all times. Take advantage of opportunities to compete for fellowships, leaves and visiting scientific exchange arrangements in the United States or abroad. Don't immediately say "No, I couldn't leave my department because they will need me next year for committee 'X' or course 'Y'." Do remember *NO ONE IS INDISPENSABLE.*

Strategy Number Ten

The last point and strategy I'd like to suggest concerns the passage of the bill in Congress (Bill #583) on (1) the development of technologies, methods and instructional materials at the undergraduate level to strengthen skills in science and mathematics and to increase student awareness of career opportunities requiring scientific and technical skills, (2) the training and retraining (including inservice training) of faculty, counselors, administrators, and other appropriate personnel at the undergraduate level to improve the ability of such personnel to (a) strengthen the skills in science and mathematics of students whose primary field of study is not scientific or technical, (b) increase student awareness of career opportunities for women in science, particularly in the fields in which women are most seriously underrepresented, and (c) increase student awareness of career opportunities for women requiring basic scientific and technical skills; (3) the awarding of graduate and post-graduate fellowships, and career development grants, directly to individuals and to institutions for award to individuals, without regard to when the individual received an undergraduate degree; (4) research participation, traineeships, work-study, and internship programs; or (5) projects to encourage individuals interested in scientific and technical fields to continue in and complete courses of study leading to degrees in such fields.

Under newly announced budget cuts, we cannot expect all of these programs to be adequately funded in the years ahead. Therefore, we will all have to consider alternative methods for carrying out these programs. They are very important.

References

Ehrhardt, A. A., and H. F. L. Meyer-Bahlburg. 1981. Effects of prenatal sex hormones on gender-related behavior. *Science* 211: 1312-18.

Ernest, J. 1976. *Mathematics and sex.* Santa Barbara: University of California.

Jensen, A.R. 1969. How much can we boost IQ and scholastic achievement. *Harvard Educational Review* 39: 1-123.

Lambert, H. 1978. Biology and equality: A perspective on sex differences. *Signs* 4: 97-117.

National Assessment of Educational Progress. 1978. *Final reports.* Denver, Colorado: Education Commission of the States.

Schockley, W. 1971. Negro IQ deficit: Failure of a 'malicious coincidence' model warrants new research proposals. *Review of Educational Research* 41: 227-28.

Women Scientists and Engineers
in Academe

Academic Career Mobility for Women and Men Psychologists

Rachel A. Rosenfeld

The ideal-typical career in academia involves going as quickly as possible up through the academic ranks at high prestige universities to the goal of being a widely recognized, full professor at a top school. In the process, one's achievements at each step serve to increase one's achievements at the next. Those with a tenure track position at a top university have the colleagial contacts and resources to do research. Since academia purports to be meritocratic and since merit is judged primarily by one's scholarly output, rather than by such other criteria as the quality of one's teaching, one's productivity then serves to increase the probability of promotion. It also increases one's reputation, enhancing one's attractiveness as a potential colleague at a still more prestigious institution. Those with "good track records" and at good universities have better chances of getting research grants and the research assistance and time off from teaching that grants can give. Thus, productivity leads to further productivity and advancement. In the sociology of science, such "accumulation of advantage" has been widely recognized (Allison and Steward 1974; Cole and Cole 1973; Cole 1979).

In comparing men and women as groups, one sees inequality by sex in the extent to which this type of career is followed. Not all men have careers of the ideal-typical kind, but women are even less likely to have them. Academic women are at the lower ranks and at lower prestige institutions than men, and it is precisely at the top institutions that women are least likely to be in the higher, tenured ranks (Howard 1978; Kilson 1976; National Academy of Sciences 1979). Further, in general it takes women longer than men to reach the top ranks (Harmon 1965, 1968; Reagan and Maynard 1974; Robinson 1973), and they have lesser reputations than men (Cole 1979). Such comparisons, how-ever, do not tell us why there are these differences in career outcomes. In this chapter I try to provide more insight into these differences by reviewing the literature on the stages of academic careers and on the ways in which men and women differ at each stage. In addition, at points I use data that I have collected on a sample of male and female academic psychologists (the APA sample), who received Ph.D.'s in 1955-62. The literature on career differences by sex within academia has burgeoned, but the most extensive career data are on scientists, social and otherwise. Therefore, most of the descriptions I give are for academic scientists.

The career stages and processes I examine are as follows: graduate school; the first position; career mobility over the career, including pro-motion up the tenure track ladder; and the roles of productivity and recognition. At each step, I examine how women compare with men and with the ideal-typical career and whether women accumulate advantages to the extent that men do. Since it has long been argued that women's traditional roles in the family preclude involvement in a demanding career (Graham 1978), an additional concern in this review is the extent to which being married and having a family contribute to or distract from women's, and men's, careers.

For the most part, I do not examine sex differences in salary. For one thing, rank is a very strong predictor of salary (Bayer and Astin 1975; Reagan and Maynard 1974), and, to a large extent, differences by sex in salary are explained by differences in rank (Bayer and Astin 1975; Cole 1979; Gordon, Morton, and Braden 1974). There is even some evidence that there is a *negative* relationship between one aspect of a "good" position and salary; that is, that those at the "best" places are paid less than elsewhere, perhaps because of the other advantages offered by such academic institutions (Hansen, Weisbrod, and Strauss 1978). This is not to say that purely economic rewards are not impor-tant. Men and women work, at least in part, to support themselves and their families. Beyond this simple fact, since, in many places at least, some of one's salary level is determined by the distribution of discretionary funds (merit pay), the distribution of economic rewards, especially within a department, could be a very sensitive indicator of women's place in academia. For the moment, however, a focus on broader career patterns seems more useful.

This chapter accepts, for the most part, that the ideal-typical career is the ideal career. In the conclusions, though, I briefly consider the desirability of following such a career, for either men or women, and alternatives to it. Further, one needs to keep in mind that careers take place within a structure of opportunity, the academic labor market, and that conditions in this market are not constant. Most of the research I review has used data on the academics themselves. Very little research has been done on the process of hiring and promotion by universities. Thus, the nature of the data can sometimes give to descriptions of careers the impression that the trajectory a career takes is within the control of the individual. This, of course, is not the complete truth. The number and nature of positions open and the extent to which they are open disproportionately to members of one group or another are crucial at any given time and also vary over time. Descriptions of what individuals do serve as a basis for speculation about what institutions and departments are doing. I return to this issue as well in the conclusions.

Getting the Ph.D.

Much of the literature I review here is in the sociology of science. It is assumed that a person has a Ph.D., the minimum credential required to follow the ideal-typical career. Of course, there are academics without a Ph.D. (though perhaps decreasingly so), but in general it has been difficult to attain the "best" positions without one. Indeed, women have been at a disadvantage in academia because they disproportionately lacked Ph.D.'s (Brown 1967). Getting a Ph.D. is part of a larger educational process. Although women have been more likely than men to finish high school, until about 1975 they were less likely to go on to college (Heyns and Bird 1982). When women have gone on to college, they have been less likely to go on to graduate school; when they have gone to graduate school, they have been less likely to obtain a Ph.D. (Cole 1979, 85; Graham 1978; Heyns and Bird 1982; Zuckerman and Cole 1975, 88-9). For most of the remainder of this paper, I use "academic" and "doctoral scientist" interchangeably, assuming that the academic begins a career with a Ph.D.

The difficulty of combining a family and a career is apparent even in graduate school. Using a 1969 national sample of graduate students,

Feldman (1973) found that women graduate students were less likely than men to be married, but that when they were married, the women were less likely to be full-time students than single women or married or single men (which would imply that it would take them longer to finish if they ever did), and more likely than married men to say that pressure from their spouse would or might cause them to drop out of school. The most committed graduate students in this sample were divorced women.

In past cohorts, women who *have* gotten their Ph.D.'s have taken longer than men to do so and have been older at the time they finished (Centra 1974). They were therefore at a disadvantage as compared with men in achieving the ideal-typical career, since, on average, they could not reach the higher ranks at the normative age or younger (Caplow and McGee 1958, 111; Cole 1979). However, this does not seem to be the case for recent Ph.D. cohorts in most fields (National Academy of Sciences 1979).

Getting a Ph.D. is the first step toward having a "good" academic career. As is true of academic positions in general, the quality of the institution at which one studies is as important as finishing the degree. The quality of one's graduate department affects the prestige of one's later employing institutions and productivity (Cole 1979; Long 1978; Reskin 1979). Going to a more prestigious graduate school may mean getting better training, being in contact with the more eminent members of the field (who provide apprenticeships, examples, and references and contacts), having as peers other graduate students who will later be leaders in the field, and acquiring some of the prestige of the school itself. Reskin's (1979) analysis, for example, separated overall prestige from sponsor's eminence and found continuing effects of both variables on careers of male chemists. Even though young women high school students now go on to college in proportions at least equal to those for men, they continue to go to less prestigious undergraduate institutions (Hearn 1981; Heyns and Bird 1982; Rosenfeld and Hearn 1982). Given the association between selectivity of undergraduate school and prestige of graduate institution (Reskin 1979), one could hypothesize that women, when they do go on, go to graduate schools of lower quality. This, however, does not seem to be the case. Women and men seem to receive their degrees from top departments in their fields in about the same proportions (Cole 1979,

79-80; National Academy of Sciences 1979).

An additional explanation for the effect of prestige of graduate institution on later productivity and location is the "selection" argument; namely, that the best students are selected into the best schools, and that it is the effects of intelligence and ability that appear later. One consistent difference between men and women at departments of all qualities, however, is that the women have somewhat higher I.Q.'s and other measures of ability (Cole 1979; Harmon 1965; National Academy of Sciences 1979). Thus if the selection argument holds, women from the best schools should later do at least as well as men.

Although men and women go proportionately to the same sorts of schools, they might still have different experiences there. The documentation for this is somewhat sketchy. One argument for the idea that women do not get the same training and other benefits as men at given graduate schools is that women do not get sponsorship to the extent that men do (Schwartz and Lever 1973). Centra (1974, 120-21), though, did not find differences in the extent to which men and women found faculty members who took an interest in them not only in graduate school but also afterwards. To the extent that the quality of the graduate experience differs for men and women (Centra 1974, 124-27; Zuckerman and Cole 1975) in other ways, women could be expected to be at a disadvantage in beginning their careers. Feldman (1973), for example, found women students in general, but especially married women students, more likely than men to say they saw "almost none" of their fellow graduate students socially. About one-fifth of the men said this, but from one-quarter (single) to almost half (married) of the women responded this way. This could lead to a weaker collegial network for women later.

First Job

Although men and women start their careers from approximately the same sorts of graduate institutions and women even have an edge with respect to tested intelligence and ability, they differ considerably in the types of jobs they hold right after graduate school. The first columns of table 1 show the first jobs of the people in the APA sample.[1] Given that the sample chosen were academic psychologists, it is not surprising that most of the men and women start their postdoctorate careers in academia.[2] The women, though, are somewhat more likely than the men to take a first position in an academic institution--seventy-three percent of the women as compared with sixty-six percent of the men.

Table 1. Distributions over Types of Jobs by Sex for Academic Psychologist Ph.D.'s: First Job after Receiving the Ph.D. and Job Held Eight Years Later

	First Job		Eighth Year Job	
Type of Job	Men	Women	Men	Women
Instructor	19	33	8	7
Assistant Professor	60	45	28	52
Associate Professor	13	11	99	71
Full Professor	10	3	37	24
Postdoctoral Fellow	10	16	2	1
Other academic nontenure track	25	43	16	33
Nonacademic	69	43	16	15
No job reported	1	13	1	4
Total N	207	207	207	207

The tendency of women doctorates to be more likely than men to have academic employment has been documented elsewhere as well (Centra 1974; National Academy of Sciences 1979). With respect to prestige of the institution at which they held these jobs, women had, if anything, a slight advantage; nineteen percent of the women compared with thirteen percent of the men were in departments rated "distinguished" in Cartter (1966a). Within the academic category, however, women were in the *types* of positions that are less likely than others to provide the potential for career building. In fact, their seeming equality with respect to prestige of employer may simply reflect that it is at the highly-regarded large research universities that there are more of the marginal positions women tend to hold.

Within academia, there are a number of kinds of positions. The ranks of assistant professor, associate professor, and full professor are generally considered the tenure track ranks, with tenure usually accompanying promotion to associate professor.[3] At some institutions, the rank of instructor is a tenure-track position, leading to promotion or even directly to tenure (Abramson 1975; Howard 1978, 23). Usually, though, instructor is off-tenure track, although it is sometimes the rank one holds until finishing the Ph.D., with promotion to assistant professor automatic when the degree has been earned. Generally, by moving up the academic ladder one gains job security and other benefits.

Nontenure track positions vary in prestige and reward. Especially for this sample, academic administrative positions, which are usually "good" positions, are temporary, because of the teaching criterion used to select the sample. Other positions, such as adjunct or clinical professional ranks, tend to be somewhat marginal with respect to the academic hierarchy of an institution. Postdoctorate fellowships are a means of advancement, not end positions in themselves. Positions such as lecturer and research associate tend to be marginal positions not leading to higher positions (Bernard 1964, 212-13).

The APA women with academic positions after receiving their Ph.D.'s are found more often than men to have started in the marginal nontenure track situations, and the men tend to hold the more prestigious nontenure track positions (e.g., administrator). Women are slightly more likely than men to have held postdocs right after graduate school (National Academy of Sciences 1979; Reskin 1976). These positions can give one additional time to concentrate on research and learning before going on to a regular academic appointment. However, as Reskin (1976) points out, postdoctoral fellowships vary in prestige and implications for career building (as discussed later), and in her sample of 1955-61 Ph.D.'s in chemistry, women held postdocs, on average, that were lower in prestige than the men in their field and cohort.

More men in the APA sample than women held academic ladder positions, and they held higher rank: forty-nine percent of the men in the sample and forty-four percent of the women held tenure track positions in their first jobs after completing their Ph.D.'s. When ranks were coded from instructor $= 1$ to full professor $= 4$, women had a mean rank for their first jobs of 1.8, slightly below assistant professor; the mean rank for men was 2.1, just above assistant professor. The sample of women includes twice the proportion of instructors and less than one-third the proportion of full professors, although the women full professors are, on average, younger than the men.

One way in which the accumulation of advantage occurs is by the influence of the prestige of one's graduate institution on one's first job. Men and women here have different sorts of positions after graduate school, but to what extent does this represent a difference in the ability to accumulate their advantages?

Looking just at prestige of institutions, which, as we have already seen, disguises differences between men and women in the types of positions they hold, Cole (1979), with data on 1957-58 science Ph.D.'s who were academically employed in 1965, found that the prestige of graduate department if anything correlated slightly higher with prestige of first employing institution for women than men, net of intelligence. Welch and Lewis (1980), in contrast, did find differences in the effects of graduate school prestige on the prestige of the institutions where women and men held their first jobs. Using data from 1976-77 Ph.D.'s in sociology, they found among those who had first academic jobs interactions of sex, graduate school prestige, and first job prestige. Women from lower ranked schools were more likely than men to end up in similar (i.e., lower ranked) graduate departments, while men were more likely to end up teaching in non-elite undergraduate departments. Women from the high rank departments, though, suffered considerably more downward mobility just in terms of prestige of school than did men.

With the APA data, I examined some of the determinants of *type* of first position (tables 2 and 3).[4] Here, for both men and women with academic first jobs after receiving the Ph.D, holding a first job at a high-ranking school decreased the probability of being on tenure track, perhaps because, as I speculated before, many postdocs and other temporary positions are open at larger research universities, which are ranked, by the scheme I used, higher than other sorts of institutions. Although prestige of degree-granting institution did not affect whether one held an academic position (analysis not shown, Rosenfeld 1974) or the academic rank one held, if one did have an academic position, it did affect the probability of being on the academic ladder for men, but not for women. Men coming from higher ranked departments were more likely to be instructors, assistant professors, associate professors, or full professors in their first jobs after the Ph.D. Reskin and Hargens (1979), though, using data on 1955-61 chemistry Ph.D.'s and controlling for a different set of variables, did not find significant effects of graduate school prestige on getting on tenure track for either men or women. Some of the difference in results may be due to the difference in how careers are structured in the physical and social sciences. In the physical sciences, postdoctoral fellowships are a much more crucial step

Table 2. Regression of Type of Academic First Post-Ph.D. Position on Personal Characteristics, Degree Characteristics, Location and Mobility for APA Sample in Academic First Positions

Independent Variables	Unstandardized Regression Coefficient	
	Men	Women
Subfield[a]	-.119	.023
Marital status[b]	-.011	-.192*
Age when received Ph.D.	-.009	.007
Ph.D. granting institution[c]	-.061*	-.025
Year received Ph.D.	.003	.019
Urbanized area size of place of first position[d]	-.002	-.006
Employing institution of first position[e]	.052*	.051*
Move made or not to first position[f]	.197*	.081
Constant	.629	-1.006
R^2	.250	.220

Note: The dependent variable is a dichotomy with tenure track position (instructor, assistant professor, associate professor, professor) = 1; non-tenure track academic position = 0.

[a]1 = clinical interest
  2 = nonclinical career

[b]1 = married
  0 = not married
d.k. = proportion married

[c]1 = distinguished psychology department, rated by Cartter
  2 = top half of strong departments
  3 = second half of strong departments
  4 = good departments
  5 = adequate plus departments
  6 = ACE rated University I
  7 = ACE rated University II
  8 = ACE rated University III

[d]1 = less than 100,000
  2 = 100,000-250,000
  3 = 250,001-500,000
  4 = 500,001-750,000
  5 = 750,001-1,000,000
  6 = 1,000,001-2,000,000
  7 = over 2,000,000

[e]same as (c) plus:
  9 = ACE rated College I
  10 = ACE rated College II
  11 = ACE rated College III
  12 = Junior College

[f]1 = Urbanized area same as one in which Ph.D. earned
  2 = geographic move made to urbanized area of 1st position

*$p = .05$

Table 3. Regression of Academic Rank of First Post Ph.D. Position on Personal Characteristics, Degree Characteristics, Location and Mobility for APA Sample on Tenure Track for First Position

Independent Variables	Unstandardized Regression Coefficient	
	Men	Women
Subfield [a]	-.085	.124
Marital status [b]	.161	-.095
Age when receiving Ph.D.	.076*	.041*
Ph.D.-granting institution [c]	-.075	.050
Year received Ph.D.	.080*	.020
Urbanized area of location of first position [d]	.013	-.071*
Employing institution of first position [e]	.035	.030
Move made or not to first position	.131	.211
Constant	-5.344*	-1.354
R^2	.370	.340

Note: The dependent variable of rank is coded as instructor = 1; assistant professor = 2; associate professor = 3; and professor = 4.

[a]1 = clinical interest
  2 = nonclinical career

[b]1 = married
  0 = not married
d.k. = proportion married

[c]1 = distinguished psychology department, rated by Cartter
  2 = top half of strong departments
  3 = second half of strong departments
  4 = good departments
  5 = adequate plus departments
  6 = ACE rated University I
  7 = ACE rated University II
  8 = ACE rated University III

[d]1 = less than 100,000
  2 = 100,000-250,000
  3 = 250,001-500,000
  4 = 500,001-750,000
  5 = 750,001-1,000,000
  6 = 1,000,001-2,000,000
  7 = over 2,000,000

[e]same as (d) plus:
  9 = ACE rated College I
  10 = ACE rated College II
  11 = ACE rated College III
  12 = Junior College

[f]1 = Urbanized area same as one in which Ph.D. earned
  2 = geographic move made to urbanized area of 1st position

*p = .05

in the career and probably more likely to serve as first positions, on which one would build in going to the first regular appointment (National Academy of Sciences 1979). In the same study, Reskin and Hargens (1979) found that the prestige of a postdoctoral fellowship increased the chances of being on tenure track on the first regular job for men but not for women.

In her closer examination of postdoctoral fellowships (which, for most of those who held them, were first positions after receiving the Ph.D.), Reskin (1976) did find differences in the effects of graduate department quality on men's versus women's placement. While graduate school prestige did not affect whether one took a postdoc for either men or women, it affected the prestige of the postdoc for men but not for women. In fact, women were not able to transform any of their predoctoral characteristics into a prestigious postdoctoral fellowship.

It may be that one reason women are less able than men to accumulate advantage at this stage of their careers is related to movement to the first post-Ph.D. job. Often, in academic careers, one cannot obtain the optimal first job by staying at the institution where one received the Ph.D., and changing institutions usually involves changing geographic location. In looking at the APA sample, I found that over half of the women made geographic moves to their first positions, but over two-thirds of the men did so. Further, whether women moved or stayed, they were located in urban areas larger than those of men of comparable mobility status. The academic market is a national one. Those who do not accommodate their choice of geographic location and willingness to move to their careers may lose out.

Family status could affect women's geographic mobility. Women who are married may be constrained in their choice of geographic location by their spouse's career. Professional women who are married are usually in a dual-career marriage.[5] Although a wife's career could be as great a constraint for a man, there is evidence that when the needs of two careers conflict, the decisions are still usually made to further the man's career (Astin 1969, 68; Bryson and Bryson 1980; Centra 1974, 115-17; Feldman 1973; Ferber and Huber 1979; Ferber and Kordick 1978; Reagan 1975; Wallston, Foster, and Berger 1978). The perception of women as immobile or tied to a husband's career can also lower their bargaining power with employers (Abramson 1975; Reagan 1975, 103). Even single women, though, may be constrained in their geographic mobility, preferring to limit themselves to larger urban areas for social reasons (Astin 1969; Creager 1971; Maxwell, Rosenfeld, and Spilerman 1979; A. Rossi, personal communication 1973). Of course, marriage could constrain women's careers in other ways than by affecting geographic mobility. Given that the division of household labor is often by traditional sex roles, women may have less unrestricted time and fewer blocks of time to devote to a career (Pepitone-Rockwell 1980). The lower proportion of female Ph.D.'s who are married, as compared with both male Ph.D.'s and women in general, could reflect an anticipation of these constraints. In my sample, only sixty-two percent of the women listed in American Men of Science (AMS) were shown as ever married, compared with eighty-six percent of the men. The arguments above, of course, apply to constraints on later career mobility as well as to movement to first job and will be explored in the next section also.

In the APA sample, mobility and marital status did have different effects on the types of positions men and women held after receiving the Ph.D. (tables 2 and 3). While only clinical interest for men and women and age at Ph.D. for men significantly affected whether the first position was academic or not (regression not shown, Rosenfeld 1974), moving increased the probability that a man with an academic job held a tenure track rank right after graduate school. Being married decreased this probability for women, but had essentially no effect for men. The size of the urbanized area where women held their first positions was negatively related to the rank they held; women who were in the larger cities held lower rank, net of the other factors, including marital status.

While Reskin (1976) did not present information on geographic mobility, she showed that the sex differences in probability of holding a postdoc and in the prestige of the postdoc were due in large part to the propensity of married women to hold such positions. Further, more women than men held multiple consecutive postdocs, consistent with the idea that for women holding a postdoc often represents a lack of other job opportunities. However, while the National Academy of Sciences (1979) showed that there were increases in the proportion of women holding postdocs and decreases in the proportions of men holding them between 1973 and 1977, it did not find that marital status was consistently related to the probability of planning a postdoc for women. In most fields, it was single men who planned on a postdoc. Further, the National Academy of Sciences (1979, 50) did not find recent evidence that postdocs are a holding status for women.

At the first step in their careers beyond graduate school, women are already found in lower ranks and in positions that are less likely to give them the chance to develop their academic careers. Further, there is already evidence at that point that they are not as able as men to build on any advantages that come from going to the top graduate schools. There is some support for the idea that this is because women are more constrained than men in their geographic mobility. There is also some evidence that married women are at a disadvantage even net of their mobility; that is, married women were somewhat more likely to hold academic nontenure track rather than tenure track positions, even controlling for their mobility and geographic location. However, this effect was not strong.

Later Jobs and Job Shifts

The first position in a career is not as important as how far and how fast one advances, except insofar as first job defines the range of positions in which mobility can take place. Most advancement within a career occurs in discrete steps, as one changes positions. With absolutely free mobility, shifts in position would be made for gain in some area--income, prestige, work situation. The academic labor market structure forces some shifts by younger nontenured faculty. For persons at the assistant professor level, free (i.e., personally determined) mobility and compulsory (i.e., structurally determined) mobility are maximized. For an associate professor, both are minimized. For a full professor, compulsory mobility is at a minimum and free mobility is limited by the market situation (Caplow and McGee 1958, 42-3). When people move, they do switch between departments of different quality, and this has been noted as a way in which "promotion" and "demotion" occur, at least for men, since while one can go down in quality of department, one rarely goes down in rank over the career. At the same time, both Caplow and McGee (1958, 107) and Brown (1967, 30) note that members of high-prestige departments are more geographically mobile than those in lower ranked departments, perhaps because of their greater visibility and resources for mobility.

Being off-tenure track can hurt in the mobility process. Even at the best institutions, being off-track can lower one's visibility and access to other resources. According to the National Academy of Sciences (1979: 76, 79), "such positions may be a holding pattern for people they (the department) would like to keep until a more promising appointment becomes available. More frequently, however, they are marginal jobs, fluctuating with enrollments, unexpected leaves of regular faculty, and other exigences......In virtually all cases with which we are familiar, people in such off-ladder positions are not permitted to apply for outside research support, thus eliminating any chances they might have to establish independent research records and improve their prospects....Traditionally, they have been viewed as opportunities to continue professional activity for women scientists who were ineligible for regular positions because of nepotism rules or overt sexist bias, or who temporarily preferred less demanding commitments for personal reasons." Women academics, I hypothesize, are limited in the gains they can receive from their job shifting, both because of the personal constraints on their mobility, noted in the previous section, and also because of their early location in nontenure track positions.

We can use the APA data to look directly at the job-shifting that takes place over the early career. A job shift is defined as, at minimum, a change of title or a change of institution. The career histories of the APA sample--from 1955-62 to 1970--were broken down into pairs of jobs, with a job defined as a given title held at a given institution. Thus, if a person moved from assistant professor at one school to assistant professor at another, and then to associate professor at the latter school, he/she would have two job shifts--assistant professor to assistant professor and assistant to associate.

The men and women in this sample made approximately the same average number of job shifts over the time they were in the sample, that is, .19 per year, not counting shifts into and out of the labor market. Again, as was true for first job, women were less likely than men to move geographically to a new job; specifically, thirty-five percent of the job shifts made by women and fifty percent of those made by men included a change of location. This varied somewhat by marital status. Among those for whom marital status was known, thirty-four percent of the married women, forty-two percent of the unmarried women, fifty-one percent of the married men, and fifty-eight percent of the unmarried men made a geographic move from the first to the second of a pair of jobs. Single men were the most mobile, while even single women moved less than men.

With this transformation of the career histories, we can look at the types of jobs to which people go from the different types of positions. Table 4 shows the probability of moving from one type of job to another with a job shift for women and men. That is, across a given row is the proportion of people starting from a given type of position ending a job shift in the type of job denoted by the column heading. For example, of all shifts from assistant professor made by women, sixty-six percent led to an associate professor position. Note that the numbers on the diagonal are for "movers" also--for example, moving from assistant professor to assistant professor at another school. Women's probabilities of moving up with a job shift were lower than men's, except for moving from instructor to assistant professor. Furthermore, women were more likely than men to end any shift (except from instructor) in a nontenure track position, and they were especially likely to go from one nontenure track position to another, consistent with the National Academy of Sciences (1979) description of such jobs as temporary. Men, in contrast, were more likely than women to go from nontenure track positions to tenure track. Thus, women moved up the tenure track ranks more slowly than men, as has been found elsewhere by researchers using both institutional data and panel data on cohorts (Cole 1979; Robinson 1973). Women also held the non-tenure track positions for significant parts of their careers.

In other analyses with these data, I found that, for women, making a geographical move with a job shift increased the speed with which almost all moves were made--up, down, sideways, across categories; for men, geographical mobility was important only in the speed with which they moved between assistant professorships, from associate to full professor, and from nontenure track to associate. Where geographic mobility affected the speed of a move for men, it was more important (i.e., had a bigger effect) than for women. Net of geographic mobility, marital status had no effect (using only cases where marital status was known). Thus, for women, even single women, geographic mobility seemed less well coordinated with career mobility (Marwell, Rosenfeld, and Spilerman 1979; Rosenfeld 1974; Rosenfeld 1981). Consistent with what has been found elsewhere, when looking

Table 4. Probabilities of Types of Job Shifts by Sex for APA Sample.

Second Position of a Pair of Positions	Instructor	Assistant Professor	Associate Professor	Professor	Academic Non-tenure Track	Non-Academic	Row Total [a]	Row Total N	Index of Dissimilarity Between Men and Women's Transition Probabilities
First Position of a Pair of Positions				Women					
Instructor	.07	.57	.14	0	.16	.07	1.01	44	14
Assistant Professor	.01	.16	.66	.02	.12	.04	1.01	112	7
Associate Professor	.02	.06	.30	.56	.06	.02	1.02	54	18
Professor	0	1.00	0	0	0	0	1.00	2	62
Academic non-tenure track	.05	.27	.10	.05	.38	.15	1.00	130	34
Nonacademic	.06	.23	.13	.07	.34	.16	.99	82	24
First Position of a Pair of Positions				Men					
Instructor	0	.50	.13	0	.17	.20	1.00	30	
Assistant Professor	0	.19	.69	.04	.06	.03	1.01	135	
Associate Professor	0	.03	.19	.73	.03	.03	1.01	77	
Professor	0	0	.08	.85	.08	0	1.01	13	
Academic non-tenure track	.01	.35	.31	.11	.16	.06	1.00	68	
Nonacademic	.15	.19	.13	.03	.19	.31	1.00	124	

[a]Totals differ from 1 because of rounding.

at all job shifts over the career, prestige of graduate department did not affect the different types of mobility rates, nor did prestige of employing institution in general.

As others have noted, women tend to diverge more and more from men over their careers. That is true in the APA sample, as one can see by comparing the distribution of year one and year eight of the post-Ph.D. careers (table 1). The quality of employing institution diverges more as well, perhaps because women have moved to teaching positions from nontenure track positions. For those in academic positions, thirty-eight percent of the women and thirty-three percent of the men are in colleges, four percent of the women and three percent of the men are in junior colleges, and thirteen percent of the women and twenty-three percent of the men are in distinguished or strong departments. The rest are in other university departments.

How marital status, mobility, geographic location, and earlier career characteristics affect the types of positions held in the eighth year by academic men and women is shown in tables 5 and 6. Men accumulate advantage from their graduate school prestige, in that coming from a better school increases the probability of having a tenure track appointment (although the absolute magnitude of this effect is somewhat smaller than the effect on first job). Men gain from the moves they have made as well: the more moves they have made, the more likely they are to hold a tenure track position. With respect to the rank they hold if they are on tenure track, men gain in rank if they are not clinical psychologists (probably because many clinical psychologists are not pursuing a strictly academic career). Net of other characteristics, those who began in academic positions or who are older are also at higher rank, due in part at least to the seniority aspect of promotion. But being in a larger urban area, where there would be more jobs available for a two-career couple, decreases men's chances of being on tenure track and of holding higher rank.

The patterns for women are similar to those for men, except that they gain less than men from factors that carry advantage and are hurt more by factors that depress career advancement. They do not gain at all from their mobility. With respect to the rank that they hold, they suffer more from being in a larger urban area. Controlling for other factors, they gain less from beginning their careers in academia than men, less from older age, and not at all from their graduate school prestige. Further, there is evidence in tables 5 and 6 that women have more difficulty in being on tenure track and holding high rank in better schools; that is, while prestige of employing institution has no effect for men, being in better schools for women significantly decreases the chances of being on tenure track and depresses the rank they hold when they are on tenure track (Cole 1979, 57). While marriage *per se* does not have a significant effect net of all the other variables (perhaps because the substitution for missing values by the mean attenuates the associations), it does have a consistently negative effect for women.

Reskin and Hargens (1979) also looked at type of job early and later in the career and found important effects of first position on later positions for women, indicating that women are perhaps at a disadvantage with respect to their careers because of where they begin them. Having a tenure track position as a first job had a much stronger connection with being tenured at the end of the decade after receiving the Ph.D. for women than for men. Indeed, further analysis of this link indicated that virtually all women who were tenured a decade after the Ph.D. began their careers in tenure track university positions. In contrast, the men in Reskin's sample often moved from first jobs that were not tenure track university positions to tenured positions in universities a decade later. Thus, women are not only more likely to go off tenure track, but also more likely to be hurt by doing so in their careers, consistent with what I found in the analysis of the APA job shifts.

Over the first eight years of their post-Ph.D. careers, thirteen percent of the women in the APA sample had a period without reported employment. Although this is a relatively small percentage compared with women in general, it is much larger than the almost zero percentage for men. These women are committed to their careers (at least in the sense of fairly continuous employment), but still have more breaks than men (Astin 1969; Centra 1974; Ferber and Huber 1979). Reskin suggests that interrupted employment for women is a reaction to lack of opportunity for advancement. "Career continuity might reflect professional commitment....., but opportunities for advancement undoubtedly affect both career continuity and commitment. In fact, among academic chemists, women whose first jobs were not on the tenure track were more likely to interrupt their careers than were women on tenure track" (Reskin 1978, 1241). Interruptions in employment, of

Table 5. Regression of Type of Academic Position Held Eight Years After Receiving the Ph.D. on Personal, Degree, Career and Location Characteristics for APA Sample

Independent Variables	Unstandardized Regression Coefficient	
	Men	Women
Subfield [a]	-.042	.227*
Marital status [b]	.092	-.099
Ph.D.-granting institution [c]	-.030*	-.024
Year received Ph.D.	.010	.024
First position academic (1) or nonacademic (0)	.076	-.023
Age 8 years after Ph.D.	.004	.003
Employing institution 8th year [d]	.002	.022*
Urbanized area location in 8th year [e]	-.022*	-.025*
Total moves over 8 years	.048*	.008
Total number of periods without reported position	----	-.115
Constant	.213	-1.005
R^2	.14	.20

Note: The dependent variable is a dichotomy with tenure-track (instructor, assistant professor, associate professor, professor) = 1; nontenure track = 0, academic 8th year position for those with more than one position in the eight years.

[a] 1 = clinical
  2 = nonclinical
[b] 1 = married
  2 = not married
d.k. = proportion married

[c] 1 = distinguished department as rated by Cartter
  2 = strong (1st half) rated by Cartter
  3 = strong (2nd half) rated by Cartter
  4 = good departments
  5 = adequate plus departments
  6 = ACE rated University I
  7 = ACE rated University II
  8 = ACE rated University III

[d] same as (c) plus
  9 = ACE rated College I
  10 = ACE rated College II
  11 = ACE rated College III
  12 = Junior College

[e] 1 = population less than 100,000
  2 = 100,000-250,000
  3 = 250,001-500,000
  4 = 500,001-750,000
  5 = 750,001-1,000,000
  6 = 1,000,001-2,000,000
  7 = over 2,000,000

*$p = .05$

Table 6. Regression of Academic Rank Eight Years after Receiving Ph.D. on Personal, Degree, Career and Location Characteristics for APA Sample on Tenure Track in 8th Year

Independent Variables	Unstandardized Regression Coefficient	
	Men	Women
Subfield [a]	.304*	.395*
Marital status [b]	-.138	-.294
Ph.D.-granting institution [c]	-.016	-.037
Year received Ph.D.	.024	-.027
First position academic (1) or nonacademic (0)	.563*	.364*
Age 8 years after Ph.D.	.052*	.025*
Employing institution 8th year [d]	.003	.050*
Urbanized area location in 8th year [e]	-.056*	-.095*
Total moves over 8 years	.026	-.037
Total number of periods without reported position	----	-.217
Constant	-1.018	2.853
R^2	.41	.32

Note: The dependent variable of academic rank is coded as instructor = 1; assistant professor = 2; associate professor = 3; and professor = 4, for those on tenure track in 8th year who have had more than one job in the eight years.

[a] 1 = clinical
2 = nonclinical
[b] 1 = married
2 = not married
d.k. = proportion

[c] 1 = distinguished department as rated by Cartter
2 = strong (1st half) rated by Cartter
3 = strong (2nd half) rated by Cartter
4 = good departments
5 = adequate plus departments
6 = ACE rated University I
7 = ACE rated University II
8 = ACE rated University III

[d] same as (c) plus
9 = ACE rated College I
10 = ACE rated College II
11 = ACE rated College III
12 = Junior College

[e] 1 = population less than 100,000
2 = 100,000-250,000
3 = 250,001-500,000
4 = 500,001-750,000
5 = 750,001-1,000,000
6 = 1,000,001-2,000,000
7 = over 2,000,000

*p = .05

course, can be simply a reaction to a lack of any position (National Academy of Sciences 1979; Weissman et al. 1972). These interruptions, in turn, can affect one's advancement (Bayer and Astin 1975, table 6), in part at least because these interruptions are "time-out" from the minimum time at a given position it usually takes to be considered for promotion.

There is another aspect of women's career patterns, not yet mentioned, that can also affect their rate of promotion. This is the effect of working part-time. Women are more likely than men to work part-time, sometimes because they have chosen to be employed less than full-time, but sometimes because full-time jobs are not available (Centra 1974; Howard 1978; National Academy of Sciences 1979). Often those with part-time appointments are not even on tenure track (Howard 1978, 23). When they are on tenure-track, they still usually advance more slowly, again because they accumulate seniority in a given position more slowly than someone employed full-time over the same time span.

Not surprisingly, family situation affects the extent to which women are unemployed or part-time employed. For example, Centra found that (1974, 47-8)"...the majority of reasons given by women for unemployment deal with their marital status and family life responsibilities." This includes "no suitable jobs being available in husband's locale" and "anti-nepotism policy." "In addition, many of those who said they did not want to work preferred to stay home with their children rather than seek domestic help, even if it was available." Ferber and Huber (1979) also found evidence that being married to a highly educated man and having children decreased the percentage of time women had worked since getting their Ph.D.'s.

Tatnall, Macke, and Houseknecht (1980) examined the effects of women's family status on several types of underutilization, including unemployment and part-time employment. Using a sample of women who received professional degrees from one large university between 1964 and 1974, they found that being married, having more children, and moving for a husband's career all increased the probability of part-time work. Further analysis of the ever-married women suggested that it was those with a greater expressed commitment to working who worked part-time. For these women, the timing of their marriages relative to that of their degrees also had some effect, but number of children did not. Marital status, number of children, and husband's mobility again affected the probability of unemployment. Those who said they were less committed to working were more likely to be unemployed as well. Among those ever-married, though, only marital status, timing of marriage, and work commitment affected the probability of unemployment, while, among ever-married women with children, husband's mobility once again entered the scene. Additionally, for ever-married women with children, having children before the degree increased the probability of working part-time, while number of children *per se* had no effect. Since the timing variables were included only in the analysis of ever-married women, it seems that some of the negative impact of having children is related to the timing of their births relative to the woman's career stage (Perun and Bielby 1980).

In summary, then, women over their careers continue to move to nontenure track positions, and they move less easily from them than men do. When women are on tenure track, they move up less quickly than men, especially at the better departments. They are hurt by their geographic mobility patterns and geographic locations. They are less likely than men to gain from having gone to a better graduate school. Some women (though not a large number) have interruptions in their employment, some have part-time employment, and both of these work patterns hurt their chances for further advancement. The causes of these aspects of women's career patterns are linked to their family situations.

As mentioned above, the relatively low level of interruptions in employment for academic women can be taken as one measure of their high level of commitment to their careers. Even when their careers do not develop over time as do men's, women still consider themselves to be having careers, not just jobs. Reagan (1975, 105) looking at a 1974-75 survey of economics Ph.D.'s who had been employed at least one year as economists, reports that "ninety-one percent of the women see their work histories as a development of a career rather than just a series of jobs. The corresponding proportion for males is only a little higher, ninety-five percent; this is not a statistically significant difference."

Productivity and Recognition

So far, I have focused on geographical and family constraints as possibly affecting women's career patterns. Yet, productivity and recognition also intervene between type of position held at one time and later advancement. How does this link work for women as compared with men? And how does family situation affect it? Long (1978) has shown that prestige of position affects productivity more than productivity affects prestige of position. Blackburn, Behymer, and Hall (1978), Crane (1965), Hansen, Weisbrod, and Strauss (1978), and Reskin (1977) provide other evidence on the importance of organizational context for productivity. At the same time, publications (and good publications) are generally a criterion for promotion, at least at the better departments (Bayer and Astin 1975; Cole 1979; Katz 1973; Yoels 1973).

One question is whether women in fact publish less than men. Given that different studies have used data from different disciplines and varied in the criteria used to delimit the samples (Ph.D. or not, etc.), it is not surprising that there is not a clear consensus on the issue. Research showing women publishing less than men includes Astin (1969, 85); Astin and Bayer (1972, 103); Blackburn, Behymer and Hall (1978); Centra (1974); Cole (1979); Katz (1973, 474); and Reskin (1978). Those finding no difference or differences in favor of women include Ferber and Loeb (1973); Robinson (1973); and Simon, Clark, and Galway (1967). Perhaps the safest general conclusion is that the difference in publications by sex is relatively small, certainly smaller than differences in career patterns by sex.

What about the effects of women's positions in families on their productivity? It has been assumed that one reason women produce less is that those who are married, given traditional division of labor within the family, have less time and energy to devote to producing scholarly publications. The evidence in favor of this hypothesis is either weak or lacking. In a sample of graduate students who planned to be university or college teachers, Feldman (1973) did find that married men were more likely to have published a paper (twenty-three percent) and married women less likely (thirteen percent). Yet, both single men and women published less than their married peers (sixteen percent of the single men and twelve percent of the single women had published an article). Being single did not seem to increase productivity for either men or women. The highest producers among the women were divorced women (eighteen percent had published one article), while divorced men also published more than never-married men (twenty percent). While Feldman found that women published less than men across marital status, he did not find that being unmarried gave women an advantage. Reskin (1978) also failed to find strong effects of marital status and having children on productivity. For continuously employed women, as for men, these variables had no significant effect on productivity, net of other factors. For all women, they had a weak negative effect. Having any unemployment, which was shown in the previous section to be linked to family factors, had only a small, weak effect on publishing.

Other research, by both Reskin and Cole, helps explicate the weakness of the influence of marriage on publishing. Cole (1979) found that controlling for marital status and number of children did not decrease the association between sex and productivity. Although women published less than men in each marital status category, the patterns across family types were the same for men and women--those who were single were low producers, those who were married without children were the highest producers. Having more children, though, offset the advantage of being married, for both women and men. Cole (1979, 66) speculates that marriage provides a certain measure of balance and "social integration" to life, although "as Durkheim suggests, there clearly seems to be an optimal level of social integration." Hargens, McCann, and Reskin (1978), using a sample of Reskin's chemists who were in university and government research jobs, also found that, while women tended to publish less than men across family types, having more children lowered productivity for both men and women. The effect of having children on both men and women is consistent with findings based on time-budgets (Meissner et al. 1975) that when husbands help in a household they are most likely to be involved with child care.

Further support for the idea that marriage offers some benefits for productivity to both men and women comes from a study of dual-career couples. Looking at psychologist couples (not all of whom were in academic settings), Bryson and Bryson (1980) report that, while women published less than men in both the dual-career couples and in the control group, the women in dual-career couples published more than other women (and were more likely to receive large grants). The highest producers (and most likely winners of large grants) were the husbands in the two-psychologist couples (Butler and Paisley 1980). However, the women in the dual-career couples had jobs that paid less and were more likely to be part-time or nontenure track. "The effects of dual career status for the husband seem uniformly positive. For wives, however, the effects of dual career status are more mixed" (Bryson and Bryson 1980, 252). Ferber and Huber (1979) found that having a highly educated spouse decreased the number of articles by both male and female Ph.D.'s, but also found hints of a positive effect on husbands' productivity from having a wife in the same field.

Marital and family status do not seem to explain sex differences in productivity. On the basis of their institutional locations, though, one would expect women to produce less than men. In their national sample of faculty (with either Ph.D.'s or Master's degrees at four-year colleges and universities), Blackburn, Beyhmer, and Hall (1978, 138) initially found a small association between being male and having higher productivity. However, when they controlled for the types of positions and activities of the faculty, the difference by sex disappeared. They report that "much of what we see on the surface as sex differences in productivity can be explained by examining the sex differences in variables which most strongly correlate with productivity. For example, it was found that women are less interested in research, generally graduate from less prestigious schools, work in less prestigious schools (especially in four-year colleges in contrast to research oriented universities), more often are untenured, hold lower rank, teach undergraduate courses, and are more often found in the humanities and less often in the natural sciences. In contrast, exactly the opposite characteristics most often correlate with high productivity."

Others have also found that the type of position a woman holds affects her productivity, sometimes more than a man's. Reskin (1976), looking at the effects of holding a postdoctoral fellowship on later productivity, showed that having a postdoc, especially a more prestigious one, increased the productivity of both men and women equally. In a different analysis, Reskin (1978) found a somewhat greater influence of postdoctoral fellowship prestige on productivity for women, and a much greater effect of having a tenure track position as the first job after the Ph.D. For men, the important dimension of first job was whether it was in a university or not. "University employment automatically entered men in the contest regardless of initial rank, and they performed accordingly" (Reskin 1978, 1239). However, prestige of Ph.D. department, net of other variables, another locational resource, had a greater impact on men's productivity.

Cole (1979, 68) did not find effects of location on productivity for women, but he was using only prestige of the department, reporting that, "In short, academic men scientists are more productive than their female colleagues in universities just as they are in colleges." He admits, though, that he lacks other data on the nature of the positions women hold.

Productivity and recognition are supposed to be the major criteria by which academics are judged. Do women translate their productivity into higher career positions to the extent that men do? No. Although Cole finds that for men, as for women, publications lead to recognition by colleagues, productivity and reputation do not lead to promotion for women to the extent that they do for men. Further, while productivity and number of citations to work were more important than sex in predicting the quality of the department in which a person worked, controlling for productivity and citations did *not* reduce the association between rank and sex. Productive women were just as likely as men to be in the top departments, but they were there at lower ranks. Reskin's (1976) results also show that women, in contrast with men, were unable to translate productivity in graduate school into prestigious postdocs and the productivity they got from prestigious postdocs into tenured positions a decade later. Further, the effect of the fellowship on later job outcomes was actually weaker for single than for married women. Using citations as an indicator of quality of performance in another analysis, Reskin and Hargens (1979) found that citations to the work of men significantly increased their chances of having a tenured position ten years after they received their Ph.D.'s. It had no effect for women. Perun (1980) presents similar results; namely, while more time spent in research and teaching led to publications among an earlier cohort of academic women, their productivity did not affect their rank or the prestige of their employing institution at the time they were sixty.

Cole has suggested that the *level* of women's productivity may be too low to influence their promotion, that the high producers among women do not match the level of productivity of high male producers. However women nonproducers do worse than male nonproducers (Zuckerman and Cole, 1975). Women's publishing histories show less continuity than men's. The lack of continuity may affect the extent to which women get returns from productivity because departments may not feel they are able to use the publishing records of women as predictors of later performance. Still, productivity and recognition do not seem to be the missing links between gender and lower status in academia.

Conclusions

This review has shown that women's academic careers are not like men's. Throughout their careers, women academics are less able than men to accumulate advantages, to build upon what they have achieved at each stage in their careers. At the same time, there is some accumulation of disadvantage. Women Ph.D.'s start out from graduate institutions of the various prestige levels in the same proportions as men, but they do not get the returns from the prestige of their graduate institutions that men do. In their first jobs, they are already more likely than men to be in the lowest academic ranks and the marginal nontenure track academic positions. Over their careers, these nontenure track positions play a more important role for them than for men, and they are more difficult for women to leave to go onto the academic ladder. Further, some women have periods of less than full-time employment that at a minimum slow down their progress. When women get into positions that give them the opportunity to publish, the position gives them an advantage with respect to productivity at least as great as it gives a similarly placed man. However, this productivity does not translate for them into further advancement. At least some of the differences in career patterns seem to be related to the constraints on women that prevent them from maximizing their career advancement with geographic moves and employment decisions. These constraints result in part from women's roles in their families, although men also gain some advantages and suffer some disadvantages with respect to their productivity from support they get from and the time they give to a family. support they get from a family. However, it is more than this. Single women, while more like men than married women, are still found to differ from men in their career patterns, geographic mobility, and productivity. While married women have more demands on their time and greater constraints on their career decisions than single women, academic single women, too, are at a disadvantage, even compared with single men. Given the propensity of women to marry and to date up in age and status, single women would be more likely to find suitable male companions--and other single women like themselves, as well--in larger cities. They might, therefore, choose to go to less than optimal positions to avoid small, family-centered cities and towns. In the past, at least, such women may have had difficulty even in collegial interactions with men, by virtue of their single and female status, and thus have had problems in networking, problems different from but perhaps of almost the same magnitude as those of married women.

As I indicated in the introduction, one must take care to avoid thinking that it is *just* the individual who is building the career and who determines where he or she will go. There are other actors involved. One important set of these other actors is the academic institutions and departments, and these actors may discriminate on the basis of sex. One particularly insidious form of discrimination is statistical discrimination (Phelps 1972). In this form of discrimination, the employer discriminates against all members of a particular group on the basis of what he (or she) knows about that group on average. Thus, knowing that women are constrained in their geographical mobility and location and perhaps publish less, and knowing that married women tend to follow their husbands' careers, departments could decide not to risk hiring and promoting any women, especially married women, or even to make them offers of positions. The flaws in this logic have to do with the nature of information search and risk. Economists say that this sort of discrimination usually occurs when the cost of getting information about an individual and the risk from hiring the "wrong" individual are very high. However, before an individual is hired in academia a very thorough search for information occurs. At each stage on the career ladder, more information is presented, so that the risk of hiring someone who is not "appropriate" or who does not live up to his or her promise is low; there are several stages at which to release someone. Thus, statistical discrimination is not economically rational in academia. *Some* women do not publish as much as men or follow their husbands or whatever, but not *all* women do, and one can find out about who these women are with relative ease.

Another problem with discrimination is that it can result in the attitudes upon which discrimination is supposedly based. If women are blocked from certain positions, and then not rewarded even when they do publish, they may lose the motivation to pursue a career to the extent that men do. Thus discrimination could in the end justify itself. We do not have much more than anecdotal information on the extent to which this is true (Kanter 1977a; Nielsen 1979).

One reason that people discriminate is that they feel more comfortable with people like themselves. Women have been a minority in most of academia. They are not men and often have gestures, speech patterns, etc. which differ from men's. Acting like men does not work for women, either, since the discrepancy between how they are trying to act and their obvious sex is also disturbing. As anyone who has been involved with hiring, tenure, and promotion decisions in academia knows, these decisions are not always made strictly on the basis of merit. Many random and idiosyncratic factors enter in. It is here that conscious and unconscious feelings of unease with someone who is different in some obvious way could have an effect. One solution is to have more women around, so that they are no longer tokens. There are obvious problems in actualizing this solution, especially without the intervention of affirmative action.

The extent to which there have been positions open to anyone in academia has been changing. The demand for academics has declined. In the 1960's, the academic market was a seller's market and an expanding market. A paper published in 1966, for example (Cartter 1966b), responded to concern about whether there would be *enough* college teachers in the next decades. When there is a large demand for academics, the chances are greater that at least some women will be hired--somewhere. By 1970, the market was a buyer's market and a contracting one. Buyers can be more choosy. In May 1970, Landers and Cicarelli (1970, 15) wrote, "Women, the last in and the first out, will find the job market all but impenetrable unless they are willing to accept greater salary differentials." Thus, in the 1970's, as more women were getting Ph.D.'s, the number of openings was not keeping up with the number of job candidates.

At the same time, a third set of actors, the federal government and some state governments, has altered the legal right of employers to discriminate against women. In 1972, a watershed year, the Equal Employment Opportunity Act and Executive Order 11246 as amended by Executive Order 11375 made institutions of higher education in the U.S. responsible for correcting discrimination practices and effects. Title IX of the Education Amendments Acts of 1972 also prohibited sex discrimination in any educational institution receiving federal funds, although this has since been interpreted as applying only to students rather than as including employees generally (U.S. Commission on Civil Rights 1980). There is some evidence that since 1972 more women have been hired into assistant professor positions, thus getting their feet on the academic ladder (Howard 1978; National Academy of Sciences 1979). Some of these women seem to be not only new Ph.D.'s but also women who have had careers outside the usual tenure track and who have been given regular appointments so that institutions could meet quotas (National Academy of Sciences 1979). At the same time, Reagan (1979, 145), in a study of the "stocks and flows of academic economists" says that "although....the pattern of affirmative action (or the converse) is far more complex, increases in women faculty tend to occur only when total faculty increases." Further, in some cases, these seemed to be "revolving door" appointments, in that women were disproportionately released from these positions (Reagan 1979).

Although the laws exist, enforcement of them is difficult (Abramson 1975). It will be interesting to see how affirmative action laws work in a tight market and a conservative political climate. One limitation of the review in this paper is that the most extensive career data (Cole's, Reskin's and mine) are of Ph.D. cohorts from the late 50's and early 60's who were followed only until around 1970. Careers since 1972 need to be followed, something I plan to do in future work.

Raw hiring patterns are not sufficient evidence of discrimination. People turn down job offers, or fail to look for them, as well as accept them. On the supply side, the situation of academic women, and men, has been changing recently. More women Ph.D.'s have been marrying and finding themselves in two-career families, while at the same time they are delaying childbearing. Men, too, are more likely to be in two-career families. Thus, more women and men academics find themselves constrained in their mobility. This situation, in connection with affirmative action laws, might actually make it more difficult for academic women to advance in their careers than previously. In theory, at least, affirmative action laws make it more difficult for universities to hire a husband and wife as a package (Moore 1980). The extent to which it is *fair* for universities to deal with couples as such, perhaps filling positions that would go to a one-career family or single person, is not clear. A colleague of mine, though, has cynically said that if only one member of a couple can be hired, it is better that it be the woman, that the predominately male department would not be able to stand for long the sight of another academic male unemployed because of his wife's career. Indeed, there have been recent cases of universities going all out to get a position for the husband of a woman they wanted to hire. Whether this happens more than efforts to find positions for a wife is not clear.

So far, this chapter has the implicit assumption that it is a good thing to follow the ideal-typical academic career. That is obviously a value judgment. The extent to which any individual accepts this varies. A long-standing argument against the ideal-typical career is it deemphasizes teaching. Because women have been overrepresented in teaching, large numbers of them have failed to achieve ideal-typical careers. However, there is considerable intrinsic reward for teaching, and it is not only women who are concerned about its lack of prestige in the academic career. Further, following the ideal-typical academic career (as is true of careers in general) requires considerable dedication of time, often taken away from family life. Whether such a situation is desirable for anyone is debatable. At minimum, it works against equalitarian family life if one member of a couple sacrifices everything for a career--and it has usually been the woman in the family who drops her career work and fills in for the husband at home. It is possible that as more men and women find themselves in two-career families, there will be a trend toward more equalitarian careers, with both members of the couple at times passing-by an opportunity to optimize his or her career advancement in favor of finding the best situation for the family as a whole (Lawe and Lawe 1980). To a certain extent, institutions can help couples when they make these decisions by making sure that for both men and women, off-tenure track and part-time positions are not dead ends, and by allowing both maternity and paternity leaves. At the same time, especially in a society that is not equalitarian with respect to roles played by men and women, it will take considerable commitment on the part of the couple. Social attitudes have changed so that it is much more acceptable now than before for a woman to have a career, but less has changed with respect to helping her balance this career with a family.

It is my hope that from my depiction of the academic careers of women as a group and of the changing conditions in which these careers take place, individual women will have a greater awareness of the consequences of the decisions they make as well as of the points at which they might try to change the structure of academia and women's roles.

Notes

1. The data on career histories of women and men academic psychologists were taken from the 1970 American Psychological Association *Biographical Bulletin* (1970). The sample of two hundred seven women includes all the women listed in the APA (1972) 1971-72 Survey of Women Members who had received their Ph.D.'s from 1955 to 1962, listed teaching as one of their principal activities in 1970, were employed in 1970 in an academic institution, and had sufficient career information listed in the APA Bulletin to reconstruct their careers. The sample of two hundred seven men met the same Ph.D. date and teaching criteria as the women and was matched proportionately to the women by age at receiving the Ph.D. (over thirty-five or not), by interest within psychology (clinical or not) and by quality of graduate institution ("distinguished," "strong" or "other," as rated in Cartter (1966a)). The APA Bulletin did not contain any information on children or marital status; this information was obtained from American Men of Science (1962; 1965) for seventy-three percent of the men and fifty-six percent of the women. In regressions, missing data on marital status are replaced with the mean by sex. In other types of analysis, "missing data" is treated as a separate category. The distributions over marital status and number of children by sex for those for whom data were collected agree well with those in other sources (Astin 1969; Harmon 1968).

2. Of course, for at least some of these people, these are not their *first* academic jobs. Some, especially those who are older, may have gotten a Ph.D. to advance in a career that they had begun earlier. Since the sample was chosen so that age as well as quality of degree-granting institution and clinical interests were proportionately the same by sex, differences in the characteristics of first post-Ph.D. position should not represent differences in career stage by sex. Centra (1974,28) found that in general over forty percent of the women and almost half of the men in his sample continued after the Ph.D. in a job they had held while working on the degree.

3. The National Academy of Sciences (1979, 62), however, cautions that even the traditional tenure track ranks may no longer be such. There has been a trend also toward granting associate professor rank without tenure.

4. The tables show results from ordinary least squares regression analysis. In these tables, each coefficient shows the change a one-unit increase in a given explanatory (independent) variable brings about in the variable to be explained (dependent variable), controlling for everything else included among the independent variables. The R^2 gives the proportion of the variance in the dependent variable explained by the whole set of independent variables. These analyses are simple to interpret and comparable to other analyses of men's and women's positions in academia. There are, however, statistical problems with the procedures used here that should be kept in mind. The first dependent variable, that of being on tenure track or not, is a dichotomy. Strictly speaking, when one has such a dependent variable, and especially if the distribution across the categories is skewed, one should not use OLS regression but a procedure, such as logistic regression, that involves assumptions appropriate to categorical data. Hanushek and Jackson (1977) provide a good discussion of this problem. Further, for both types of dependent variables, a subsample of the APA sample has been selected. For example, in table 3, only those with tenure track academic positions are included. Such selection can lead to selectivity bias (e.g., Berk 1983). The OLS results, then, should be taken as tentative and illustrative.

5. The trend may be for *both* men and women to be increasingly in such families. For example, for their sample of married 1958-63 and 1967-71 Ph.D.'s in a range of fields, Ferber and Huber (1979, 319)

report that thirty-five percent of the men and seventy-seven percent of the women in the first cohort were married to Ph.D.s compared with forty-one percent of the men and eighty-one percent of the women in the second cohort. See, also, Astin (1969); Centra (1974); and Rosenfeld (1974).

References

Abramson, J. 1975. *The invisible woman.* San Francisco: Jossey-Bass.

Allison, P. D., and J. A. Stewart. 1974. Productivity differences among scientists: Evidence for accumulative advantage. *American Sociological Review* 39: 596-606.

American Men of Science. 1962. *Physical and biological sciences.* 10th ed. Tempe, Arizona: Jacques Cattell Press.

——————. 1965. *Social and behavioral sciences.* 11th ed. New York: R. R. Bowker.

American Psychological Association. 1970. *Biographical bulletin.* Washington, D.C.: American Psychological Association.

——————. 1972. *Survey of women members of the American Psychological Association (1971-72).* Washington, D. C. American Psychological Association.

Astin, H. S. 1969. Sex discrimination in academe. *Educational Record* 53: 101-18.

Astin, H. S., and A. E. Bayer. 1972. Sex discrimination in academe. *Educational Record.* 53:101-18.

Bayer, A. E., and H. S. Astin. 1975. Sex differentials in the academic reward system. *Science* 188: 796-802.

Berk, R. A. 1983. An introduction to sample selection bias. *American Sociological Review* 48: 386-98.

Bernard, J. 1964. *Academic women.* University Park, Pennsylvania: The Pennsylvania State Univ. Press.

Blackburn, R., C. Behymer, and D. Hall. 1978. Research note: Correlates of faculty publications. *Sociology of Education* 51: 132-41.

Brown, D. 1967. *The mobile professors.* Washington, D.C.: American Council on Education.

Bryson, J., and R. Bryson. 1980. Salary and job performance differences in dual career couples. In *Dual career couples.* ed. F. Pepitone-Rockwell, 241-59. Beverly Hills, Calif.: Sage.

Butler, M., and W. Paisley. 1980. Coordinated career couples: convergence and divergence. In *Dual career couples*. ed. F. Pepitone-Rockwell, 207-28. Beverly Hills, Calif.: Sage.

Caplow, T., and R. McGee. 1958. *The academic marketplace*. New York: Basic Books.

Carnegie Commission on Higher Education. 1971. *A classification of institutions of higher education (technical report)*. New York: McGraw-Hill.

Cartter, A. 1966a. *An assessment of quality in graduate education*. Washington, D.C.: American Council on Education.

——————. 1966b. The supply of and demand for college teachers. *Journal of Human Resources* 1: 22-38.

Centra, J. 1974. *Women, men, and the doctorate*. Princeton, N. J.: Educational Testing Service.

Cole, J. R. 1979. *Fair science: Women in the scientific community*. New York: Free Press.

Cole, J. R., and S. Cole. 1973. *Social stratification in science*. Chicago: Univ. of Chicago.

Coleman, J. 1964. *Introduction to mathematical sociology*. New York: Free Press.

Crane, D. 1965. Scientists at major and minor universities: A study of productivity and recognition. *American Sociological Review* 30: 699-714.

Creager, J. A. 1971. *The American graduate student: A normative description*. Washington, D.C.: American Council on Education Research Reports 6: 5.

Feldman, S. 1973. Impediment or stimulant? Marital status and graduate education. *American Journal of Sociology*. 78:982-94.

Ferber, M. and J. Huber. 1979. Husbands, wives and careers. *Journal of Marriage and the Family* 41: 315-25.

Ferber, M. and B. Kordick. 1978. Sex differentials in the earnings of Ph.D.'s. *Industrial and Labor Relations Review* 31: 227-38.

Ferber, M. and J. Loeb. 1973. Performance, reward, and perception of sex discrimination among male and female faculty. *American Journal of Sociology* 78: 995-1002.

Gordon, N., T. Morton, and I. Braden. 1974. Faculty salaries: Is there discrimination by sex, race, and discipline? *American Economic Review* 64: 419-27.

Graham, P. A. 1978. Expansion and exclusion: A history of women in American higher education. *Signs* 3: 759-73.

Hansen, W. L., B. A. Weisbrod, and R. P. Strauss. 1978. Modeling the earnings and research productivity of academic economists. *Journal of Political Economy* 86: 729-41.

Hanushek, E. A. and J. E. Jackson. 1977. *Statistical methods for social scientists.* New York: Academic Press.

Harmon, L. 1965. *Profiles of Ph.D.'s in the sciences: Summary report on follow-up of doctoral cohorts, 1935-1960.* Career Patterns Report 1. Washington, D.C.: National Academy of Sciences.

————————. 1968. *Careers of Ph.D.'s: Academic vs. non-academic.* Career Pattern Report 2. Washington, D.C.: National Academy of Sciences.

Hargens, L., J. C. McCann, and B. Reskin. 1978. Productivity and reproductivity: Professional achievement among research scientists. *Social Forces* 57: 154-63.

Hearn, J. C. 1981. Reconceptualizing equity in postsecondary participation patterns. Paper presented at the annual meeting of the American Educational Research Association at Los Angeles, California.

Heyns, B., and J. A. Bird. 1982. Recent trends in the higher education of women. In *The undergraduate woman: Issues in educational equity,* ed. P. Perun, 43-69. Lexington, Mass.: D. C. Heath and Co.

Howard, S. 1978. *But we will persist: A comparative research report on the status of women in academe.* Washington, D.C.: American Association of University Women.

Kanter, R. M. 1977a. *Men and women of the corporation.* New York: Basic Books.

————————. 1977b. Some effects of proportions on group life: Skewed sex ratios and responses to token women. *American Journal of Sociology* 82: 965-90.

Katz, D. 1973. Faculty salaries, promotions, and productivity at a large university. *American Economic Review* 63: 469-77.

Kilson, M. 1976. The status of women in higher education. *Signs* 1: 935-42.

Landers, C. E., and J. S. Cicarelli. 1970. Academic recession. *The New Republic* 162: 14-16.

Lawe, C., and B. Lawe. 1980. The balancing act: Coping strategies for emerging family life styles. In *Dual career couples*, ed. F. Pepitone-Rockwell, 191-203. Beverly Hills, Calif.: Sage.

Lewis, L., R. Wanner, and D. Gregorio. 1979. Performance and salary attainment in academia. *American Sociologist* 14: 157-69.

Long, J. S. 1978. Productivity and academic position in the scientific career. *American Sociological Review* 43:889-908.

Marwell, G., R. A. Rosenfeld, and S. Spilerman. 1979. Geographic constraints on women's careers in academia. *Science* 205: 1225-31.

Matthews, J. R., and L. H. Matthews. 1980. Going shopping: The professional couple in the job market. In *Dual career couples*, ed. F. Pepitone-Rockwell, 261-81. Beverly Hills, Calif.: Sage.

Meissner, M., E. Humphreys, S. Meis, and W. Scheu. 1975. No exit for wives: sexual division of labor and the cumulation of household demands. *Canadian Review of Sociology and Anthropology* 12: 424-39.

Moore, D. 1980. Equal opportunity laws and dual-career couples. In *Dual-career couples*, ed. F. Pepitone-Rockwell, 229-40. Beverly Hills, Calif.: Sage.

National Academy of Sciences. 1979. *Climbing the academic ladder: Doctoral women scientists in academe.* Washington, D.C.: Report of the Committee on the Education and Employment of Women in Science and Engineering, Commission on Human Resources.

Nielsen, L. 1979. Sexism and self-healing in the university. *Harvard Educational Review* 49: 463-76.

Pepitone-Rockwell, F. 1980. *Dual-career couples.* Beverly Hills, Calif.: Sage.

Perun, P. 1980. Career attainment and the academic woman. Wellesley College. Mimeo.

Perun, P. and D. Bielby. 1980. Structure and dynamics of the individual life course. In *Life Course: Integrative theories and exemplary populations*, ed. K. Black, 97-119. Washington, D.C.: American Association for the Advancement of Science.

Phelps, E. 1972. The statistical theory of racism and sexism. *American Economic Review.* 62: 659-61.

Reagan, B. 1975. Two supply curves for economists? Implications of mobility and career attachment of women. *American Economic Review* 65: 100-07.

—————————. 1979. Stocks and flows of academic economists. *American Economic Association, The academic labor market for economists* 69: 143-47.

Reagan, B., and B. J. Maynard. 1974. Sex discrimination in universities: An approach through internal labor market analysis. *American Association of University Professors Bulletin* 60: 13-21.

Reskin, B., 1976. Sex differences in status attainment in science: The case of the postdoctoral fellowship. *American Sociological Review* 41: 597-612.

—————————. 1977. Scientific productivity and the reward structure of science. *American Sociological Review* 42: 491-504.

—————————. 1978. Scientific productivity, sex, and location in the institution of science. *American Journal of Sociology* 83: 1235-43.

—————————. 1979. Academic sponsorship and scientists' careers. *Sociology of Education* 52: 129-46.

Reskin, B. and L. Hargens. 1979. Scientific advancement of male and female chemists. In *Discrimination in organizations,* ed. R. Alvarez, K. Lutterman, and Associates, 100-22. San Francisco: Jossey-Bass.

Robinson, L. 1973. Institutional variation in the status of academic women. In *Academic women on the move,* ed. A. Rossi and A. Calderwood, 199-229. New York: Russell Sage.

Rosenfeld, R. A. 1974. Sex differences in geographic and career mobility among academic psychologists. Master's thesis, Department of Sociology, University of Wisconsin, Madison.

—————————. 1981. Academic men and women's career mobility. *Social Science Research* 10: 337-63.

Rosenfeld, R. A., and J. C. Hearn. 1982. Sex differences in the significance of economic resources for choosing and attending a college. In *The undergraduate woman: Issues in educational equity,* ed. P. Perun, 127-57. Lexington, Mass.: D. C. Heath and Co.

Schwartz, P. and J. Lever. 1973. Women in the male world of higher education. In *Academic women on the move,* ed. A. Rossi and A. Calderwood, 57-77. New York: Russell Sage.

Simon, R., S. Clark, and K. Galway. 1967. The woman Ph.D.: A recent profile. *Social Problems* 15: 221-36.

Tatnall, P., A. Macke, and S. Houseknecht. 1980. The underutilization of professional training among highly educated women: A role conflict perspective. Paper presented at the annual meeting of the American Sociological Association, New York, New York, August.

U.S. Commission on Civil Rights. 1980. *Enforcing Title IX.* Washington, D.C.: U.S. Government Printing Office.

Wallston, B., M. Foster, and M. Berger. 1978. I will follow him: Myth, reality or forced choice--Job seeking experiences of dual career couples. *Psychology of Women Quarterly* 3: 9-21.

Welch, M. and S. Lewis. 1980. A mid-decade assessment of sex bias in placement of sociology Ph.D.'s: Evidence for contextual variation. *The American Sociologist* 15: 120-27.

Weissman, M., K. Nelson, J. Hackman, C. Pincus, and B. Prusoff. 1972. The faculty wife: her academic interests and qualifications. *American Association of University Professors Bulletin,* 58: 287-92.

Yoels, W. C. 1973. On 'publishing or perishing': Fact or fable? *The American Sociologist* 8: 128-30.

Zuckerman, H. and J. R. Cole. 1975. Women in American science. *Minerva* 13: 82-102.

Responsibilities of Women Faculty in Engineering Schools

Mildred S. Dresselhaus

Introduction

The life of a woman in academia in one of the science or engineering departments of a university is a multifaceted venture. There are of course the traditional responsibilities that are common to all faculty members: teaching, research, thesis supervision and administrative responsibilities of various types. In addition there are the *extra-curricular* activities upon which I focus here.

For a woman to be a successful faculty member in the overall academic enterprise, top priority must be given to the traditional academic responsibilities, and this cannot be overemphasized. It is on the basis of the traditional responsibilities that promotions are made and international reputations are established. Success in the traditional faculty activities is necessary for establishing professional credibility as an individual and for the community of women scholars in general. For this reason the primary emphasis of women faculty must be on professional excellence in teaching and research. It is important for women to demonstrate to the academic community, including faculty members and students of both sexes, that women *can* contribute effectively in the faculty role. I would even go as far as to say that if this function is done well, a major contribution is made to the advancement of the status of women in science and technology.

The Extra-Curricular Activities

I now come to the topic of the *extra*-curricular activities of women in academia. Although it is not essential for every woman faculty member to participate in extra-curricular activities as I describe them, it is vital for women collectively to make such a contribution. And in fact it is probably necessary for women to organize themselves so that this function is carried out as effectively and efficiently as possible. Extra-curricular activities encompass several subareas of activity, which I classify in terms of local activities and national activities. Local activities are directed toward improving the work environment at the university for students, professionals and employees, especially women. National activities are directed toward increasing the opportunities and visibility of women in science and engineering on the national scene.

First, I focus on extra-curricular activities that are student related. Then, I address extra-curricular activities related to the concerns of faculty and staff. Finally I mention extra-curricular activities which occur at the national level.

At the Purdue Conference, we heard statistics giving evidence for substantial progress by women in academia in the fields of science and engineering. We still have a long way to go before women are making the level of contribution that we are capable of making. It is my opinion that attention to extra-curricular activities in some organized way will enable us to make more efficient and effective progress in this direction.

Student-Related Activities

Many people have stressed the importance of role models for women students for enhancing the professional contribution they will make in later life. Though it is by no means essential that role models for women students be female, it is well recognized that all factors being equal, women role models are more effective than are men. I can say from my own experience as a professor, that the role model function that I have provided has been vital to the success of many undergraduate and graduate students.

Firstly, a woman professor acts as a role model by providing an existence theorem for professional achievement. Beyond that, women students seek professional women for career counseling and for advice on how to combine their professional lives with marriage and family. These counseling functions range from casual encounters to acute appeals for help. And when women faculty are approached for help of this kind, it is natural for them to respond.

Many women students suffer from lower aspiration levels and have less self confidence than do men with equivalent talent and accomplishment. Inspiration by women professionals assuring students that they "can do it too" is often essential. Also important are practical tips on how to be self-assertive and to do so in socially acceptable ways. The offering of practical advice on how to handle social problems in a research situation is another area where women faculty members contribute importantly to the effectiveness and to the retention of women graduate students.

Another role played by women faculty is that of advocate for women students. Women faculty who command the professional respect of the faculty and administration are in a strong position to speak up on behalf of the needs of women students. Every such woman faculty member is in an advantageous position to effect changes in practices which are discriminatory to women. From my own personal experience, I can say that this kind of activity has had a major impact on improving the academic and social environment of all students, and women students in particular. Women faculty can be expected to play an important role both in identifying issues requiring attention and in recommending mechanisms for addressing these issues. Let me illustrate this function of women faculty with some specific examples from my personal experience at MIT.

In my early years at the Institute, I was heavily involved (in my extra-curricular activities) with establishing the principle of equal admissions standards for men and women students. Once the principle was formulated, methods for the evaluation of equivalent standards were specified, and methods for implementation were identified, there was effectively no opposition to instituting this important change. The adoption of an equal admissions procedure soon led to an increase in the percentage of women students by a factor of three.

A second example where the advocacy of women faculty played an essential role was in providing improved access of women students to athletic facilities. An area in which I am now working concerns the improvement of housing options for women students. Although changes to improve the environment of women students occur without the intervention of women faculty, the speed and effectiveness of the changes are significantly enhanced when women faculty are advocates for the cause.

Another area where women faculty can be especially helpful to women students is in providing leadership in creating student networks. Once such networks are operating effectively, women faculty are only needed for occasional support and encouragement. When the number of women in the science/technology area is small, interactions between groups of women are important. These interactions may occur through group meetings that are department based, or through meetings organized on a larger scale by the Engineering School, for example. Student chapters of the Society of Women Engineers represent another mechanism for creating a basis for interactions among women students facing common experiences, concerns and problems.

Women faculty can also be called upon to contribute to the advancement of the academic needs of women students in the science/technology area. As the number of women students increased at MIT, it became clear that many of them had less exposure than their male counterparts to experiences with woodworking, machine shop tools, electronics and computers. To provide a means for students to gain experience in some of these practical areas, two women professors (a friend and I) started a low-key freshman offering to address these issues. The offering was very successful in general, and especially attractive to women who wanted to become more comfortable in the setting that constitutes an institute of technology.

Faculty/Staff Related Activities

It is realistic to assume that, for some time to come, the rank distribution of women faculty and professionals in the science/technology area will be different than that for men. Specifically, more women will be found concentrated in the junior faculty ranks as compared with their male counterparts. In this context I will cite a few areas where senior women faculty will be called upon to provide leadership.

When a new faculty member or professional is hired at any institution, it is to the advantage of all concerned that this person succeed. Despite the importance of hiring women faculty and professionals to contribute to the large variety of extra-curricular activities that must be carried out, it is also important that appointments be made to people who are well qualified for the job. It is in this context that affirmative action makes sense. More specifically, the new people often need mentors, "to show them the ropes," to help them, "over the rough spots," and to serve as their advocates. In this context, networking organizations provide an important mechanism for offering help, encouragement and technical know-how. To provide such a function, about ten years ago I founded the Women's Faculty Luncheons at MIT. This luncheon group meets once a month during the academic year. The major topics of discussion focus on professional issues such as the promotion process, how to write grant proposals, the annual faculty member review with her department head, strategies for affirmative action, strategies for increasing the number of women faculty, staff and students. The women's faculty group also undertakes projects of various types as an advocacy group and makes presentations, as for example to the search committee for a new President and a new Dean of Engineering. Many of our women faculty members feel quite isolated and thus welcome this opportunity to make contact with other women at the Institute. What is perhaps of greatest importance is the role played by the women's faculty group in organizing extra-curricular activities.

The concept of the Women's Faculty Lunch has been so useful, that there is now a women's postdoc group that meets monthly. This group focuses on issues of primary concern to women postdocs and has been very successful.

Although network groups are vital to the success of many women professionals, the primary responsibilities for organizing and administering these groups fall on the senior women faculty, who have both the job security and resources to operate such efforts successfully. It is completely unrealistic to expect junior women faculty to have the time to organize and administer networking groups. Junior women faculty must give highest priority to their own professional careers. It is my opinion that the provision of a modest budget for speakers and refreshments for a networking group is a good investment by a university in the career development of its personnel. As I indicated earlier, it is in everybody's best interest that each employee succeed to the fullest possible extent, compatible with his or her talent.

Women faculty also are called upon to represent the interests of women on a variety of university committees. Since women faculty tend to be relatively few in number, their service on committees tends to significantly exceed that of men at comparable levels. And we also know that there is little professional reward for committee service at universities. Nevertheless, it is important in many cases for women to serve and for the women's viewpoint to be heard. It is often through committee service that women faculty can act as advocates on behalf of women, including women students, staff and professionals.

In a related vein, women faculty play important roles when serving on departmental admissions committees for graduate students, personnel committees for faculty promotions, and search committees for hiring faculty, professional staff and administrative leaders such as department heads and deans. Although highly time-consuming, such activities are important for the overall advancement of women at an institution. It is of course also obvious that the presence of men and women in senior academic positions who are sympathetic to women's issues is vital for the overall advancement of women at an institution.

Before leaving the topic of extra-curricular activities on behalf of women faculty and professionals, let me also emphasize the important leadership role that women faculty must play in looking after the interests of women employees at all levels. We all recognize that the success of every major institution depends on the dedication of the rank and file employees, many of these employees being women. In the case of women employees, it is often women faculty who must assume a position of leadership and advocacy. In this connection, I may cite the founding of the Women's Forum as a networking organization started by women faculty at MIT on behalf of women employees. This organization was founded in 1971 and has met weekly or biweekly over the years and has provided an effective vehicle for discussion and professional development for women employees.

The National Scene

The extra-curricular activities of women faculty do not end on campus. The presence of women in influential positions in the professional societies has been very important for gaining professional recognition of women by their colleagues, and for establishing networking organizations within the professional society to help women help each other. These activities have led to increased visibility of women in the societies, with highly beneficial impacts on young women joining the profession.

Participation of women on national committees (such as committees and boards of the National Research Council) and in studies sponsored by these committees has increased the visibility of women in science and technology and has given them increased input into national planning in these areas. In a similar vein, the participation of women on national selection committees for prizes, major appointments and promotions provides an important area for input to the decision making process. Other important areas for decision making are provided by advisory committees to funding agencies and university visiting committees to academic departments; and the participation of women in these areas has been increasing steadily. Consulting arrangements with industry and memberships on industrial boards of directors are other areas where women have recently started to penetrate.

Summary

The responsibilities of a woman faculty member in the traditional academic areas already represent more than a full time job. The additional responsibilities of the extra-curricular activities represent an additional burden which we must all bear collectively for the time being. This is a burden we must learn to share until such time when women will have equal opportunities and access, and there will be no further need for affirmative action.

Alternative Science-Based Careers

Alternative Development of a Scientific Career

Esther A. H. Hopkins

To understand the topic of an alternative development of a scientific career, we need to consider the meanings of the word "career," the conventional route to a scientific career, the range and scope of alternative routes, and then some details on one specific alternative development, my own, so that you can see why I call myself a chemist and why I see what I do as a scientific career. This is not a road map for anyone to follow but, rather, some personal observations you can use while you are assessing who you are, what career you want, and how you are going to go about getting it.

First, let us look at the word "career." In Webster's *New Collegiate Dictionary*, there are four definitions for the word, the first two of which are not particularly pertinent here: (1) is a course, a passage; full speed or exercise of activity; (2) is an encounter or charge; (3) is a field for, or pursuit of, *consecutive, progressive* achievement, especially in public, professional, or business life; and (4) is a profession for which one trains and which is undertaken as a *permanent* calling. Both definitions (3) and (4) make me a little unhappy, since (3) says that unless one moves consecutively, progressively toward more and more achievement, one doesn't have a career; and (4) says that one is in it for life. The word "permanent" carries the sense of "continuing or enduring without fundamental or marked change."

But let us give the term "career" the option of allowing the topping out at various points for various people, and let us allow a small number of career changes without destroying the concept of permanence.

A "scientific career," then, is one of relating to, or exhibiting, the methods or principles of science. These careers may be in academic, governmental, industrial, or not-for-profit areas. A scientific career, based as it is on possession of knowledge as distinguished from ignorance or misunderstanding, does not, *a priori,* presume a moral, principled input, yet any scientific career requires an ethic. A scientist, no matter what substance comprises the daily working material, needs consideration of certain principles in order to defend the integrity of science and to pursue and communicate scientific knowledge while maintaining absolute respect for basic human rights and human dignity.

The conventional development of a career can usually be equated to the path successful men follow to the pinnacle of success in the various arenas. In the academic area, for a chemist, for example, when one has obtained the Ph.D. (at a recognized school) and has completed postdoctoral training (at a different but comparable school, under a recognized researcher), one obtains a tenure-track appointment at a major university, usually as an assistant professor. One then does research, obtains grants, does the obligatory committee functions, teaches, and in the fullness of time is promoted to associate professor, full professor, distinguished professor, professor emeritus, and late professor, while perhaps serving at some point as head of department or in other collateral administrative positions.

Governmental agencies usually have a similar, scheduled listing of the way jobs lead to further jobs.

In the industrial arena, a chemist gets a job, without any promise of lifelong tenure: in fact, the usual employment contract calls for a month's notice on either side. In our company, that entry-level job for a bachelor's degree holder has the title "assistant scientist." Satisfactory performance, which means a performance rating of excellent or outstanding, can result in promotions to associate scientist, scientist, and then a branching. One branch leads the individual contributor to senior scientist and research fellow; and the other branch, into management, leads to research group leader, manager, senior manager, and division manager. The latter course has led at least one white male chemist to vice president, senior vice president, and executive vice president. The steps for the consecutive, progressive achievement are there, have been followed by some men, and are not, *per se,* closed to women. It should be recognized, however, that all the steps are not taken by all the men. No scientific company can have all the assistant scientists become executive vice presidents, just as no university can have all the assistant professors become distinguished professors. The progression is possible but not assured.

Since these, then, are what I call conventional development, we consider next what sort of range and scope is involved with alternatives.

We should look at the career development of two major groupings of people: those who of themselves do not buy into the "get ahead syndrome" and those who by virtue of their shape or color of their skins are not allowed to be in that system. Women should realize that not all men buy into or are successful "in the system." For those who want to and do not make it, there is the numbing realization that they do not have the external excuse of discrimination. Discrimination can range from the historic and blatant to the subtle and seemingly decorous. Blatant discrimination historically kept black people from certain fields where no one was hired or trained, so, obviously, no one was ever ready; for example, the discrimination that kept Percy Julian, the eminent black chemist, from working for one particular industry, because the labs were located in a fairly isolated community that had a law forbidding anyone to house a Negro overnight. An example of subtle discrimination is the grouping together of all the women in a laboratory to work for one woman who is allowed to progress only so far. These are the so-called "harem labs."

Can you avoid discrimination in building your career? No. The blatant forms are generally outlawed these days. If you run into them, you can fight, if you care to. The subtle forms are all around us but are evaporating. (You can tell this was written on one of my optimistic days, but, even on rereading it and trying it out for feel, I still say that, in general, the subtle forms are evaporating.) Each success of each woman, each good job done by a minority person thins out that persuasive cloud that surrounds us. I look forward to the day when young women, black and white, yellow, brown, and red, can do whatever they choose, whatever they have abilities to do.

There is a subgroup of women who do not stay in the usual career progression, because of life events that introduce breaks in the progression -- events such as, for example, childbirth or family moves based on a career development other than that of the woman herself. Meanwhile, if your shape or skin color keeps you from the consecutive, progressive achievement in professional life that *you* want, don't let that lower your perception of who you are and how valuable *you* are.

The other group, the ones who do not buy into the usual progression, include some people I've referred to in the past as having a certain restlessness. They use their science and scientific training in fields not usually recognized as pure science. I have described them as women scientists much like the others any of us knows: disciplined, trained, intelligent, thoughtful, with that restlessness that pulls them out of the continuum that flows from the laboratory to the classroom and into a different dimension. I have talked with some men who insist that the restlessness is not confined to women and that I should broaden that description to include men scientists also.

What do these people do? They are in business, in law, in administration, in health agencies, in literature. They are deans and presidents of schools and universities. They lead the development and management of new products. They consult, they write science and science fiction. They prosecute patents.

I have said that a scientist needs to pursue and to communicate scientific knowledge. Simply telling people of discoveries, however, is not often the best way to use that knowledge for progress. Someone, at some point, needs to take advantage of that knowledge for the benefit of everyone.

Our economic system is such that the incentive for using knowledge is often the money one can obtain by making the knowledge available. If I discover something new and beneficial that may be worth a hundred million dollars to the people of the nation but it would cost me ten million dollars to do all the development work, the setup, and market development, I have little incentive to give that knowledge broadly to just anyone. If I keep it to myself, progress in that area is not made.

Our Constitution proposes to promote progress in science by securing for limited times to inventors the exclusive right to their discoveries. Our nation says to scientists, "Help progress by telling us what you have discovered, and we will give you protection from others' making, using, or selling your invention for a definite period of time. We'll see that you have a head start in getting to the market before others can use your invention; however, you must tell us precisely and accurately exactly what you've discovered and its usefulness in exchange for that protection." The patent embodies that agreement. It describes in detail what was found new and useful, in language such that anyone skilled in the art may reproduce the invention, and it signifies that for seventeen years from the date of issue no one else may make, use, or sell it without the owner's permission. Patent attorneys present the case to the government in order to secure the agreement. To present the case, the patent attorney needs to have the background in science or engineering to be able to understand and describe, to defend and explain. In other words, the patent attorney needs enough scientific background to be of use to the scientist in presenting the case.

Not all scientists are articulate. Some wave their arms around a lot and make sketches on blackboards when explaining things. Some use jargon and codes, abbreviations, or even make up their own terms. The patent attorney must listen to all this, watch it, sense it, and reduce all of it to writing, in English, in words that are clear and universal, so that first the patent examiner and then those in the field can read it, understand the point, recognize the newness and usefulness, and reproduce the invention if necessary. The patent attorney must be a scientist also -- not doing the research, not making the discoveries, but interrelating to the laboratory scientist to bring forth the words that define the invention and prosecuting the agreement to fulfillment. People react differently to that word "prosecute," reading into it only its meaning of pursuing for redress or punishment. Its first meaning is to follow to the end or pursue until finished, and that is what the patent attorney does. He or she pursues the development of the idea to the end. The end is a piece of intellectual property, valuable as other property is valuable. The owner can then use it to create something for the market. A business can be built; a product can be sold, and humankind can earn a benefit. Over four and a quarter million patents have been granted by the United States up to March, 1981. Not all, of course, are equally valuable. All *do* say someone has found something new and useful and has shared that knowledge with the nation. Progress has been made; at least two scientists have communicated scientific knowledge.

As you probably suspect, mine has not been a conventional career in either the sense of consecutive progressive movement or a permanent direction. Because I see what has happened to me as being both pro-active and re-active, it probably has little in terms of direct pattern development for any readers, but it may have tremendous indirect

importance when you translate the factors in my life and the responses
I found possible to the factors in your life and the range of responses
possible for you. From the time I remember a serious direction in
terms of what I wanted to do, it was to have a career in medicine. Oh,
I had always enjoyed mathematics and music, loved them, in fact; but
I really had no idea anyone could make a living at something that was
so utterly, personally delightful. I had no role models whatsoever for
those two fields, and my interests in them have always remained collateral and something I do *for me*. Medicine was something I saw people
earning community respect and money at doing. I even knew a woman
doctor who was a graduate of Boston University Medical School, and I
pored over her college and high school year books to obtain information concerning her leadership activities, courses and outside interests
in order to follow in her footsteps. My one serious college application
was to Boston University. Although Yale gave a scholarship to a graduate of my high school, I wasn't eligible; the principal explained to
my mother that, had I been a boy .... I was accepted to Boston
University College of Liberal Arts. Perhaps I should indicate that college was not the usual path in my family. My brother and I, in the
same public school grade, were the first in my family to earn high
school diplomas. My degree from Boston University, with a chemistry
major, was the first degree in my family, ever. The chemistry major
came as a decision that clicked into place one morning in a sophomore
organic chemistry class when the premedical curriculum and my delight
in the orderliness of organic chemistry came together and, since most
premeds majored in a scientific field, I saw chemistry as the one I preferred. I took the professional chemistry major and the biology courses
needed for medical school application and applied to Boston University
Medical School, for that was the reason for all of it.

Reality hit when I was told that the Medical School took in two
black applicants a year and that a male veteran and a woman with an
advanced degree were ahead of me. I cried for a week and remember
to this day the psychic effort necessary to keep my life together, to
make some positive plans for salvaging something out of the devasta-
tion that hit me that spring, thirty-four years ago. What could I do?
Well, that chemistry major was there, and the math and physics.
When pressed for a positive response and an end to the wringing of
hands, I said I would go to graduate school and add to the liberal arts

"philosophy of life" degree some graduate training, so I could get a job as a chemist. Somehow, a different medical school to an M.D. did not seem the path for me. If the B. U. quota kept me out, what chance did I have at any other school, where I was a complete stranger?

I applied for and was accepted to Howard University Graduate School, in the Chemistry Department which was accredited by the American Chemical Society for the training of chemists, although Boston University at that time was not.

A Master's degree there, then a year in the Department of Physiology at the Howard University Medical School as a research assistant, and three years teaching chemistry at Virginia State College followed. Each of these moves was a reaction, a way of allowing things to happen to me, rather than choosing what I wanted and going after it. After all, I had wanted Boston University Medical School so much, had worked so hard for it, and had it removed so irrevocably that I feared wanting anything else that much, and I accepted what was offered. So, I tried in this place, and I tried in another. I was a control chemist in a pharmaceutical house, a medical technologist in a hospital lab in Connecticut, a graduate student in physical chemistry at Boston University, an organist at various churches of various denominations in Virginia, in D. C., in Connecticut, a biophysicist at a medical research institute in Connecticut, and a research chemist at a major industrial concern in my home town. That part of my résumé is difficult to write even today. What was I doing? I don't know. I certainly wasn't planning anything. Pulling out of that phase required effort. With my husband as sympathetic supporter, I looked at what I was, where I was, what I would probably be doing for the rest of my life and decided that I would work. There was no life of leisure or moneyed indulgence on the horizon. I also decided that I would do something satisfying to me that was not a routine, nine to five putting in time, but something I could sink my mind into. I would stop dallying and be a chemist. This required the union card, the Ph.D., so I set out to earn it in order to give validity to my abilities. You can get the chance to do the job if you have the educational credentials to get the interview and the person hiring is willing to take the risk.

I applied for and was accepted for admission to Yale Graduate School. I took quite seriously the stated requirements about placement exams and language exams. My son, who went to the nursery school at Yale Divinity School, and I were perhaps Yale's oddest couple. As those years fade into my past, they acquire a patina of pleasantness. They were difficult, long, challenging, stimulating, and have given me an abiding impatience with shoddy thinking. You know, exercising your mind is like exercising your body. It starts tiring and exhausting, but continued use leads to conditioning and to the feeling of exhilaration and an addiction to thought. You sense what you can do, and you enjoy trying it. You look for the opportunity each day. You want challenge in your work.

Anyway, there were tears in graduate school but also delight. Remembering, for instance, that one of your committee members for your thesis said, "I liked the way you handled the math." Then came the job. Industry? A medical school research position? Teaching? I had not enjoyed the teaching earlier, when I taught nonscience majors general and organic chemistry. They seemed to lack the fire to want to learn, and somehow I couldn't kindle it in them. Because I didn't feel that I could handle being a black person in a white world, *and* a woman in a man's world, *and* a Ph.D. in an M.D. world at the hospital in New Haven, I looked at industry.

I found this strange company with an *esprit de corps* that was humanizing and that urged people to look at inventive things they could do. While it was certainly not perfect, it tried different ways of providing a worklife for people which allowed them to continue to grow. I became a member of Polaroid Corporation, in the research labs, and spent seven years there as a chemist in the analytical labs and as a supervisor in the black and white lab. (Black and white refers to the photographic emphasis as opposed to color and not to the ethnic mix.) However, I was feeling no real sense of consecutive, progressive achievement. Then I had an occasion to talk with an engineer with whom I had interacted on a company matter, an engineer who was currently going to law school. And I heard myself say, "Were I to start over, I'd be a lawyer." That verbalization shocked me, but I thought about it and realized that, of course, we cannot start over but, if we want something, we should try for it. I decided that if I really wanted law I should try for it. I transferred into the patent department, on a career exposure (a program Polaroid has that allows one to experience a different field without making a final commitment to it). I applied for evening law school, prepared for the law school admissions test, and on acceptance went to law school after work three or four evenings per week.

It took three calendar years to finish. Half-way through, right at the end of first-semester, second-year exams, I was injured in an automobile accident and had a broken foot, broken back, and broken jaw; but I did not stop, because I feared that the loss of momentum might make it impossible to start again. I learned some things then; for example, how to maneuver through the turnstile at the law library on crutches, with a cast on my leg and a brace on my back. But I also learned that thinking about human reactions can be as stimulating as thinking about reaction mechanisms and that the two can be complementary. During work, I did the sorts of things described earlier as the role of a patent attorney. I worked with scientists from our research labs, people I had worked with earlier as a colleague. They knew I understood them. I knew what they were saying. It was a tremendously satisfying mental interaction.

I passed our state bar and the Patent and Trademark Office bar and became a patent attorney. There I wish to stop this story, for what I'm doing now is in another direction, a tale for another day, not completed, still forming.

What has it all meant? Has it been satisfying? I can't elaborate on all the meanings, but let me tell you of just one moment that was satisfying, one very recent moment. This year Nabisco has published a poster on "Famous Black American Scientists." Both Dean Jewel Plummer Cobb and I are in it and are two of the three women portrayed. The poster has had rather broad circulation, and one day about a week ago I received a set of letters from a fourth-grade class at a science and music magnet school in Houston, Texas. One of the letters read:

Dear Mrs. Hopkins,

When I grow up I hope to be just like you, have a good education, study a lot, and maybe get two degrees. We learned that if we try hard we might be able to accomplish what you have done. I hope you come and visit us some time.

Love,
Desireé Durousseau

You can imagine my delight and my sense of responsibility as a role model. You can imagine the very warm glow of recognition that my life had meaning for youngsters who could desire to follow.

Were *one* of you to be encouraged or inspired, or just more accepting of herself, I would say I have my reward and that it is worth it.

Scientific Sexism: The World of Chemistry

Anne M. Briscoe

This chapter deals partly with sexism in chemistry in general, partly with one career, my own, as a particular illustration, and finally with a program of action for women individually and collectively.[1] The story of my career may have some historical value as an example of institutional barriers that can be overwhelming if they are encountered at very crucial stages. First, it must be pointed out that a summary of my present activities obscures a lot of my personal and professional history. To explain where I am "coming from," I am one of the senior people at the Purdue Conference, having been born before women had the vote in this country. The nineteenth amendment was sent to the states for ratification in June of 1919 when I was six months old and ratified in August of 1920, somewhat before my second birthday. So, I was a child in the twenties. Edith and Archie Bunker described those days as "you knew where you were then -- girls were girls and men were men," and all the standards were double. If you read a biography in American Men and Women of Science, a person is born and then there's no more information until she graduates from college. I'll get to the point where I received my doctorate. That was in 1949. I had been at Yale four years, and I think that would be viewed favorably by Dr. Hornig as a respectable length of time in which to do it. When people talk about first-class institutions, I think Yale compares fairly favorably, and the Department of Biochemistry in those days had many very distinguished people.

I had goals at the time -- career goals. First, I did a post-doctoral year at the University of Pennsylvania because a representative from NIH came to Yale (in those days they came around to see the fellows) and said he felt that I needed a post-doctoral year. I took that as a compliment. A year later, in 1950, when I finished my post-doctoral year, I decided to look for a job. I did this at something called the annual FASEB meetings. FASEB stands for Federation of American Societies for Experimental Biology, and it includes the six major societies in the biomedical sciences. FASEB runs a job bureau every year and I registered with it. There were many jobs in 1950 and the young men who had graduated with me were getting twenty-five interviews with offers of tenure-track positions. I got three interviews. Although on paper I should have looked as capable as any of the men, I was apparently the wrong sex. The three positions I was offered were not really what I wanted. That is to say, I had the idea that I would teach biochemistry to medical students as I had done as a teaching fellow at Yale. I would also teach graduate students, and I would have a teaching appointment in a department of biochemistry of a medical school. I would do basic research in biochemistry. Well, I have never had a teaching appointment in a department of biochemistry and the best research opportunities that I have had have not been in basic research. Rather, they have been in clinical research. However, I don't think that I am unusual in not having been able to achieve the career goals that I had when I first emerged. Many men don't achieve their career goals and have to adapt their ambitions to reality. I was just thinking today about what had happened to the young men who were fellow students. Two of them didn't achieve their career goals because they died young. Two or three others have had undistinguished careers, as I have had, and the fourth one, who did the most pedestrian research, is a university president.

I am going to leave that subject of my individual experience for a moment because the sub-title of this chapter is, "The world of chemistry." I know you have seen a lot of statistics but a few more may not be out of order. When I remembered that I had given a very specific title for this chapter I was appalled that I had done so since I had no recent data. But there is a woman's network and I tapped into it. I phoned Sister Agnes Ann Green who is retired and living in Los Angeles, because I remembered that she had done a survey of women in chemistry for the Women Chemist's Committee of the American Chemical Society a few years ago. I thought even five or six-year-old data might be better than none, but it turned out that she had done a very recent update from 1978-79. That is about as recent as you can get unless you are Betty Vetter or Lilli Hornig. Sr. Agnes had the following sources for her material: the fourth edition of *College Chemistry*

Faculties, that is put out by the American Chemical Society (1979b); *The directory of graduate research* (American Chemical Society 1979a); a publication of the National Academy of Sciences (1979a) called *Climbing the academic ladder: Doctoral women scientists in academe* and the *Survey of doctoral recipients* of the National Academy of Sciences (1979b). Let us first consider institutions that confer only a B.S. degree, or a B.S. and M.S.; that is, the ones that do not have doctoral programs. There is an interesting chart in *College Chemistry Faculties* that gives the data by states. It contains the total number of chemistry professors, or chemistry faculty in each state, and the number and the percentage who are women.

I will begin with the most important state at the Purdue Conference: Indiana. In Indiana there are thirty-three different institutions that are in this category of granting only a B.S. or just B.S. and M.S. and in which one wouldn't think that research was all that important in getting appointed anyway. Teaching in those thirty-three institutions in 1977-78 were one hundred sixty-three men and ten women. The percentage of women was six. In comparison with the rest of the United States, there are twenty states that are worse; that is, they have a lower percentage of women on the chemistry faculty, and there are twenty-nine that are better. Thus, Indiana almost makes it to the middle. But how many of these institutions had *no* women at all? Out of the thirty-three, twenty-five did not employ any women and that is seventy-six percent. Again, comparing Indiana with the rest of the United States, to give you a little food for thought, only four states had a larger absolute number of colleges which did not employ women in chemistry but three of those had so many more institutions that their percentages are better. Only TEXAS had a higher percentage of colleges that excluded women.

Now let us examine universities that offer doctorates in chemistry and we shall consider data from '78-'79. Sister Agnes got responses from one hundred eighty-eight institutions. I think there are actually one hundred ninety-six but it does not change the picture if you include the rest of them. Collectively, they employ somewhat over four thousand faculty. Out of the actual four thousand two hundred fifty-three, there are only one hundred twenty-nine women teaching chemistry in the research institutions that give Ph.D.'s in chemistry, or three percent. In that year fourteen percent of the doctorates, or two hundred fourteen, went to women. There were twenty-eight full professors out of the one hundred twenty-nine. They were teaching at Auburn, Howard, Delaware, Toledo, West Virginia, Louisville, Illinois, Wyoming, Cleveland State, Arizona State and Kent State -- good institutions, but not great. You have to do down to the assistant professors to find names such as Purdue, Duke, Harvard, Dartmouth, Brown, MIT, Cal Tech and Wisconsin.

Has the picture changed any from '71-'72 to '78-'79? Well, it depends on how one looks at it. The percentage of women teaching in a chemistry department at this type of institution increased from one and one half percent to three percent. In terms of percentage it is a one hundred fold increase, but by the end of the decade there were still ninety-five institutions that had no women on their chemistry faculties. Against this, Purdue does not look so bad; it had two out of forty-nine full-time faculty in '78-'79. This represents an increase of two women in eight years since there were none eight years ago. I don't know if anybody has been appointed since. At that time and now, Indiana University has no women in its Chemistry Department. Two, it turns out, is above the national university average. You can count on the fingers of one hand the institutions in the United States that have more than two women in their chemistry departments: American University has four; Rutgers has five; Polytechnic of New York has four, and the University of Maryland has three.

Suppose you never wanted to do that sort of chemistry -- inorganic, organic, physical, analytical, colloid, polymers. Rather, you wanted to do biochemistry. How hospitable is that sub-specialty? Actually, it is a little better. In that year ('78-'79) approximately ten percent of the people teaching biochemistry were women. Those figures exclude the women with doctorates in biochemistry who are appointed to the clinical departments of the medical schools. That is probably where most women in biochemical research are employed. Many of them have titles such as "Senior Scientist:" appointments that do not lead to tenure, do not entitle one to sabbatical leave, and have no opportunity for upward mobility. The full professorships for women in biochemistry were found at more prestigious institutions than were the professorships in chemistry, but not at Purdue. They are at Columbia, Cornell, Yale, Pennsylvania, New York University, Case Western Reserve, Baylor, Pittsburgh, and Ohio State. The overall increase in biochemistry women faculty between '76 and '78 was one and two-tenths percent. At that rate it might take eighty years for us to achieve parity. In 1979, twenty-nine departments had no women at all: that is twenty-one percent. This is better than the fifty-one percent of chemistry departments that exclude women. The scientific establishment, with a little help from sociologists like Jonathan Cole (1979), contend that women get their fair share of the jobs. The argument is that the numbers appointed represent the proportion of, I hate to say this, "qualified women;" that there just are not any more to be found. There is another spurious argument that women are less productive, publish fewer papers, papers of lesser quality. Some say they must be of lesser quality because they are cited less often by other authors, (as judged by the number of biographical citations). I looked in the references of *Fair Science* to see if Cole cited a book that I edited. I was co-editor of the New York Academy of Sciences annal that resulted from the 1978 Conference, *Expanding the Role of Women in the Sciences* (Briscoe and Pfafflin 1978), and it wasn't mentioned. But I allowed that perhaps the publication of ours and his were too close in 1979, and that he wasn't aware of it. However, I looked to see whether Ruth Kundsin's annal on *Successful Women in the Sciences* had been cited because that was published in 1973. There was no reference to it. In fact a number of other books of which I think he should have been aware are not cited.

Let us consider the size of the pool, that allegedly small pool from which women might be selected for faculty appointments. Dr. Bernice Sandler, Director of the Project on the Status of Education of Women of the Association of American Colleges, has current, authoritative data. Her most recent figure taken from a 1981 supplement to *Professional Women and Minorities* (Scientific Manpower Commission 1981) is that since 1960, Ph.D.'s in chemistry were granted to 3,260 women. How many of them have we accounted for in faculty positions? We found five hundred and two in schools that do not give a Ph.D. and one hundred thirty-two in the Ph.D. granting institutions for a total of six hundred thirty-four, or about one-fifth. Where are the other 2626? Some work in industry, but all available data show that far fewer women work in industry than in academia. Some are employed in government laboratories. Still others are working in fields other than chemistry, and some may have dropped out of the job market altogether. Note that the total figure of three thousand two hundred sixty does not include biochemistry and thus the two hundred twenty-seven women who have appointments in biochemistry departments are not included in my estimate of the number of Ph.D. chemists we can account for. It does seem, however, as if the pool of women chemists qualified for academic appointments is far larger than the total of six hundred thirty-four implies. A reasonable conclusion is that there must be widespread discrimination and institutional sexism in chemistry departments.

Let's look at another subfield in chemistry, namely clinical chemistry. I am a member of the American Association for Clinical Chemistry. Its directory lists five thousand members, but doesn't tell how many are women. You have to go through and count them up as well as you can but I DID IT! Twenty-three percent of the members have identifiable feminine names. There are some that just don't have any gender connotation for me so I left them out, but at least eleven hundred women are listed there. Undoubtedly there are women working in clinical chemistry who have not joined the society but there is no way of knowing. Now, how many of the eleven hundred have a doctorate? Thirty-three percent or three hundred eighty-three.

Since I wanted to know more about clinical chemistry, I phoned the National Office and was duly connected to the Assistant Executive Director. It turns out that he is not only the Assistant Executive Director, but also the Director of Finances and Accounting. When I asked him about women, he immediately said he could tell me about their salaries. He wanted to know why I was interested and I said I had noticed that there were no women editors among the twenty men on the Board of Editors of the official journal called, *Clinical Chemistry*. On the Advisory Boards, there were two women out of twenty so that is two out of forty, or five percent. I told him that a lot of talent was being wasted because women generally write well and are good editors. He said he would send me the 1978 salary survey, and it arrived on March 17 with this note, "Here is the survey. I hope it is useful. I didn't realize that women excelled in writing and verbal ability. I thought it was just cooking and cleaning and stuff. Thanks for the tip. I do look forward to meeting you. Cheers!"

This is what his data show. For male clinical chemists who have bachelor's degrees, the average salary in 1978 was $20,000 a year. For women it was $18,200. With a master's degree, the average salary was $23,000 for a man, and $19,000 for a woman, and these figures are a little further apart. When you get to the Ph.D. level, the average man was earning $32,000, and the average woman was earning $26,290, which is a difference of $5,710. That is only confirmation of the idea that the divergence is greater with the years; as men get older, and, I think, equally senile, they are considered to be worth more. Private labs and industrial employers pay the highest salaries, of course, as in other fields, indicating that this is an area where there is some opportunity. But if you think about what you have been told and what I have been saying, one must ask the question, "Why should a nice girl go into chemistry?" She might be better off to go into one of those womanly traditional fields like teaching or library science. The answer to that is that those fields do not pay well either. The salaries in clinical chemistry are at least as good as those that teachers and librarians get. A woman does not get to be the school principal or the head of the library. Even in nursing, a very large percentage of the directors of nursing services are men. You may as well choose a field that interests you, and for which you feel suited intellectually and emotionally. If you work harder than most men, you will probably have a career and you will earn less unless you have the kind of qualifications that say, somebody like Esther Hopkins has, that is, double qualifications; or Janet Berry, another superwoman who, like Hopkins, has a Ph.D. in chemistry and a law degree and who is President of the American Institute of Chemists. I don't think that really tells you very much about changes in chemistry, but it may represent a change in the American Institute of Chemists.

Well, I left off in my biography at the point where I took a job. I was appointed to a prestigious institution -- Cornell University Medical College but *not* in the Department of Biochemistry. I was the biochemist in the Department of Psychiatry where I had no biochemical colleagues, where I was really isolated. This was at a very crucial stage, just when I had finished my post-doctoral fellowship and should have been working where there was a very lively research group of people from whom I could learn. That was not the case.

I wrote letters to four or five chairmen of biochemistry departments. I spoke to two of them, and I was told that my credentials were very good; but each said he didn't want a woman. That was

1950-51 when sex discrimination was legal. I had no opportunity to teach at Cornell. I wanted to teach; I liked teaching. I went over to Hunter College which was just four blocks away and applied for a position to teach at night in the chemistry department. I was told that the chairman did not want a woman. I went to the physiology department since a biochemist is somewhat of a biologist and physiologist and was hired. I taught at Hunter College for a total of seventeen years: fourteen at night while I was working in the daytime and an additional two years as an adjunct in the School of Health Sciences. I also taught in the nursing school at our hospital. I helped to develop a hospital-based physicians' assistant program and taught in it. I have supervised laboratories for several generations of house staff physicians; and I have had a continual series of laboratory technician-trainees from the New York City High Schools and prepared them for licenses as Clinical Laboratory Technicians.

Going back in the saga of my personal history, I suddenly got married in the summer of 1955. I mean it looked sudden to other people. I was married in London and when I came back and announced that I had gotten married, it did seem a bit sudden. Then I relocated twice because of my husband's career and came to Columbia nearly twenty-five years ago. When I left Cornell, I was an assistant professor of biochemistry. When I came to Columbia, the chairman of the Biochemistry Department said he could not possibly make me an assistant professor and I didn't see what I could do. I spent the next sixteen years doing clinical research in the Department of Medicine. My title was Associate in Biochemistry, and for sixteen years I was not promoted. I was publishing, but I felt invisible in the medical school. Much of the dissatisfaction I felt in the laboratory and in the general situation in the Department of Medicine was offset by the teaching because I had wonderful students, and if you like to teach, that makes up for a great deal.

All those years, I really thought that there was something wrong with me: I had not worked hard enough; I was not smart enough. It just didn't occur to me that that American Dream was not correct: the dream or myth that if you worked hard enough, you would get there. That is what everybody of my generation was brought up to believe. What changed me from a conformist to an activist was not something that happened overnight. It began at one of those FASEB meetings I described earlier. I had attended them since 1946 but had never seen very many women. But in 1966 I got an invitation to something that was called, "The Women Scientists Champagne Mixer." Of course to some people "Mixer" means men. I thought it looked interesting and I went. What amazed me was how many women there were in these societies. Perhaps we were very much outnumbered by the men, but there were a lot of women. They were doing very important work, and they had the same sort of low ranks and lack of recognition in their institutions as I had. The gathering was organized by Dr. Virginia Upton, who at that time was on the periphery of Yale. She worked in the West Haven V. A. Hospital. She is now a Vice President of Wyeth International, one of the world's major drug companies. She single-handedly got the names of all the women who had attended those meetings the year before and invited them to this Champagne Mixer and got a sponsor to pay for the champagne. It took us years to form what is now the Association for Women in Science. We met in 1966, '67, '68, and '69 and nothing seemed to happen; but the Women's Movement was incubating. In 1970 the late Judith Pool of Stanford University suggested that we discuss the problems of women scientists instead of just meeting socially. Thus, we had a more formal type of meeting in 1970 after the champagne or before, I'm not sure which, but we still did not get organized. We circulated something that said, "If there were an organization, would you join?" But we didn't form it until 1971. The tenth Anniversary of the founding of the Association for Women in Science or AWIS, as we call it, was April 13, 1981. Once we got going, once we had an organization and a conviction that this was something we needed, that this was something that might help to improve the status and the opportunities for women in the sciences, we began to do a lot of different things. Among them, and one of the first things when we were not yet a year old, was to institute along with some of the other women's advocacy groups, a lawsuit against NIH and the Department of Health, Education and Welfare (AWIS v. Richardson 1972) charging them with violating the executive order to appoint more women to the public advisory committees, the committees that give out the research money. While the suit was in the courts, the percentage of women on these committees went from about two to twenty. The executive order, or at least the order from the head of NIH, was that no more men should be appointed until the committees were thirty-three percent women. When they got to be twenty percent, the men began to say that there weren't enough qualified women. The backlash came and I doubt if it ever went beyond twenty percent. However, it does make a difference that there are more women on these committees.

AWIS publishes a bimonthly newsletter with information about its members, activities of its chapters, legislation pending in Congress, deadlines for research grant applications, employment opportunities and feminist issues. In addition, a job list is mailed every three weeks to members who request it. AWIS has a computerized registry of women scientists in its Washington office that serves as a resource for employers and for nominations for public advisory committees. It represents a constructive answer to those who claim that there are "no qualified women" to explain why they are not in compliance with affirmative action requirements. Membership is not restricted to women nor is it restricted to those with degrees. Students comprise about twenty-five percent of the membership. An open invitation to join is extended to all who are students, faculty or just persons who would like "to promote equal opportunities for women to enter the professions and to achieve their career goals," the statement of the mission of AWIS.

Another lawsuit that was instituted (WEAL v. Weinberger 1974) was on the basis of discrimination in hiring and employment at educational institutions and in the failure of the Office of Civil Rights to look into formally filed complaints within a reasonable length of time. That suit was joined with another lawsuit that involved race discrimination and the case was won in the sense that the judge ruled that we had standing to bring the suit. If you are not a lawyer, you may not understand that. However, after that, the judge asked us to draw up a timetable for a complaint to be heard and a judgment to be rendered. The plan and timetables were agreed to between our lawyers and the government lawyers in 1977, and then the President transferred those regulations from the Department of Health, Education and Welfare (now HHS) to the Department of Labor. That's where it sits. I do not know how it is doing now, but there was a brief period when the Director of the Office of Civil Rights, who was appointed by President Carter, was Eleanor Holmes Norton. She was able to get him to increase her budget by a very large amount and therefore to increase the staff and to get at the backlog of some of those cases.[2]

There are chapters of AWIS in sixteen cities that are effective support groups for women. Perhaps women at Purdue should think of forming a chapter in West Lafayette because Chicago is too far. Looking at the chemistry data here, I think Purdue needs an active and visible chapter on campus.

Active participation in an AWIS chapter may influence your career. It may help you to deal more effectively with institutional sexism. I found that participation in the women's movement not only changed my perspective of myself, but also my leadership role unexpectedly impressed my colleagues, many of whom had not noticed me before. In 1972, Columbia University promoted me to assistant professor, eighteen years after my first assistant professorship at Cornell. In 1976, twenty-five years after I joined the faculty, I was given a tenured appointment. Did I achieve my career goals? No, but I survived professionally. Moreover, salaries in clinical departments are much higher than those in the basic sciences. And in the last decade, I turned my energy and commitment away from research and have devoted my efforts to the professional women's struggle for equal opportunities. I have had the great privilege and immeasurable satisfaction of guiding AWIS, of helping other women toward their goals, and of participating in the effort to crack the male monopoly of power in the scientific establishment.

It is an effort that is more a hope than a reality at present. There are two aspects to the challenge, one being their deficiencies and the other being our own. The scientific establishment is not composed of male saints. They are ordinary men who control the means of science. They are not different from men in government, in business or in labor unions. They are not different with respect to morality, politics, fair play, or even the degree of objectivity of which they are capable. They are, however, the people who control who gets the fellowship, who gets the research grant, who gets to present the paper at the meeting, who gets the visibility presiding over the scientific session, or whose papers get published in the prestigious journal. In other words, one point I wish to make is that we have a lack of power. The real point is that we lack power in society generally, and we are not going to improve this situation until we wake up the sleeping giant of fifty-one percent of the population -- women -- and exercise our potential power at the polls. We have little or no representation in the legislatures and law courts at all levels; we are taxed and governed without representation; and we are co-conspirators in our own subjugation because we have the means of changing the balance of power and we do not use it. We all should be giving a lot of time, effort and money to the women's advocacy groups. We have to continue to support the concept of affirmative action for everyone, not just our own special interest groups. Enforcement of affirmative action requirements has not been good; nevertheless, it has made a difference that employers must say they are "equal opportunity employers." It has propaganda value; it has the effect of water wearing away the stone. There is more acceptance of it than is immediately apparent. We must try very hard in this interlude of a conservative tide in Washington to hold on to what we have and at the same time to work through political and women's organizations to win back some of those seats in the House and Senate. WE COULD CAUSE A SOCIO-ECONOMIC REVOLUTION IN THE UNITED STATES JUST BY GETTING ENOUGH WOMEN TO VOTE.

Notes

1. This chapter was the luncheon address delivered on the second day of the Purdue Conference.

2. In August of 1982 the Reagan administration requested the Department of Education (which inherited the pertinent equal opportunity regulations from HHS) and the Department of Labor to phase out by 1985 the mandated time limits on resolving complaints about discrimination. Lawyers for both the Women's Equity Action League and the National Association for the Advancement of Colored People argued in court against the elimination of time tables. Early in 1983, Judge John H. Pratt, of the U.S. District Court of the District of Columbia, who had mandated the original time tables, issued a new order reimposing time limits. He ruled that the federal agencies had not proved that deadlines were no longer needed. This new order should lead to stepped-up enforcement of civil rights laws at educational institutions and also to resolution of some longstanding complaints by students and faculty. -eds.

References

American Chemical Society. 1979a. *American Chemical Society directory of graduate research.* Washington, D.C.: American Chemical Society.

———. 1979b. *College chemistry faculties, fourth edition.* Washington, DC.: American Chemical Society.

AWIS et al. v. Elliott Richardson and Robert Q. Marston. 1972. C.A. 594-72, District of Columbia.

Briscoe, A. M., and S. H. Pfafflin, eds. 1979. *Expanding the role of women in the sciences.* New York: New York Academy of Sciences.

Cole, J. R. 1979. *Fair science: Women in the scientific community.* New York: Free Press.

Kundsin, R. B., ed. 1973. *Successful women in the sciences: An analysis of determinants.* New York: New York Academy of Sciences.

National Academy of Sciences. 1979a. *Climbing the academic ladder: Doctoral women scientists in academe.* Report of the Committee on the Education and Employment of Women in Science and Engineering. Washington, D.C.: Commission on Human Resources.

National Academy of Sciences. 1979b. *Survey of doctoral recipients.* Washington, D.C.: National Research Council.

Scientific Manpower Commission. 1981. *Professional women and minorities. 1981.* A Manpower Data Resource Service of the Scientific Manpower Commission, 2nd edition supplement. Washington, D.C.: Scientific Manpower Commission.

WEAL, et al. v. Caspar W. Weinberger, et al. 1974. C.A. 74-1720, District of Columbia.

You've Come a Long Way Baby:
The Myth and the Reality

Naomi J. McAfee

Equal Pay for Equal Work?

Throughout history profound remarks have been made by men about the influence and impact of women on society; but history has also shown that the more prolific and high sounding the rhetoric about women and their special place in society, the lower the status of women in that society. How does that apply to us today? We are being told that women are beginning to be accepted in all areas of society and in the workforce; that equal pay for equal work is a reality; and that there is no longer a need for legislation to protect women or to ensure that in the eyes of the law, as guaranteed by the Constitution, women are equal.

As can be seen from table 1, almost thirty four-percent of all women over the age of sixteen were working in 1950, and the percentage has steadily increased since then. Today nearly fifty-two percent of all women over the age of sixteen are in the workforce and it is projected that by 1990 fifty-three percent of all such women will be employed outside the home.

Women in today's workforce, however, typically work in areas that are known as predominately female fields (clerical, secretarial, and so forth), which have a low monetary return. Consequently, in 1979, a woman, on the average, earned only fifty-nine cents for every dollar earned by a man (U.S. Bureau of the Census 1981).[1] Most of the high incomes are earned by people in the male-dominated professions. Women have been in these professions, in small numbers, for many years and, as shown in table 2, they constitute a small albeit increasing minority even now. Of note is a significant disparity between women

Table 1. Participation Rates for Women Over 16 in the Workforce

Year	Percentage in Workforce
1950	33.9
1960	37.9
1978	50.0
1980	51.6
1990 (Projected)	52.9

Source: U.S. Bureau of Labor Statistics. 1980. *Handbook of Labor Statistics.* Washington, D.C.: U.S. Government Printing Office.

in the professions and women in management. Using engineering as an example, one would expect at least four percent of the engineering managers to be women, and yet only 0.05 percent of engineering managers are women.

Table 2. Women in the Professions, 1980

Professions	Percentage Women
Medicine (MD's)	13.4
Legal	13.0
Accounting	36.2
Management	26.1
Engineering	4.0
Dentistry	4.3
Engineering Managers[a]	0.05

Sources: U.S. Bureau of Labor Statistics. 1981. *Employment and Earnings.* Washington, D.C.: Superintendent of Documents, January, 1981; Engineering Manpower Commission. 1976. *Engineering as a Profession for Women.* New York: Engineers' Joint Council.

[a]This data was obtained from a survey made by the author.

What is the reason for the difference? Many factors come into play. One major reason given is that it has been only recently that significant numbers of women entered the engineering field, and it takes experience on the job before one can be promoted into a management position. Figure 1 shows the growing number of women enrolled

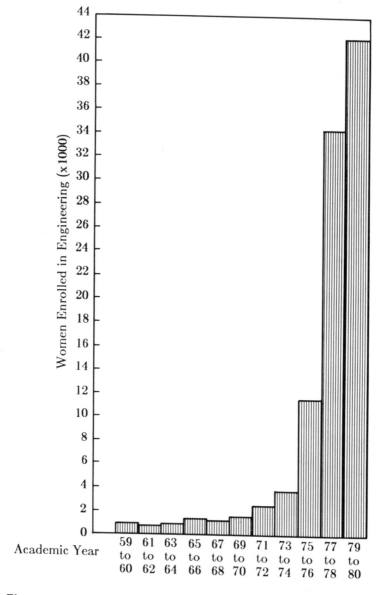

Figure 1. Growing Number of Women Enrolled in Engineering Schools, 1959-1980.

Source: Society of Women Engineers. 1980. *Report on Women Undergraduate Engineering Students, 1959-1979.* New York: Society of Women Engineers.

in engineering schools from 1959 through 1980.

The Society of Women Engineers has conducted a survey of its members for a number of years to try and define the salary, responsibility level, and job title, that is, the "Profile of the Woman Engineer." Responses about responsibility levels are shown in table 3 for the years 1974, 1977 and 1979. Of the approximately eight thousand society members in 1981, five thousand are students, and four hundred sixty-two answered in 1974, 1,109 in 1977 and 1,318 in 1979. For each year shown, at least five percent of the respondents indicated that they were managers or supervisors providing direct supervision over components ranging from teams or small units to major organizations. This contrasts with the survey (table 2) which shows that only 0.05 percent of engineering managers were women, because these latter data were based on job titles and women did not hold management titles.

Table 3. Management Responsibility

	1974	1977	1979
None	37%	40%	40%
Indirect or Staff Supervisor	23	23	23
Supervisor of Team or Unit	14	12	13
Project/Section Manager	13	16	14
Major Department or Program Manager	8	5	6
General Manager of Organization	5	2	2
	100	98[a]	98[a]

Source: Society of Women Engineers. 1980. *A Profile of the Women Engineer.* New York: Society of Women Engineers.

[a] For years 1977 and 1979, figures add to 98 percent because two percent of respondents to the survey did not answer this question.

The difference between holding the job and having the job title is usually significant when it comes to pay. Is there a difference in pay, or does equal pay for equal work really exist in the engineering field? One way to decide is to compare salaries of men and women in the field. Therefore, the results from the Society of Women Engineers survey are compared to results of a similar survey conducted by the American Association of Engineering Societies (AAES) in figure 2. The

AAES data cover all engineers, including women. Although it was impossible to remove the women from the AAES survey, their numbers are so small when compared to the total that their inclusion probably has only a minor effect on the data. In the beginning, women engineering graduates with bachelor's degrees are given higher salary job offers than men with the same degrees; that is, women earn twenty-three dollars more a month than men according to a 1980 College Placement Council Survey (College Placement Council 1980). Two years after the degree award, women's salaries are still slightly ahead of men's, but at three years the lines cross; from then on, with only one exception, women engineers consistently earn less than their male counterparts.

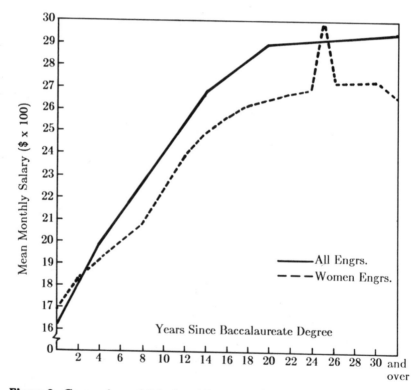

Figure 2. Comparison of Salaries of Female and All Engineers.
Sources: Society of Women Engineers. 1980. *A Profile of the Woman Engineer,* New York: Society of Women Engineers; Engineering Manpower Commission. 1980. *Professional Incomes of Engineers,* New York: American Association of Engineering Societies.

At twenty-five years the exception occurs, but it consists of only five data points (i.e., only five responses from women engineers). After the twenty-five year point, salaries slope down for both men and women. How far have we really come if sex differences in salary persist in a field that is presumably one of the best for women to enter?

Myths About Women

Among the many factors holding women in traditional jobs are myths or "old husband's tales," -- I don't think old wives would have told these -- listed below.

1. *Men won't work for women.* If I can be slightly facetious--men have *always* worked for women. The difference is that now women are asking for a piece of the action and part of the power, and as a result, men are saying, "No way!"

2. *Women won't work for women.* Unfortunately, in this case, I think that women may be their own enemies because, typically, when surveys are conducted, women say they really don't want to give another woman a chance to be supervisor, and they'd rather work for a man. A Gallup poll taken in 1976 asked, "If you were taking a new job and you had a choice of boss, would you prefer working for a man or for a woman?" Three out of every five women said that they preferred to work for a man (American Institute of Public Opinion 1976, 45). Now if we really believe in parity, and that women are equally as capable as men, then we as women have got to start giving other women a chance.

3. *Women won't travel.* Often what happens is a male supervisor makes a decision that she won't travel. The individual woman never has a chance to say yes or no, but she is held responsible for the results. It then becomes a self-fulfilling prophecy.

4. *Women aren't mobile--they can't change job locations.* Again, this becomes a self-fulfilling prophecy because the theory is that a wife follows her husband, not the other way around. The other day, I happened to be in a situation, which after a while, got to be rather hilarious. A couple, both engineers, had left the company. In fact, she had decided to leave and he went with her. All the male managers were bemoaning the loss of this good male engineer and nothing complimentary was being said about her --

she was a malcontent, and so forth. It finally dawned on me that the thing that was bothering them wasn't the fact that we had lost two good engineers, but the fact that sex roles had been reversed. She had left, and he had gone with her. These male managers just couldn't quite take that. When I confronted them with this, there was a blank stare. Somebody told me I didn't understand the situation. Obviously I didn't, and we changed the subject. However, quite often women aren't offered promotions because men, who are in positions of power, feel that women's places are with their husbands and the opportunity to exercise a judgement or make a decision is not given to the individual involved. The individual is held responsible for the decision even though it wasn't hers.

5. *Women are too emotional and can't stand pressure, crisis or conflict.* That may be true. There are emotional women; there are also emotional men. It's very interesting when one gets into a discussion with a male and all of a sudden he says, "Well, if you're going to get emotional, I'm not going to talk to you about it!" People are beginning to recognize that both sexes are emotional, some individuals more so than others and that situations like this do arise. There are some people who can handle crises; there are some people who can't. There is a perception that women don't like conflict. There is also a perception that some women enjoy starting it. Confrontation is one of the modes that management uses for solving problems. It's an interesting technique, more so for a woman than for a man, because people really don't expect a woman to stand her ground--or pound on somebody's door. It is a very effective technique. As far as standing pressure, people stand pressure depending on what the circumstances are. If you look at where most crises and pressures are generated, it's in the home, which is woman's domain, with kids who have to be rushed to the hospital for split lips, broken heads from falling out of trees, and so forth. So, the myth becomes obvious when you look at it in its true light.

6. *Women can't make decisions or enforce discipline.* Anybody who says that never had a mother, school teacher, or possibly even an older sister. Women can make decisions and they can enforce discipline. They do it as required. As far as enforcing discipline in a

professional work force, there really shouldn't be a lot of discipline that has to be enforced. Professionals should work as professionals. But when it's required, the idea is to make sure that it's done very effectively and very professionally.

7. *Women subtly influence men.* Well, there are two heads to that coin, too. If you turn that around, that characteristic in a male executive is called leadership. So, yes, leaders subtly influence people. Our good chemist friend, Prime Minister Thatcher, has proven that a woman can lead equally as well as a man.

8. *Women make very poor corporate images.* What is the typical image of a corporate leader? Somebody who is very tall, very strong, very virile, very macho, instead of somebody who is very intelligent and compassionate.

These myths are what we are fighting today and we will have to work very hard to overcome the barriers they generate. Until we can change these stereotypic perceptions, women in the workforce can expect to remain in low-paying jobs and be promoted at a slower rate than men.

Where Are We and Where Are We Going?

Now, where are we, and where are we going? We have been told that in November, 1980, there was a mandate issued about what was going on and that in the future all of the gains women have made are going to change. The backlash really has already started. I'm hearing things now that I would not have heard when I started to work in 1956; for example, there is the joke about the "women's libber" who went out to a meeting and when she came home she told her husband that she wasn't going to fix dinner, that she was going to another meeting. This happened two or three times, and he finally asked her, "What happens if you don't *see* me for three or four days?" She said, "Ah, that wouldn't be bad." He said, "Well, take your pick, three or four?" And she said, "three". Three days later, she got one of her black eyes opened enough to see him just a little. That story wouldn't have been told fifteen years ago, ten years ago or even a couple of years ago.

Another interesting argument that has surfaced is, "All societies have developed as being male dominated and therefore it must be right." That comes from people who appear to be very much in the forefront of allowing equal opportunity. The affirmative action backlash, the Bakke Case (Regents of the University of California v. Bakke 1978), is another example; the Weber vs. Kaiser Case (United Steel Workers of America v. Weber 1979) is another one. Interestingly enough, the people who complain the most about affirmative action are not the youngsters, the twenty to thirty-year-olds or the thirty to forty-year-olds; it's the forty to fifty-year-olds and beyond. It's ironic that they're complaining about affirmative action because when they were making their way up through the ranks and were really having to compete, there weren't enough women out there to even matter. Their competition was other white males and they couldn't make it. Thus, they rationalize their lack of success by putting blame into an arena which didn't exist then. What's happening in government is also frightening. In 1980 there were over four hundred women in top level government jobs. By count, as much as I could determine yesterday afternoon, there are now less than thirty. A large percentage of those thirty are busily dismantling all the things that we put together to try to get to where we are today.

So, where are we? We are dealing with the perceptions. We've come a long way. For example, there's a movie out today called, "Rosie, the Riveter." If you get a chance to see it, do so; it's almost as good as the movie, "Nine to Five." It shows what happened in the late 1930's and early 1940's when the U.S. got into World War II. It documents how those women were encouraged to enter the work force to keep the war effort going; and, then, after the war was over, and all the work had been done, and Johnny came marching home, the massive propaganda effort that went on to put them back into the bedrooms and kitchens. This movie is based on a novel of the same name (Frank, Ziebarth, and Field 1982). I hope the 1980's will not be a recycling of the late 1940's and early 1950's because I *do* think we've come a long way. I think we've come a long way with just being able to get people together like this to talk about it, to discuss it, and to have the nerve to attend a conference like this. The myth still outweighs the reality because we haven't come as far as the myths would have us believe. The reality is that we are moving and we're not going to stop.

Note

1. According to the Spring 1983 issue of the *National Voter,* published by the League of Women Voters (see page 7), women earned sixty-four cents for every dollar earned by men in 1955, and in 1983 the figure is fifty-nine cents. -eds.

References

American Institute of Public Opinion. 1976. Women in America. *The Gallup Opinion Index Report 128;* Princeton, N.J.: American Institute of Public Opinion.

College Placement Council. 1980. CPC salary survey, final report. Bethlehem, Penn.: The College Placement Council.

Field C., M. Frank, and M. Ziebarth. 1982. *The Life and Times of Rosie the Riveter.* Educator's Edition. Emeryville, Calif.: Clarity Educational Productions.

Regents of the University of California v. Bakke, 438 U.S. 265, 98 S. Ct. 2733, 57 L. Ed. 2d 750 (1978).

U.S. Bureau of the Census. 1981. *Current Population Reports.* Washington, D. C.: U.S. Government Printing Office.

United Steel Workers of America v. Weber, 443 U.S. 193, 99 S. Ct. 2721, 61 L. Ed. 2d 480 (1979).

Women's Views of
Scientific Views of Women

Early Socialization:
Causes and Cures of Mathematics Anxiety

Patricia F. Campbell and Susan C. Geller

Introduction: What is Math Anxiety?

Mathematics avoidance refers to the "voluntary" decision by a large number of people to cease study of quantitative topics. The factors which contribute to this avoidance are many. One of the better known factors is termed mathematics anxiety -- an almost irrational dread of mathematics or quantitative study. It must be noted that anxiety in general is not an illness that must be cured. Rather it is an "essential and complex feeling that does not always function in a totally facilitating manner" (Reyes 1980, 168) Although the issue of mathematics anxiety has received much attention in the last five years, it was the subject of a survey of 704 college students as far back as 1957 (Dreger and Aiken 1957). This survey estimated that thirty-five percent of the sampled college population exhibited mathematics anxiety.

People tend to choose to do the things with which they feel comfortable, to accept those challenges which they are confident they have the ability to meet. As noted by many researchers (Betz 1978, Fennema 1978) high math anxiety is associated with lower achievement in mathematics; and, beginning in adolescence, females exhibit higher anxiety levels than males. This is not to say that mathematics anxiety and mathematics avoidance are exclusively female characteristics. However, with adolescence, females seem to lose confidence in their ability and avoid mathematical study more than males.

Mathematics anxiety is a widespread problem. Some researchers suggest that everyone will at some point in his/her life fear some aspect of mathematics. The concern is when this anxiety over mathematics is not simply an occasional experience but an impediment. As a group, females tend to exhibit deeper and more incapacitating fears than do males (Betz 1978). However, females are typically more open about their emotions than are males; and some researchers believe that the higher anxiety reported by women is a consequence of this openness (Maccoby and Jacklin 1974). Since it is socially acceptable for women to do poorly in mathematics, they are not encouraged nor challenged to overcome their mathematical problems. As the awareness of the phenomenon known as "mathematics anxiety" spreads, two distinct reactions may occur. On one hand, many people may come to recognize their avoidance behavior and to realize that they can work to meet this anxiety without it becoming debilitating. As they cease to be anxious and experience success in mathematics, these people may realize that their self-perception of a lack of mathematical ability was imagined and not actual. However, there is also the danger that others will use "mathematics anxiety" as still one more rationalization to justify avoidance of mathematics.

Another factor influencing math avoidance is the fact that many young women do not see mathematics as useful for their future roles or careers (Fox 1977). Avoidance of mathematics at this stage carries with it a heavy price. Failure to study sufficient mathematics in high school to permit enrollment in calculus upon entrance to college will at the least delay entrance into science/engineering fields and at worst permanently discourage students from ever attempting a major requiring the study of calculus. Thus the study of high school mathematics rather than mathematical ability may be acting as a "critical filter" for many occupations (Sells 1976).

Causes

The causes of math anxiety are varied. Included may be a prior low level of conceptual understanding of mathematical topics, a poor attitude toward mathematics, idealogical issues (e.g. "Mathematics is a male domain"), and inadequate or inappropriate teaching.

Attitude and achievement in mathematics have generally been found to have a low, but statistically significant, correlation. A very strong negative or positive attitude may affect achievement, whereas in the middle range of attitudes, aptitude is a more powerful predictor than attitude (Jackson 1974). The relationship of self-image or self-confidence to attitudes is not clear (Harway et al. 1976).

The extent to which math anxiety is fostered by the sex-role stereotyping of mathematics as a male domain is not documented. This stereotyping by students does not occur until the adolescent years, which is when females begin to exhibit more math anxiety than males (Stein 1971; Stein and Smithells 1969). It may be that this leads to the acceptance of math anxiety in females as being either inevitable or irrelevant. Fox (1977) asks if this causes girls to learn to attribute failure to their lack of ability, while males learn to attribute failure to factors beyond their control. In that case, adolescent girls are learning to avoid situations where they may fail, while adolescent boys are learning to try harder. A recent study (Wolleat et al. 1980) investigating students' causal attributions of performance in mathematics presented evidence consistent with Fox's hypothesis. This study noted that whereas males were likely to attribute their success in mathematics to ability, females were more likely to attribute their success to effort. When asked to explain failure in mathematics, females were more likely to cite a lack of ability and task difficulty than were males.

Sex-role socialization may also have an impact on the interaction between teachers and students in the classroom. Evidence of differential treatment in high school mathematics classes has been published. Becker (1981) noted that male students received more teacher attention, reinforcement and affective contact than did females. She hypothesized a three-step pattern that seemed to shape teacher-student interaction. First, teachers have differential expectations for students based on sex. Teachers then treat students in a manner which is consistent with their sex-role expectations. Finally, the students tend to behave in a manner which is in accordance with the expectations of their teachers. Becker concluded that whereas males were provided "a good cognitive and affective environment in which to learn mathematics," the females seemed to be treated with "benign neglect." One can only speculate the extent to which this socialization in the mathematics classroom may lead young women to conclude that their pursuit of mathematical learning is a waste of time and effort for all involved. Such differential treatment may also lead to a loss of self-confidence and an increase of mathematics avoidance in the future. If feelings of anxiety toward mathematics are already present, this lack of positive interaction may further its development.

It may be that math anxiety fostered by an inadequate conceptu-alization of mathematics is related to either inadequate or inappropri-ate teaching for that student at a prior level. For example, Lazarus (1974) questions whether math anxiety has its roots in the early years of schooling. She notes that an elementary school student may view mathematics as a collection of arbitrary rules, but seems to be making satisfactory progress due to proficiency in using a memorize-what-to-do approach. As demands of time and effort increase in high school, the student is subject to increasing strain. Unfortunately, since it has been some time since the student has understood the mathematical concepts, the change in approach to actually comprehending the material is impossible without a complete re-education in mathematics.

Cures

The increase in mathematics anxiety clinics and remedial programs attests to the popular claim of cures for math anxiety. For example, the University of Minnesota has a mathematics anxiety program in its continuing education division (Hendell 1977); the University of Missouri-Kansas City offers a special section of its introductory mathematics course for the math anxious student (MacDonald 1976); the Mills College Program prepares students to enter calculus after a one-semester course, no matter what their entering background (Blum and Givant 1980). These programs operate on the implicit assumption that societal factors coupled with a lack of understanding have led to the anxiety and that through a relaxed, classroom/workshop setting the student will experience success, learn mathematics, and gain self-confidence. In contrast there are clinics which emphasize the individual's psychological problems, with anxiety and fear as the focus of attention (Richardson and Suinn 1972). The emphasis on psycholog-ical therapy to the exclusion of mathematical study in these clinics seems to have a major fault. These clinics cannot be preparing the student to attempt more advanced study of mathematics. Other clin-ics offer intervention programs which combine counseling with mathematics instruction leading to a desensitization of the anxiety. In particular, a mathematical autobiography is produced and sessions pro-mote a reappraisal of the student's perception of error and intuition (Tobias 1978). In this combination approach a counselor and a mathematics teacher work together. The teacher attempts to clear up misconceptions about mathematics content, while the counselor aids the teacher in avoiding instructional techniques which may promote anxiety.

The following are some techniques that instructors could follow to help individual students or entire classes learn mathematics and overcome some or all of their anxiety. As much as possible instructors should try to lessen the stress of a testing situation. For example, it may be possible to give examinations that are not timed or to give anxious individuals a test in a room separate from the class. There may be situations where partial credit is appropriate. In addition, the absence of the perception of intimidation in the classroom is mandatory. Teachers must be very careful not to censure a student for making mistakes or for asking a "stupid question." In general the classroom should have an encouraging, reassuring, accepting and supportive atmosphere. Teachers should take an objective look at the environment in their classes.

Discussion

A recent paper of Benbow and Stanley (1980) has led to widespread diffusion of the claim in the media that evidence has been collected which indicates that women are mathematically inferior to men for genetic reasons. In their article, Benbow and Stanley reviewed SAT-Math data collected by the study of mathematically precocious youth over the last eight years from large samples of highly gifted seventh and eighth graders. In each of the six studies cited, males scored higher than females and a larger percentage of males than females scored above 600. One should be critical not of the data presented but of the interpretations of the data offered by Benbow and Stanley.

In particular, Benbow and Stanley (1980, 1262) concluded that since the students had "received essentially identical formal instruction in mathematics," the hypothesis of differential course-taking in mathematics as a cause of sex differences in achievement was not supported. However, they favored the hypothesis that "sex differences in achievement in and attitude toward mathematics result from superior male ability" (1980, 1264). These purported causes of the sex-differences cited are suspect, and one should question some of the implicit assumptions of the article. These assumptions included: (1) the generalizability of results from a highly selective sample to an entire population; (2) the adequacy of the SAT-Math test as a measure of inherent mathematical ability; and (3) the presumption that the sampled girls and boys had identical mathematical experiences prior to the seventh or eighth grade. In addition, the authors failed to compare and defend these results with other research studies on sex differences and mathematics involving the impact of socialization. It has been pointed out that Benbow and Stanley admitted that other conclusions may be drawn from their data. In fact, Fox and Cohn (1976) carried out an analysis on the same data and concluded that the socialization process may start quite early and have a pronounced effect by early adolescence. A formal reply to Benbow and Stanley was presented in *Science* by Schafer and Gray (1981).

It is worthwhile to note that sex differences in specific measures of mathematical achievement as well as the frequency of mathematics anxiety are present. One should be concerned that articles such as Benbow and Stanley's may promote the belief that these sex differences will exist forever. If these differences are perceived to have genetic causes, the implication is that the differences are perpetual. If sex differences are perceived as being a result of early and continuing socialization, then the implication is that through responsible modification of these social forces the differences may be reduced and eventually eliminated. The impact of Benbow and Stanley's article has been unfortunate as it has been used to support and encourage the continuation of inequity. The social implications of its publication may prove to be catastrophic.

References

Becker, J. R. 1981. Differential treatment of females and males in mathematics classes. *Journal for Research in Mathematics Education 12:* 40-53.

Benbow, C. P., and J. C. Stanley 1980. Sex differences in mathematical ability: Fact or artifact. *Science* 210: 1262-64.

Betz, N. E. 1978. Prevalence, distribution and correlates of math anxiety in college students. *Journal of Counseling Psychology* 25: 441-48.

Blum, L., and S. Givant. 1980. Increasing participation of women in fields that use mathematics. *American Mathematical Monthly* 87: 785-93.

Dreger, R. M., and L. R. Aiken. 1957. The identification of number anxiety in a college population. *Journal of Educational Psychology* 48: 344-51.

Fennema, E. 1978. Sex-related differences in mathematics achievement: Where and why? In *Perspectives on women and mathematics*, ed. J. E. Jacobs, 1-20. Columbus, Ohio: ERIC/SMEAC.

Fox, L. H. 1977. The effects of sex role socialization on mathematics participation and achievement. In *Women and mathematics: Research perspectives for change*, ed. L. H. Fox, E. Fennema, and J. Sherman, 1-77. (NIE Papers in Education and Work: No. 8) Washington, D.C.: National Institute of Education.

Fox, L. H., and S. J. Cohn. 1976. Sex differences in the development of precocious mathematical talent. In *Women and the mathematical mystique*, ed. L. H. Fox, L. Brody, and D. Tobin, 94-111. Baltimore: The Johns Hopkins Univ. Press.

Harway, M., H. Austin, J. Suhr, and J. Whitely. 1976. *Sex discrimination in guidance and counseling.* Washington, D. C.: National Center for Educational Statistics, U.S. Department of Health, Education and Welfare.

Hendell, D. D. 1977. *The math anxiety program: Its genesis and evaluation in continuing education for women.* Minneapolis: Univ. of Minnesota, Measurement Services Center (ERIC Document Reproduction Service No. ED 156 727).

Jackson, R. E. 1974. The attitudes of disadvantaged students toward mathematics (Ph.D. diss., Indiana University, 1973). *Dissertation Abstracts International,* 34: 3690A. (University Microfilms No. 74-380).

Lazarus, M. 1974. Mathophobia: Some personal speculations. *National Elementary Principal,* 53: 16-22.

Maccoby, E. E., and C. N. Jacklin. 1974. *The psychology of sex differences.* Stanford, California: Stanford Univ. Press.

MacDonald, C. T. 1976. An experiment in mathematics education at the college level. In *Women and the mathematical mystique,* ed. L. H. Fox, L. Brody, and D. Tobin, 115-37. Baltimore: The

Johns Hopkins Univ. Press.

Reyes, L. H. 1980. Attitudes and mathematics. In *Selected issues in mathematics education,* ed. M. M. Lindquist, 161-184. Berkeley, Calif.: McCutchan Publishing Corp.

Richardson, F. C., and R. M. Suinn. 1972. The mathematics anxiety rating scale: Psychometric data. *Journal of Counseling Psychology* 19: 551-54.

Schafer, A. T. and M. W. Gray. 1981. Sex and mathematics. *Science* 211:231.

Sells, L. 1976. The mathematics filter and the education of women and minorities. In *Women and the mathematical mystique,* ed. L. H. Fox, L. Brody, and D. Tobin, 66-75. Baltimore: The Johns Hopkins Univ. Press.

Stein, A. H. 1971. The effects of sex role standards on achievement and sex role preference on three determinants of achievement motivation. *Developmental Psychology* 4: 219-31.

Stein, A. H., and J. Smithells. 1969. Age and sex differences in children's sex role standards about achievement. *Developmental Psychology* 1: 252-59.

Tobias, S. 1978. A clinical approach to reducing math anxiety. In *Perspectives on women and mathematics,* ed. J. E. Jacobs, 113-17. Columbus, Ohio: ERIC/SMEAC.

Wolleat, P. L., J. D. Pedro, A. D. Becker, and E. Fennema. 1980. Sex differences in high school students' causal attributions of performance in mathematics. *Journal for Research in Mathematics Education* 11: 356-66.

Women Engineers in History: Profiles in Holism and Persistence

Martha M. Trescott

The Search for Information

Although this conference is oriented to women in science and social science, as well as engineering, I will limit discussion to women in engineering in American history. My comments stem from a study in which I have been intensively engaged for over a year on the history of women engineers in the United States, 1850-1975. Recently I was fortunate enough to have obtained funding from the Rockefeller Foundation so I could could make real progress on the research. However, the research has not been completed, and I'm in the process of seeking additional grant funding. Thus my remarks are still tentative and preliminary.

There have been three major methods of historical research employed in this project. First, I have interviewed over fifty individuals, in all parts of the country, having recorded interviews of forty-two on tape. Mostly, interviewees are women who have been in engineering programs and/or engineering-related work. However, I do have on tape two male engineers from the University of Pennsylvania who knew Edith Clark fairly well. In general, I have sought to interview older women engineers who have made significant contributions to theory, design, management or education, or to the history of the Society of Women Engineers (SWE), or some combination of all those things. Also, I have interviewed the very aged who entered engineering just because they could boast so many "firsts," such as the first female engineering graduate of a given school. I even have a fairly lucid interview on tape, of approximately twenty minutes, with a one hundred-year-old woman. Additionally, I have recorded a few younger women engineers who seemed to be "going places" and who volunteered to be recorded when I was in their geographic areas. Finally, I have interviewed older women who have been in engineering work or who have engineering degrees but who "dropped out" for one reason or another, in order to obtain the reflections of this group as well. I still plan to interview and record another forty or so people, mostly SWE award winners and past officers, if and when I obtain more funding.

A second major thrust of the research has been construction and administration of questionnaires. So far, the first "wave" of a projected three waves of the women engineers questionnaire has been composed and mailed to senior members and award winners in SWE, to female engineering graduates of the University of Illinois at Urbana-Champaign, and to female employees in engineering-related work in several large companies such as Rockwell International, Westinghouse, Lockheed, and a few others. Nearly 1,000 questionnaires were mailed. For the first wave, we can report an overall response rate of forty-one percent for SWE and the University of Illinois combined; some of the firms have yet to respond. The questionnaires have been answered mostly by women who were born in the 1940s and 1950s, although some respondents were born back before the turn of the century and in the first decades of this century. So, between the interviews, which have been conducted mostly with women over fifty years of age, and the questionnaires, answered mostly by women in their twenties, thirties and forties, and the survey which my research associate at Princeton, Carol Auster, has conducted of today's engineering students, we have data on several generations of women engineers.

I will relate a few preliminary results of a crude analysis of a few of the key questions on my questionnaire and will note some results of Carol Auster's preliminary analysis of her survey.

First, however, I would like to mention the other major method of research in this project, and that is the most common one of all to historians, research in the written sources in libraries and archives. In this process, I have uncovered a number of important papers, the most important collection being in West Lafayette. I am referring to the marvelous Gilbreth collection in the Purdue University library, which is supervised by Mr. Keith Dowden. This collection is one of the richest, if not the richest, I have ever seen, in terms of engineers' papers. Later on, I will discuss some of my work on this collection and my findings about the extensive and generally unacknowledged contributions of Lillian Moller Gilbreth to the establishment of modern industrial engineering.

In general, searching for the papers of women who worked in engineering-related endeavors and who lived and worked in the nineteenth and early part of this century is like looking for the proverbial needle in the haystack. (The other day that was almost literally what I was doing in a rather unique experience for me--of searching through garbage at the Urbana city dump for a scientist's papers; this is definitely *not the preferred way to do history!*) In searching for women engineers' papers, if one only turns up a few, scattered items here and there, one feels quite lucky. I have been able to locate small holdings on Bertha Lamme, Ellen Swallow Richards, Edith Clarke, Julia B. Hall, and others, at MIT, Ohio State University, Case Western Reserve, the University of Texas and Westinghouse, and to obtain some papers which have been in private hands. These have all been helpful in reconstructing aspects of the lives and work of important women engineers. However, the Gilbreth Collection is, by far, the largest I've found.

Refuting the Image

So much then, for the methods; now we shall consider some of the content of the work. Of the two themes, persistence and holism, I want first to underscore *persistence* by women engineers who came before us. At the 1979 meetings of the Society of Women Engineers, I gave a very preliminary report on this project and there emphasized the theme of my original grant project on women engineers, "Refuting the Image" (Trescott 1979). My thesis then centered around the fact that the one common denominator for all women engineers in the United States in all time periods, up through the present day, is that they have gone against the popular image of what a woman is supposed to be and do. I believe that the modern mass media have done much to actually downgrade the image of women from earlier times, especially where women and technology are concerned. Indeed, before the last one-hundred-twenty years or so, the idea of a woman technologist or engineer might very well not have been as foreign as in our own times, because mass media in this century have typically depicted women in relation to science and technology in inane ways. The negative effects of such media images on women's dignity and achievements, particularly in the professions and perhaps particularly in engineering, cannot be overemphasized. My questionnaire contains various media-oriented questions, and respondents generally seem to feel very strongly about what the media have done, in a negative light, and what the media could do to promote more positive images of women.

Be that as it may, my original idea that women in engineering have always refuted the popular image of women is a very good point of departure for a discussion of their persistence. To refute the image has often meant to go against the grain. It was not always perceived that way by pioneering women engineers, since most of them were, of course, quite independent types. Some of them had felt rather socially isolated as they grew up (though this was not always true), and often I've heard the older women engineers say that they really liked a challenge, that if someone told them they couldn't do something, that was the very thing they would do! I typically ask interviewees if they felt isolated as women in engineering, either in school or on the job. Generally, for the older ones, the answer is, not too much. As one stated last summer, "I think if I had seen just one more little girl around, I would have felt our isolation as women, but the fact that I was the only one, meant I never really thought about it." Many will add that, looking back on it now, they realize how isolated they really were. Also they will comment on their careers that, at the time, they did not perceive discrimination against them as women, but that now they can see how it operated.

Of course, there have been numerous reasons for the persistently low numbers of women engineers on both the demand and supply sides of this labor market, as economists might view it. Prejudice and social conditioning have historically operated in many ways to limit the number of women engineers.

While many of these same things explain women's low representation historically in other professions besides engineering, it is well to note that engineering cannot be viewed as a typically non-traditional field for female professionals. The percentages of women have been exceptionally low in engineering (much less than one percent of the total practicing engineering population. until the 1970's; about three percent today), as compared to law, medicine, many of the natural and social sciences, business, and other areas. Barriers over and above those experienced generally by women professionals seem to have operated here. Recent research on this problem suggests that a fundamental analysis of the "masculinist bases of engineering," in Sally Hacker's (1980) phrase, dealing with the interlocks between patriarchy and technology, may be needed.

Whatever the main reasons for the extreme underrepresentation of women in engineering (studies of pre-college students indicate that, based only on skills in mathematics and science, many more women might choose engineering than those who presently do), those who have entered engineering in the past have been *exceptionally* persistent and bright, and yet, not well-recorded. This, despite their relative visibility at the time. My questionnaire has two questions to which I wasn't sure how much credibility respondents would give. They are as follows: "In your opinion, have women who have entered engineering in the twentieth century generally been:

- more persistent than male counterparts
- about as persistent as male counterparts
- not as persistent as male counterparts."

Seventy five percent answered that women engineers have been more persistent than male counterparts, and when asked the same question about intelligence, forty-three percent answered that women engineers have been more intelligent than comparable men in engineering.

Two Profiles in Persistence

As one article on women engineers in the 1970s emphasized, and as I underscore here, the history of women in engineering is made up of "profiles in persistence" (Rubinstein 1973). I will share with you a few remarks from the transcripts of my interviews, which, of course, have to remain anonymous, but which point to great persistence. The worst I've found, in terms of engineering school experiences in the past, was related as follows. This occurred at a university in North Carolina in the 1930's, where the Dean of Engineering told my interviewee, who was then trying to enroll in engineering, "You're at the wrong school." She persisted, however, after having to attend a girls' school for over a year. She continued: "The following September, I was back....with my forty-eight and two-thirds semester hours of credit," which the Dean had told her she'd have to get before they would admit her, "and I think the 'ole' guy was shocked to see me, but they did let me in." So, she was the first female who studied engineering at that university and remained the only one to have done so for a *long* time. But that was only the *beginning* of her troubles. I asked her if she ever had felt discriminated against in grades or otherwise during school. She said, "No, not in grades, but in the work they made me do." Now, I want you to picture a very slight woman, very small, who had been somewhat frail. She continued,

> Well, for example, you know, I had to take foundry work and that sort of thing. And, after the first foundry class, Professor ---------- said he wanted me to stay after class. So, I didn't know what he wanted. And he took me out to the pattern room, you know, where they keep all the molds and patterns and things, and it was the biggest mess you ever saw. I don't think it had ever been straightened up or cleaned up since the college was started. And he said, 'I want you to clean up the foundry room, the pattern room, and get everything in order, and that's to be your job for the rest of your years here. And I want it in good shape.' So I said, 'yes, sir,' and I started in and I cleaned it up, and I kept it the whole time.

She added that the male students never had to do anything at all like that, and that they didn't really help her with the job. She said,

> They were really doing everything they could to discourage me, to get me out of there. And they kept telling me I'd never be able to get a job; nobody would hire a girl engineer. But maybe I could get a job working in a technical library or something like that, or maybe a technical secretary.

She ultimately became a very highly placed and successful engineer.

As I say, 'profiles in persistence.' Another story from the transcripts of my interviews relates to experiences on the job in a major corporation in the Pittsburgh area. This woman, who had a mechanical engineering degree, indicated that she never rose in management in the firm, although she aspired to, and although she worked for them for over thirty years in design and other areas. The management told her, although she was responsible for the design of large, rotating electrical apparatus, "I will never send you into a turbine power plant. That is no place for a woman." She said that as a matter of fact, I had been looking forward to it; in fact, my father was a tailor and he had made me two suits with slacks. But, no, we will not send you into an engineering plant. So, he immediately put that barrier up, immediately shunted me to the sideline and if something went wrong with one of my generators in the field, he would take one of the men and send him out to look at it. I could talk on the telephone and answer questions, but I was immediately put into this lower range because women do not belong in a power plant, said this manager.

So, she designed under these incredibly difficult conditions for years and only got to enter power plants, as on one occasion when she had a friend whose husband was the manager of a power plant in the Cleveland area and took her through.

Results of the Questionnaire

Persistence has been the name of the game, whether women in engineering have had as difficult a time as these two or not. Many have *not*. Although I could continue with stories from the interviews, I shall turn now to a few responses on the questionnaires to my question number fifty-seven, "Do you perceive that you were ever discriminated against as a woman in engineering at any stage and, if yes, how were you discriminated against?" Sixty-two percent indicated that they do perceive that they have been so discriminated against, in terms of sexual harrassment, sexist comments, lack of promotion, inability to find jobs, being kept from field assignments due to sex, and other forms of both overt and covert sex discrimination.

Now, although I'm emphasizing the persistence of women who have paved the way in engineering for those entering the field today, I want to indicate also that most respondents and interviewees are not generally bitter about their experiences in engineering. Quite the contrary is true. An overwhelming number are very glad they entered engineering and have found it a generally satisfying and well-paying career, considering the alternatives, and one which has given them a sense of responsibility and of helping society and the world.

A few other results from a very preliminary analysis of some of the more important questions on my questionnaire can be indicated. Some of the major points which I have not already discussed follow.

1) The first job for pay of approximately thirty-one percent of all respondents was in secretarial-clerical areas, although eleven percent held first jobs in factory work, and four percent in drafting.

2) For sixteen percent, their first engineering-related job was in government (either local, state or federal). This was the largest single employer for first engineering-related job, while the second largest was electrical and electronics manufacturing firms (fifteen percent). Third largest was schools and universities, which employed about nine percent of all the respondents.

3) The "most important" of all engineering-related positions which respondents ever held, from their own descriptions of their jobs, were managerial in nature for thirty-nine percent. Yet, many of those who answered this way were among the forty-seven percent who later reported that they had never *officially* been in management.

4) The most frequent employers of responents in their "most important" engineering-related job were government and private consulting firms of various types, followed by electrical and electronics firms, and aircraft and aerospace companies. Whether in first, "most important," or current engineering-related job, the women engineers are and have been concentrated in certain types of firms and at lower levels well into or throughout their careers.

5) Currently, thirty-nine percent of the respondents report that they hold positions which are managerial in nature. Many of them report that they have never officially been titled "management," although many have been in charge of a good many people and of relatively large teams at one time or another. Of the rest, nine percent hold technical positions as computer programmers or systems analysts; seven percent are employed in mechanical design; six percent are employed in research; six percent in electrical or electronic design; and five percent in consulting work; all with little managerial responsibility.

6) In their current positions, eleven percent work in consulting firms and another eleven percent for electrical and electronics manufacturers. Others work, in descending order, in government agencies, in schools and universities, in the aerospace industry and in the aircraft industry. About four percent work in each of the following categories: construction, telephone companies, the automotive industry, and in manufacture of heavy earth-moving and agricultural equipment.

7) When asked if they had ever competed for an engineering job which they did not get, forty-one percent answered in the affirmative. Because many of the respondents who answered "yes" here were born in the 1950s, most of the occasions cited occurred in the mid- to late-1970s, and in all geographic areas (with no one area or state predominating). Respondents often cited firms which turned them down as well as, or in lieu of, geographic area for which they had asked. Thirty-two percent indicated that they did not know the reason they failed to obtain the job sought, while eighteen percent said that overt sex discrimination was the cause. Another eighteen percent said that they were told they were not sufficiently well qualified, despite their engineering degrees, and ten percent were told that they were not well enough educated or trained, again, despite their degrees.

8) In terms of mentors who helped respondents locate jobs in any way, thirty-six percent reported that fellow students and peers helped; twenty-nine percent said that professors helped (mostly with letters of reference); nineteen percent reported that deans and/or college placement offices helped, and sixteen percent said that relatives helped. The last-mentioned is somewhat surprisingly low since sixty-nine percent said that their relatives were involved with engineering, natural science, medicine, or technology; thirty-one percent reported fathers who were (are) engineers, and fifteen percent reported older brothers as engineers. Those who reported having been helped mostly by peers and relatives were the older women, or the SWE members.

9) As stated earlier, forty-seven percent said they had never officially been in management, while fifty percent said that they had held managerial positions and that they like management. Only three percent said that they had been in management but did not like it.

10) When asked if they had ever owned their own firm, eighty-seven percent said "no," but twenty-five percent said they would like to. Of those who had founded a firm, they did so mostly in the 1970s (and 1980), and mostly in California and Arizona.

11) Forty-six percent of the respondents graduated in the top one percent of their high school class, while another thirty-seven percent graduated in the top ten percent. Eighty-three percent, an overwhelming majority, made mostly A's in their high school math courses. An overwhelming number of respondents, ninety-six percent, took natural

science courses in high school.

12) Most of the respondents, sixty-seven percent, were born after 1940, most of whom were the University of Illinois (UIUC) graduates, while thirty percent were born between 1910 and 1940, and only three percent before 1910 (most of whom were the SWE members, although a few older UIUC graduates responded).

13) A high percentage of the respondents, forty-one percent, have mothers who were immigrants and forty-three percent have immigrant fathers. Their fathers' families emigrated mostly from Great Britain (including England, Wales, and Scotland), from Germany and France, and fifteen percent came from Russia and Eastern Europe. The influence of certain ethnic cultures on daughters' decisions to enter engineering (and perhaps other professions) may have been significant in some cases, as reported by some of my interviewees.

14) As might be expected, a majority (fifty-six percent) reported that they were raised in middle class families, but a high percentage (thirty-five percent) indicated that they were from the working class. These figures would be interesting to compare with those for male engineers, and I hope to do that. Also, those from the working class tended to be older and from Eastern Europe, while the few who reported being from the upper class at times noted that this was their families' status before immigrating.

15) Finally, sixty-five percent say that they never saw a story about women engineers in books, popular magazines, professional or technical magazines, newspapers or other publications when they were growing up. The few who reported having seen such things, said coverage was typically a write-up on Marie Curie or the movie *Cheaper by the Dozen* about the Gilbreths. Today, however, according to a survey of engineering students done by Carol Auster (Auster 1981), about thirty percent have seen some reading matter on engineering which has influenced both the men and women to major in engineering. Presumably some of these materials related directly to women in engineering.

My survey also shows a high percentage of readers among my respondents, and also that they mostly did not have hobbies or toys which were oriented to science and technology as they grew up. Carol Auster has reported some other findings in her survey, the most interesting of which may be that approximately thirty percent of the women's fathers were engineers, compared with twenty-two percent for the male students. My survey found that thirty-one percent of my respondents had engineer fathers. Auster (1981, 9) also finds that "compared to the male engineering students, female engineering students were more likely to have highly educated parents with high incomes" and that "sixteen percent of women's mothers attended graduate or professional school," while only eight percent of men's mothers did so. Twenty-nine percent of Auster's women students report their mother's annual income as $15,000 or more. I am not sure how this finding will compare with my own in that area, but my general impressions and predictions are that most of the mothers of the older women engineers did not have nearly as much higher education or as high incomes. A few of my respondents and interviewees, for example, did report mothers as lab technicians and chemists and said that they served as role models.

Women Engineers as Holistic Thinkers

The questions and responses on my questionnaire relate to both the persistence and intelligence of women engineers in this century. I want to discuss not only persistence but also the intellectual acumen of women engineers in our history, for I feel that a very important characteristic of women engineers historically has been their very bright, incisive minds. In their contributions to the intellectual and practical development of many fields of engineering, moreover, they have displayed not only logical thought but also *holistic*, or systems, thinking. Of course, historically we know of many men in engineering-related work, such as George Westinghouse, Thomas Edison, Frederick Becket, Charles Martin Hall, and Benjamin Lamme, who have been excellent systems thinkers (and who, in some cases, incidentally, have been aided in such thought and design by women). Likewise, this study has found that certain women engineers have also contributed inordinately to concepts of whole, new paradigms and systems of thought in their fields. Many of these women, such as Ellen Swallow Richards in sanitary and environmental engineering, Edith Clarke in electric power systems, Kate Gleason in mechanical engineering, Emily Roebling in civil engineering, and Lillian Gilbreth in industrial engineering, are familiar names. Yet, few have acknowledged the real extent and ramifications of much of their work.[1]

One Profile in Holism

In this final section, I would like to dwell on the contributions of Lillian Moller Gilbreth, especially since we are meeting here on her own turf and where the marvelous Gilbreth Collection is located.

Dr. Lillian M. Gilbreth is perhaps the most well-known woman engineer in history.[2] She has been called "America's first lady of engineering." Yet, it is interesting that even many of Dr. Gilbreth's impressive intellectual contributions and much of their true significance have been lost to history.

Lillian M. Gilbreth has been considered important in the history of engineering by male and female engineers, and by historians to some extent. As the *SWE Newsletter* said (Society of Women Engineers 1978, 1-2), she "pioneered in the field of time-and-motion studies, showed companies how to improve management techniques and how to increase industrial efficiency and production by budgeting time and energy as well as money." She was married in 1904 to Frank Bunker Gilbreth, another pioneer in scientific management, especially noted for his very real genius in motion study. The Gilbreths worked together in scientific management--in their consulting firm, advising many companies which became the most important firms in the U.S.; in research and writing (together they authored hundreds of documents); in lectures at various companies, universities, professional societies and elsewhere; in conducting the Gilbreth summer schools on management topics; and in raising their twelve children. *Cheaper by the Dozen* (Gilbreth and Carey 1948) is their story, written by a daughter, Ernestine, and a son, Frank, Jr.

The Relative Contributions of Frank and Lillian

As one might imagine, Lillian has received far less credit than Frank by engineers and historians alike. She has been considered an *adjunct* of Frank, even though he died an untimely death in 1924, while she headed Gilbreth, Inc. for almost five decades afterward. She has been considered primarily his assistant or disciple, even though he never earned a college degree and she attained the Ph.D. Her own expertise lay in the realm of integrating psychology and considerations of mental processes with time-and-motion work, while it is recognized among their colleagues that "if Frank Gilbreth slighted any discipline in his consideration, it was psychology" (Caples 1969, 72). Also, if she is cited by historians, discussions are often limited to her contributions to domestic engineering (e.g., design of kitchens and appliances). Lillian was vigorous and professionally active almost until the time of her death in 1972, having outlived Frank by nearly fifty years. During this time, she not only headed Gilbreth, Inc. (in effect, she had been at its helm during much of Frank's lifetime, too), but also became a full professor of management in the School of Mechanical Engineering at Purdue University in 1935 (after having succeeded Frank as lecturer there in 1924), head of the Department of Personnel Relations at Newark School of Engineering in 1941, and visiting professor of management at the University of Wisconsin at Madison in 1955. She also received many honorary degrees in engineering at both the master's and doctorate levels from the 1920s on.

In short, she deserves to be recalled and viewed in her own right, not merely listed together with Frank as "the engineer, inventor, psychologist, educator Gilbreth."[3] While "engineer" and "inventor" may well describe Frank, Lillian was not only an engineer but also the psychologist and main educator of the couple. Despite the recognition and publicity of various kinds given Lillian Gilbreth in the past, the depth and breadth of her contributions to the establishment of modern industrial engineering have not been well understood or widely discussed, either by historians or by engineers. Her major contributions lie in two directions: (1) the incorporation of psychological considerations, as conceived in broad terms (problem-solving and the behavior of individuals and related topics such as incentives, the nature of the work environment, monotony, the transference of skill among jobs and industries, and so on) into time-and-motion thought and study, and (2) the establishment of industrial engineering curricula in engineering schools in this country and abroad. I will focus on the first of those here, with some comments on the second.

Contributions to Scientific Management: Industrial Psychology

With graduate studies in psychology at Brown (she obtained her Ph.D. in 1915), Lillian Gilbreth was perhaps the most well trained psychologist at the time who was also interested and working in time-and-motion study. Certainly, neither Frederick W. Taylor, in time study, who is most often cited as *the* founder of scientific management, nor Frank Gilbreth had had any special training in psychology to enable them to analyze areas dealing with psychology, work and management. Since the introduction of time-and-motion concepts and innovations was quite strongly resisted by workers the world over, it is doubtful that the work of either Taylor or Frank Gilbreth would have been widely accepted, if at all, without the shrewd application of psychology to time-and-motion work. Lillian's insights and those of her students and others (both male and female) whom she inspired, helped reduce workers' resistance, and, in fact, helped establish forerunners of the study of human factors in engineering design, along with Frank's work in physiological areas.

Of her many articles, books, reports, and lectures, her early book, *The Psychology of Management* (Gilbreth 1914), which stemmed from her Ph.D. research, is the most important in the history of engineering thought. This book was termed even by such men as George Iles (who subsumed her work under Frank's) as a "golden gift" to industrial philosophy (Iles 1917, ix-x). When the Society of Industrial Engineers made her its second honorary member in 1921 (Herbert Hoover was the first), it was commented that (Society of Industrial Engineers 1921, 2-3):

> She was the first to recognize that management is a problem of psychology and her book, *The Psychology of Management*, was the first to show this fact to both the managers and the psychologists.... Today it is recognized as authoritative.

In the literature of scientific management prior to World War I, there was little coverage of topics which Lillian treated in depth, such as the psychology of work and management; and it was in this relative vacuum at the early date of 1914 that *The Psychology of Management* appeared. It is true that others such as Hugo Munsterberg had studied industrial psychology at about the same time as Lillian. However, first of all, as Robert T. Livingston, a professor of industrial engineering at Columbia, commented in 1960, "Munsterberg's writings went largely unrecognized" for a long while (Livingston 1960, 126). Secondly, no one prior to Lillian Gilbreth in *The Psychology of Management* had brought together the basic elements of management theory, which are:

- Knowledge of individual behavior
- The theory of groups
- The theory of communication
- A rational basis of decision-making.

Although not always addressed in this modern terminology, Dr. Gilbreth dealt with these areas, some in more depth than others. I believe that the subtitle of her book, *The Function of the Mind in Determining, Teaching and Installing Methods of Least Waste,* more nearly captures the scope of her concern with just that area--industrial psychology--as we might understand that field. Indeed, she was writing in the context of scientific management which had previously focused mostly on the *physiological,* as opposed to both the mental and emotional characteristics of workers and managers. So her book deals in depth with the "function of the mind," or problem-solving, decision-making, planning, communicating, measuring and evaluating in various work and managerial environments.

In this book she has dealt as minutely with the psychology of the worker as Frank with physiology. She pioneered in considering the "individuality" of the worker, and devoted a whole chapter to that topic, commenting on individual teaching, incentives, and welfare. The approaches of Taylor and Frank Gilbreth left much to be desired in enabling each worker to feel himself or herself a unique individual. Lillian's keen insight and sensitivity to the needs of individuals had been honed by graduate work in psychology, in addition to years of raising a large family (and one gets the sense of her great insight about people in her works on homemaking and child-raising).

Throughout *The Psychology of Management,* she is able to virtually transform time-and-motion study into the rudiments of modern managerial practices. While she does draw on the literature available, including her husband's work, it is clear that her analysis represents a new point of departure in management. At various points, her analysis demonstrates her empathy with how workers feel, about which there is little in the literature of scientific management at that time. In this area, she was apparently far ahead of her generation.

From her chapter on individuality, it is easy to see her pioneering efforts in management theory, especially in "knowledge of individual behavior." Yet, not even this most obvious contribution is noted in the

American Society of Mechanical Engineers (ASME) volume covering *Fifty Years Progress in Management, 1910-1960* (American Society of Mechanical Engineers 1960). Munsterberg, Gillespie, Lecky and other psychologists are cited but not Lillian Gilbreth (who, incidentally, was co-author of the introductory, overview essay).

In fact, in 1911, Lillian Gilbreth introduced the first mention of the psychology of management at any management meeting at the important Dartmouth College Conference on Scientific Management.[4] Since this formed the basis for her dissertation, on which she had been working for years before the award of her Ph.D., it is logical to suppose that she had been among the earliest workers studying the interfaces between psychology and management--both in industry and in the home. This is true, and indeed, it is not an overstatement to term her a *foremost pioneer* in this area in the earliest days of such work.

In the Gilbreth Collection at Purdue, it is interesting to note a brief career sketch of her work, differentiating her contributions from Frank's. She wrote this in 1926 as part of her application for membership in the ASME, which, I must say, had not sought her as a member, despite her renown. Between 1904 and 1914, when Frank B. Gilbreth, Inc. "operated as a construction company," she said, "I was chiefly employed in the systems work, standardizing practice." The results were published in *Field System* (Gilbreth 1908b), *Concrete System* (Gilbreth 1908a), and *Bricklaying System* (Gilbreth 1909), all of which show only Frank's authorship. She continued:

> I was also engaged in the perfecting of the methods and devices for laying brick by the packet method, and in the design and construction of reinforced concrete work. This work had to do with the management as well as the operating end.
>
> In 1914 our company began to specialize in management work. I was placed in charge of the correlation of engineering and management psychology, and became an active member of the staff making visits to the plants systematized in order to lay out the method of attack on the problems, being responsible for getting the necessary material for the installation into shape, working up the data as they accumulated, and drafting the interim and final reports. I was also in charge of research and teaching, and of working up such mechanisms, forms and

methods as were needed for our type of installation of scientific management, motion study, fatigue study and skill study. These had to do not only with the handling of men, but with the simplification and standardization of the machinery and tools, for the use of both the normal and the handicapped. During Mr. Gilbreth's frequent and prolonged absences, both in this country and abroad, I was in responsible charge of all branches of the work. This was also the case while he was in the service, and while he was recovering from his long illness incurred therein.

Since Mr. Gilbreth's death, June 14, 1924, I have been the head of our organization, which consisted of Consulting Engineers and does work in management, and I have had responsible charge of the research, installation and the teaching, in this country and abroad.[5]

Lillian was considered an expert in fatigue study, the study of skill and its transference among industries and jobs, precision in measurement, and standardization of the work of both managers and laborers, as well as the more narrowly psychological matters. She was also known as both a researcher and teacher. *The Psychology of Management* alone shows her early interest in many of these areas, with entire chapters on measurement, standardization, and teaching; and it stemmed from her own original Ph.D. work.

As both Lillian and Frank conceived the rise of scientific management, teaching was integral for implementing and disseminating its practice. Even though instruction of employees within given firms was crucial to the spread of knowledge of scientific management, even more educational effort was needed to integrate scientific management with engineering disciplines. Specifically and most importantly, scientific management needed a brilliant researcher and teacher with a grasp of theory and practice and knowledge of the evolution of the field to represent these developments to the academic community. Such a person was Lillian Gilbreth, who was not only a teacher of methods of scientific management to workers and managers but also an academic. Additionally, as many of her colleagues noted, she had great tact and diplomacy, which served her well in integrating developments in industry and the universities.

Her upper-level undergraduate and graduate courses in management at Purdue in the 1930s and 1940s were offered in the Department of General Engineering, were "open only to graduate students and to seniors of outstanding ability" and covered "investigation of specific management problems in the fields of organization, time and motion study, industrial accounting, factory layout, economic selection and equipment, and similar topics," as described in the *Purdue University Bulletin* between 1934 and 1950.

Also, she authored papers and spoke about encouraging women to go into industrial engineering and management in this country and abroad. At the Gilbreth Summer Schools which she conducted, at least half the participants from various countries, mostly European, were women.

Indeed, Lillian's work with and on behalf of women--from the handicapped homemaker to the female worker in the factory and office to the professional manager and engineer and to women consumers in general--has not begun to be illuminated. Her efforts on behalf of women in these various roles and jobs and from different social and economic classes is a forgotten chapter in women's history.

Certainly, not only her work with and for women, but also her various contributions to industrial engineering and its precursors, spanning nearly seven decades, have been only partly and vaguely acknowledged. She, in fact, helped formulate much of the theoretical underpinnings of the field, but she has been too narrowly labeled a "psychologist." This is not to say that she did not treat such topics as the study of "psychopathic types in industry," for she did that as well. It is to say, however, that her work more nearly covered the study and measurement of a wide range of mental (and physical) processes involved in work and management. The precursors of the modern notion of "the work of a professional manager," in terms of "planning, organizing, integrating and measuring," in Harold Smiddy's conception (Smiddy 1960), can be seen in Lillian's published works, including *The Psychology of Management,* and in the records of studies she did for various firms, held in the Gilbreth Library. Yet, when Smiddy and other modern writers view the evolution of ideas about the function of the mind in management, Lillian Gilbreth's pioneering work is typically not mentioned.

After Frank's death in 1924, she continued to be a prolific writer and to participate in meetings of professional groups such as the ASME, presiding over sessions such as one on "Management Research" in 1933. Even before her husband died, the Gilbreths together authored well over fifty papers on scientific management topics, not including those written by each of them as sole author nor including their books and consulting reports. While Lillian's name alone appears on a few of these papers, it is not difficult to suppose that she was the main author on at least such works as "The Place of the Psychologist in Industry," "The Individual in Modern Management," "Psychiatry and Management," "The Relation of Posture to Fatigue of Women in Industry," and others.[6] She may well have been the principal investigator and author on articles credited to them both in the areas of fatigue, standardization, and transference of skill, but that is difficult, of course, to determine.

The fact is that her own originality has been buried by the circumstance of marriage to a man in the same general field (even though her career also obviously benefited in many ways from this close association with Frank, in terms of directions her interests took, just as Frank's work benefited from the marriage, though his contributions were not so obscured by marriage). Also, some obscurity has accrued to her work because of Frank's wish that both their names appear on all they wrote, even though this did not always happen. Yet, because her own expertise and that of her husband were so clearly differentiated in many areas, and because she outlived him by so long, establishing authority "in her own right," it is possible to resurrect her unique contributions, at least in part.

It is important that we remember the context of Lillian's work which emphasized the "human element" in scientific management. Being among the first to be so concerned with the human factor meant that she understood to explore a frontier. Many subject areas were legitimate topics of her research, since the human element is pervasive in all areas of work. As she and others who came after her worked, an increasing number of avenues for investigation were opened and a certain definition of the field evolved. *The Psychology of Management* was an entering wedge, opening whole new areas to scientific management, which have since evolved into mainstream topics in industrial engineering. *The Psychology of Management* was a departure from classical scientific management and from which much modern management theory has taken shape.

Lillian Gilbreth's path-breaking research would likely have not been as accessible as it was in molding industrial engineering had she not lived so long and been so active in so many areas of the field in its formative stages. Of the early pioneers of scientific management, Lillian Gilbreth was a key figure during most of this century among the surviving members of the pre-World War I investigators. She not only lived longer than the others, but was professionally active longer. Also, of those who lived into mid-century (and beyond), she was among the few who became outstanding and productive academicians as well as businesspersons and consultants. Thus, as a liaison for the early pioneering group of researchers to later generations and as a "gate-keeper" between academia and business of knowledge about scientific management and industrial engineering as the field evolved, she played a central role in interpreting the shape and directions of industrial engineering. In fact, because of all her work, publications, lectures, courses, workshops in so many settings, and other activities, and, therefore, her great prestige, she may have contributed more in the first four decades of this century than any other one person to the determination of what comprises industrial engineering and its major areas of investigation and analysis.

Yet, even though she did remain very active for a long time and was a prolific writer (having, therefore, left many records), it is alarming, at least to me, that history has buried many of the most significant contributions of Lillian Moller Gilbreth, "Member No. 1" of the Society of Women Engineers and perhaps the foremost woman engineer in history.

Conclusion

In conclusion, there are many, many other women engineers who, as with Lillian Gilbreth, have exhibited and are continuing to demonstrate a wide-ranging knowledge of their fields and a holistic approach to entire systems of engineering. Some researchers in psychology, philosophy and other areas, have noted women's holistic orientation and lifestyle in general.[7] It may well be, then, that those women engineers who have made substantive intellectual contributions to the theory and practice of engineering, represent historically *a highly select group of holistic thinkers.* For we find *combined* in them these characteristics of (1) persistent, independent-thinking pioneer, (2) exceptionally bright intellect, (3) engineer, who, whether male or female, often deals with systems, and (4) woman, who may have evolved a more holistic approach to life, in general, than man. With such a possible orientation, to holism, women engineers in our history may be reassessed as having contributed much more to technological change and the advancement of engineering knowledge than we might otherwise suppose from their relatively small numbers. Within the field of engineering, women have undoubtedly been outstanding thinkers and faculty members, among other roles they have filled.

Regardless of the fact that some people have told me that there is no important history of women engineers before the 1970s because their numbers were too small prior to that, I have found the history of women engineers to be an extensive and fascinating topic. As in the cases of Lillian Gilbreth, Edith Clarke and various other thinkers, women engineers have contributed greatly to the intellectual history of engineering and science. Additionally, they have contributed impressively to the history of management, to business enterprise, and, of course, to women's history. Though their numbers have been relatively small, many who have "made history" are still living. In fact, to the lone historian trying to uncover and highlight their histories, the numbers sometimes seem overpowering! As I say, I find the task a large one, the topic much more extensive than I or others had expected, and the ramifications of the project's findings very far-reaching for a variety of fields. I look forward to another phase of research and to the preparation of a book manuscript as soon as possible. To me, it has been a most fascinating, if at times heart-rending (as well as uplifting) endeavor, and I very much appreciate this opportunity to present this preliminary report.

Notes

1. See Trescott (1982a) for a discussion of the many contributions of the women noted here.

2. Trescott (1982b) contains references for the following section on Lillian Gilbreth. This section of this chapter has been excerpted from that longer paper.

3. This quotation is contained in an anonymous mimeographed paper entitled, "History of Scientific Management," and contained in file NHZ 0830-23 in the Gilbreth collection, Purdue University Library.

4. Lillian's paper can be found in the Gilbreth Collection, Purdue University. Dartmouth College Conference, file NHZ 0830-23, with typewritten note by Lillian, 2113-41.

5. This quotation is contained in an autobiographical memo, 1926 file NHZ 08301, contained in the Gilbreth Collection at Purdue University.

6. These papers may be found in the Gilbreth Collection, Purdue University Library, file NAPEGTG 0099.

7. On the subject of woman's orientation to holistic living and thinking, including comments abour her more circuitous, less linear, more systems-oriented, less fragmented (or more horizontal, less hierarchical) modes than those of men, see especially Gray (1976; 1979a; 1979b; 1982). Gray has much to say also concerning women and technology, in general.

There is a growing literature on the functions of the right and left hemispheres of the brain and of sex differences with respect to these functions, such as Harshman (1976). Yet it is still unlear just how brain function, holistic thinking and sex differences interrelate. For studies on the psychology of sex differences, much of which is relevant to engineering, Eleanor Maccoby is the leading expert. See particularly Maccoby (1966); Maccoby and Jacklin (1974); and Maccoby and Rau (1962). See also the chapter in this volume by Campbell and Geller.

References

Auster, C. J. 1981. The changing role of women in the work force: The case of women engineers. In *Final report to the Rockefeller Foundation on "Refuting the image: A history of women engineers in the United States, 1850-1975,* ed. M. M. Trescott. University of Illinois. Mimeo.

American Society of Mechanical Engineers. 1960. *Fifty Years Progress in Management, 1910-1960.* New York: American Society of

Mechanical Engineers.

Caples, W. G. 1969. Comment on "More bricks, less sweat." In American Society of Mechanical Engineers. *The Frank Gilbreth Centennial.* New York: ASME.

Gilbreth, F. B. 1908a. *Concrete system.* New York: Engineering News Publishing Company.

——————— 1908b. *Field system.* New York and Chicago: M. C. Clark.

——————— 1909. *Bricklaying system.* New York and Chicago: M. C. Clark.

Gilbreth, L. M. 1914. *The psychology of management: The function of the mind in determining, teaching and installing methods of least waste.* New York: Sturgis and Walton.

Gilbreth, F. B., Jr., and E. G. Carey, 1948. *Cheaper by the Dozen.* New York: T. Y. Crowell.

Gray, E. D. 1976. The story of a woman: Or, how I lost my faith in technology. *Proceedings of conference on public policy issues in nuclear waste management.* McLean, Va.: Mitre Corp.

———————. 1979a. Masculine/feminine dimensions of technology. Mimeo. from author.

———————. 1979b. *Why the Green Nigger?: Remithifying Genesis.* Wellesley, Mass.: Roundtable Press.

———————. 1982. Women in global society: Unique perspective, unique potential. In *Facing up to the future,* ed. J. Richardson. Forthcoming.

Hacker, S. L. Capitalistic and patriarchal elements in the organization of engineering. Paper presented at the National Women's Studies Association, Bloomington, Indiana. Mimeo.

Harshman, R. A. 1976. Sex, language and the brain: Adult sex differences. In *Conference on Human Brain Function,* ed. D. O. Walter, L. Rogers, and J. M. Finzi-Fried, Los Angeles, Calif.: Brain Information Service, BRI Publications Office, Univ. of California.

Iles, G. 1917. Introduction to *Applied motion study: A collection of papers on the efficient method to industrial prepardness,* by F. B. and L. M. Gilbreth. New York: Oxford Univ. Press.

Livingston, R. T. 1960. The theory of organization and management. In *Fifty Years Progress in Management, 1910-1960.* ed. ASME,

123-28. New York: American Society of Mechanical Engineers.

Maccoby, E. E. ed. 1966. *The development of sex differences.* Stanford, Calif.: Stanford Univ. Press.

Maccoby, E. E., and C. Jacklin. 1974. *The psychology of sex differences.* Stanford, Calif.: Stanford Univ. Press.

Maccoby, E. E., and L. Rau. 1962. *Differential cognitive abilities.* Stanford, Calif.: Stanford Univ. Press.

Rubinstein, E. 1973. Profiles in persistence. *IEEE Spectrum* 10; 52-7, 60-4.

Smiddy, H. F. 1960. Management as a profession. In *Fifty Years Progress in Management, 1910-1960,* ed. ASME, 26-41. New York: American Society of Mechanical Engineers.

Society of Industrial Engineers. 1921. Honorary member no. 2. *Society of Industrial Engineers Bulletin* 3: 2-3.

Society of Women Engineers. 1978. Lillian Moller Gilbreth: Remarkable first lady of engineering. *Society of Women Engineers Newsletter* 24: 1-2.

Trescott, M. M. 1979. A history of women engineers in the United States, 1850-1975, a progress report. In *Proceedings of the Society of Women Engineers 1979 National Convention,* 1-14. New York: Society of Women Engineers.

————. 1982a. Women in the intellectual development of engineering: Studies in persistence and holism. In *Intellectual history of women in science,* ed. G. Kass-Simon and P. Farnes, Stanford, Calif.: Stanford Univ. Press.

————. 1982b. Lillian Moller Gilbreth and the founding of the modern industrial engineering. Paper presented at the Berkshire Conference on Women's History, Vassar College.

Should Professional Women
Be Like Professional Men?

Ruth Hubbard

The question of whether professional women should be like professional men is an interesting question, and there is a lot to say. It is also a question that most professional women ask themselves at one time or another--sometimes happily, other times in deep depression. To actually discuss it without rambling is difficult, but I am going to try.

I want to start with a disclaimer. I use the terms "women" and "men" as political and not as biological categories. In this, I follow Simone de Beauvoir's (1952, 267) dictum: One is not born a woman; one becomes a woman. The same obtains for men. Obviously, there are differences between women and men that relate directly to reproduction, and some of them are entirely biological, such as whether we have two X chromosomes or an X and a Y, and some developmental events appear to follow rather straightforwardly from that difference. But to what extent obvious, reproductive sex differences, such as whether one has ovaries or testes, carry over to other than entirely reproductive facets of our lives is far from clear.

I also want to stress that, biologically speaking, women and men are far more similar than different; we are one of the least dimorphic species of mammals. Within the normal range, there are enormous overlaps between most of our physical as well as social traits. Yet, for social and political reasons, scientists tend to stress sex *differences*. For example, a current issue of *Science* (Naftolin and Butz 1981) is devoted to articles about sex differences. It would be at least as interesting, and perhaps more so, to have one on similarities. But would it be published? Would it receive attention by the popular magazines?

All of us are products of our biology and our socialization. They interact in complicated and nonadditive ways, so that one cannot look at a child or an adult and sort out what portion of any given trait derives from biology and what from social molding. This is as true of many of our physical and physiological traits as it is of our behavioral ones. Height, weight, strength, activity levels, menstrual patterns, etc., all clearly depend upon social as well as biological influences, as do our behavior patterns. That is why I think that the research program of sociobiology, to establish the biological *bases* of our social behavior, is mistaken. This cannot be done, except in the trivial sense in which it is indeed true that, because we are not able to fly and are not as good climbers as some of our primate cousins, we are not likely to structure societies around nests built in trees. But for the social behaviors that we do exhibit, it is both theoretically and practically impossible to distinguish biological from social influences and to assign primacy to either. This is just another way of stating that when I speak of women or men I am not talking biology.

Coming as women into professions whose structure and content have been shaped by men presents problems for many of us. There are the heavy demands in terms of hours, the need for total immersion in one's work, and the assumption that work comes first. Of course, there is nothing intrinsic or "natural" about any of these requirements. They result from the fact that the men who have shaped the professions have been able to count on the services of a bevy of paid and unpaid helpers, many of them women--assistants, secretaries, wives, sisters--to take care of their physical, social, and emotional needs, so as to leave them free to devote inordinately large amounts of time to their work.

Another problem for many women is the hierarchical work structures and relationships that are the rule rather than the exception in universities, industries, and other prototypically male institutions. Many women coming into the professions find them uncongenial, because women, by and large, are socialized to function primarily in the more egalitarian world of family relationships than in the hierarchically structured world of work and politics. Again, there is nothing "natural" about this. It is not in the *nature* of family or work to be egalitarian or hierarchical. Indeed, there have been much more hierarchical family structures than our present ones and much more egalitarian work situations.

However, for historical reasons, we find ourselves in a situation where the professions are much more hierarchical than are families, and many women find that uncongenial and uncomfortable. Furthermore, feminists often have ideological and political reservations about fitting into hierarchical structures. Yet, we feminists also often are the ones who push for equal access. This presents us with a dilemma: equal access to what? Are we pushing for access to professions we have had no part in building and in which we often are acutely uncomfortable?

A further problem is raised by the underrepresentation of women in the professions and by the resulting tokenism, which puts special demands on women. Rosabeth Moss Kanter (1977) has analyzed the problem very clearly in *Men and Women of the Corporation* and has interesting and illuminating things to say about what can happen to women in positions where our rarity makes us noticed not as individuals but as representatives of a group of outsiders. In such situations, our mistakes are not our own but "typical of women." Added to that disadvantage is the fact that we are often less familiar with the tools being used and with the ways in which the structures operate than are many newly entering men, because we have grown up as girls, doing girls' things, rather than as boys doing boys' things (be they repairing bicycles or radios or playing football). Therefore, we need to quickly learn skills that seem "natural" to the men in the organization. If that is so, we will find it harder to learn than inexperienced men do, because, as tokens, we are more noticed and so are our mistakes and uncertainties. Our token status therefore makes it harder for us to "learn the ropes."

I could continue about the structural problems we encounter when we enter the male-dominated professions and about the various strategies for overcoming them (such as, by affiliating oneself with a powerful man, by forming support systems with other women, by dulling one's sensibilities and going full steam ahead, by deciding it isn't worth the effort and switching into a less male-dominated field, and so forth), but I want, instead, to say some things about the problems we, as women and especially as feminists, encounter, not just with the structure but with the methodology and content of the scientific professions.

It is a truism that western science developed explicitly as a way to dominate nature, to put "her" on the rack and force "her" to give up her secrets. "Knowledge is power," said Bacon. The quotes of domination are explicit and many. Additionally, there is something very uncongenial to many women scientists, and to some men, about the Baconian warrior-scientist who goes forth to do battle with nature. Many of us have therefore been thinking and writing our criticisms of the program and content of science as much as of its social structure.

It is important to recognize that the history of science contains many examples of tensions and struggle between descriptions and explanation of natural phenomena in terms of hierarchies and unidirectional, causal paths and those that stress multiple interactions and multidirectional networks. I gave you one example earlier, when I compared the sociobiological program to find *the* biological *bases* of social behavior with more integrative models that stress the many mutual interactions between biology and society. We can also see it in the emergence of the concept of the gene as the mastermolecule from which flows the information that "determines" how all other molecules and biological structures will be shaped and will act. Lined up against this linear, causal analysis are the observations and theories that stress two- or many-way communications between different cellular components, between different cell and organ systems, between organisms.

These descriptions, explanations, and theories stem from very different views of nature and of the scientific enterprise. In the one, "man" stands outside nature and tries to understand it so as better to impose "his" will. In the other, we acknowledge that we are parts of nature and must therefore see it from inside. We must rely on its cooperation but, in turn, be respectful of it in order to try to understand nature's seamless web and our place within it. We see all too clearly that "man's" attempts at domination are producing perturbations that may end by unbalancing the entire system.

The pretense that we can be external observers of what goes on in nature, without acknowledging that we are parts of that nature and that our activities affect it constantly and profoundly, just as it affects us (indeed, that the separation between "us" and "it" is an illusion), introduces serious distortions into our scientific endeavors. Take the sentence with which my Harvard colleague, E. O. Wilson, opens the last chapter of *Sociobiology: The New Synthesis*. Wilson (1975, 547) writes, "Let us now consider man in the free spirit of natural history, as though we were zoologists from another planet completing a catalog of social species on earth." What foolishness! What is this "free spirit" of natural history? And how can we possibly imagine what hypothetical "zoologists from another planet" would notice about us, since that would depend in large measure on what they were used to "seeing" or "noticing" on "their own" planet? Would it not be much better (and more objective) scientific methodology to try to understand how the fact that one is a white, male, Harvard professor, who lives in a Boston suburb with his family and studies insect behavior in the lab, affects one's observations and ideas about human behavior than to pretend that one is an unbiased, new arrival from outer space?

I grant you that this is a rather more blatant example than many, but the myth of scientific objectivity, in general, obscures more than it reveals. How much better and more honest it is to try to identify the sources of one's *subjectivity*, to acknowledge one's position within nature and society, and to try to proceed from there. (I am sure that it has not escaped your notice that some of this century's greatest advances in physics have come out of the acknowledgment of the role of the observer in the making of measurements and out of subsequent efforts to clarify the relationship.)

What does all this have to do with women and men, with feminine and masculine styles of work in science? A great deal, I think.

My friend, Evelyn Fox Keller (1978), a physicist by training but also a profound and prolific thinker and commentator on the sociology and philosophy of science, has used a theoretical framework similar to Nancy Chodorow's (1978) and Dorothy Dinnerstein's (1976) to try to explain what she calls the "genderization" of science. By this she means the fact that science itself is perceived as male or masculine, in contrast to other endeavors in which men also greatly outnumber women, such as literature, music, or painting. According to this analysis, the phycho-developmental paths that infants and young children must take in order to differentiate themselves from their first, and often only, early caretaker--the mother or her almost invariably *female* replacement--are very different for boys and girls. Boys, Evelyn Keller argues, are much more threatened by the female presence and must learn rigidly and at all times to be *not-women*. They achieve this with greatest certainty by developing a sense of superiority and domination *over* first girls, later women. For girls, the differentiation, though perhaps personally problematic, generically is much less so. It does not threaten a girl's gender identification to have mutually accepting relations and even a sense of merging identity with her mother or another female caretaker. Girls therefore need not objectify women as "others" in order to be girls and become women. Boys do this in order to be boys and to grow up as men.

For myself, I am not altogether comfortable with interpretations of infant and childhood feelings and fantasies as a way of explaining adult behavior. Our experiences are sufficiently rich and varied to make it rather too easy to construct retrospective development explanations. Whether this particular line of argument is correct or not, it is a fact that in our society boys and men acquire more dominating, objectivizing, and aggressive styles of behavior than do girls and women, while we tend to be more intuitive, relational, and adaptable. It is also true that of the relatively small number of women scientists, a relatively large proportion has unconventional ways of conceptualizing their fields and therefore comes up with unusual questions and innovative answers. As examples, I am thinking of Barbara McClintock's (Keller 1983) observations and interpretations in genetics, of Lynn Margulies' (1982) hypotheses about the origins of life and evolution, and of Barbara Wright's (1973, 1978) models of embryonic development and differentiation, to name only a few outstanding examples in contemporary biology. These women permit themselves a more intuitive style and think in terms of relationships and interactions much more than is usual in their fields.

So, what I would like us as women scientists and professionals to think about is whether it would not be to everyone's advantage if we took pride in our female skills and acknowledged their equal, if not greater, efficacy for building successful social structures. We should have the confidence to introduce our less hierarchical ways of acting and thinking, not only into our work situations but also into the substantive content of our science and our explanations of nature. As more women and feminists enter science, it is important for us to understand and affirm that there are alternatives to the prevalent modes of scientific discovery and explanation as well as to the male-engendered structures of the scientific professions.

So, I want us to actively counter the assumption that the present practice and content of science are right, to challenge that they are givens whose structures are somehow "natural" and unchangeable and that we are the ones who must accommodate. We must understand that "the system," by which I mean both the structure and content of the scientific and technical professions, has been constructed by one particular, limited social group, composed of the economically privileged, university-educated, white men, and that it serves their needs more than ours. We must recognize that, if we are willing to accept the reigning definitions and structures and change *ourselves,* we collude in limiting women's access, for there are clear structural reasons why only relatively few women can transcend our outsider status and fit in. Though we are often assured of the contrary, our accommodation does *not* open the doors to increasing numbers of women; it only perpetuates our status as tokens and exceptions.

References

Chodorow, N. 1978. *The reproduction of mothering.* Berkeley, Calif.: Univ. of California Press.

deBeauvoir, S. 1952. *The second sex.* New York: Alfred A. Knopf.

Dinnerstein, D. 1976. *The mermaid and the minotaur.* New York: Harper Colophon

Kanter, R. M. 1977. *Men and women of the corporation.* New York: Basic Books.

Keller, E. F. 1978. *Gender and science. Psychoanalysis and Contemporary Thought.* 1: 409-33.

———. 1983. *A feeling for the organism: The life and work of Barbara McClintock.* San Francisco, Calif.: Freeman.

Margulies, L. 1982. *Early life.* Boston, Mass.: Science Books International.

Naftolin, F., and E. Butz. 1981. Sexual dimorphism. *Science* 211: 1263-1324.

Wilson, E. O. 1975. *Sociobiology: The new synthesis.* Cambridge, Mass.: Harvard Univ. Press, Belknap Press.

Wright, B. 1973. *Critical variables in differentiation.* Englewood Cliffs, N.J.: Prentice Hall.

———. 1978. What is the molecular mechanism of differentiation in the slime mould? *Trends in Biochemical Sciences* 2:N272-74.

Class, Race, Sex, Scientific Objects of Knowledge: A Socialist-Feminist Perspective on the Social Construction of Productive Nature and Some Political Consequences

Donna J. Haraway

Had we but world enough and time,
This Coyness, Lady, were no crime.

Andrew Marvel
"To His Coy Mistress"

Preface: Scientific Women and the Need for a Comprehensive Feminist Politics

Those who attended the Purdue University Conference on Women in the Professions form a group of feminist scientific workers of many kinds: engineers in universities and industries, research scientists, teachers, science writers, historians, administrators, activists. How did we get to Purdue in March, 1981; what makes this group of United States scientific female people a "we," an historical group with passionate common needs, interests, and purposes, despite our evident differences in age, rank, race, political identities, and employment? It would be reassuring to believe we exist now because of a coherent, comprehensive, feminist women's movement changing our lives over the last twenty-five years, so that we can now exercise previously forbidden skills. There is some truth in such a belief. But I build my thesis around another important material connection that produced "us" collectively: the Cold War, the nuclear arms race, and the needs of high technology industries, both military and civilian, especially the communications industries.

My Ph.D. in biology from Yale in 1972 is at least as much the result of Sputnik as it is of the women's movements with which I identify. My location in the profession of history of science owes much to that profession's historical function to justify science as progress in post- World War II militarized, science-based daily conditions. How else could an Irish Catholic girl from Denver turn into a marxist-feminist historian of biology? The women's movement did not control the money, educational institutions, and careers that made us. I suggest that most of those who participated in the conference could not have come if Sputnik had not provided the impetus to supply money for science education and if the high technology needs of modern war-based, science-based corporations for the best brain-power the nation could produce had not made even girls' brains, even some Black girls' brains, into a national resource more useful than our wombs and "low tech" domestic service.

But we came to Purdue in March, 1981, in significant collective opposition to the conditions and institutions that produced us. We have something to say about theory and practice in science and technology that might refuse to reproduce war babies, female or otherwise. I offer this chapter as a contribution to exploring two major categories with which we constitute our scientific-technical understandings of all bodies in daily life and their production: sex and labor. My purpose is to sketch what I have found to be disturbing pictures of the structures of our available objects of scientific knowledge, including ourselves. In the face of the massive anti-science practice and ideology of so much of the present women's movements, I want these explorations to help us reconstitute ourselves as scientifically, politically powerful feminist women. We profoundly need a comprehensive feminist politics about science and technology. We do not today know what such a politics might look like. This imagined political body will be birthed neither naturally nor automatically.

Finally, I want to say something about priorities, because feminists are pressed by many suitors to retreat from the politics of mere women to serve the putative universal politics of men. We are told there is no time for our sexual games; we are told to consent again. In face of the threat of nuclear war, can we really care about affirmative action, especially when scientific jobs for women, from top to bottom of our science-based society, are part of the material structure that makes modern war possible? Can we really fight for jobs for privileged, mostly white, women in the aerospace fields? My response is no, not in those terms, but because of feminism, not in retreat from it. What we need as feminists is control of the aerospace industries, not merely a few jobs with Martin Marietta or McDonnell Douglas. This utopian statement at least names a minimal program and heightens our contradictions in achieving it. As feminists with so many dangerous differences included in a fragile "we," we need simultaneously to support each other in gaining the most advanced scientific skills and in producing the most fundamental changes in the conditions of all scientific work. Not the least important consequence emerging from these dual, contradictory, minimal needs is the realization that none of us is pure, that none of us is natural. Thus, we do not want a feminist politics rooted in a search for natural purity--for the angel in the bomb. We do not want a domesticated feminism.

Introduction: Are Sex and Labor Obsolete?

Feminism and marxism have seemed both natural allies and natural enemies on almost every matter important to recent, as well as more traditional, progressive political struggles in the United States; technology, science, and development issues are no exception. Socialist-feminist theorists have repeatedly taken note of the loving antagonism and antagonistic love between marxism and feminism by calling on the imagery of failed courtship and marriage (Weinbaum 1978; Hartmann 1979). Both growing out of historically specific yet universally important social relations of oppression, these two world political movements have not, and cannot, achieve a successful union in the face of crucial unresolved disputes that go to the core of analysis and practice for both parties. At the crux of the dispute are those central categories with multiple meanings; labor and sex, production and reproduction. At issue between marxism and feminism is the formulation of politically effective analysis of the making, continuing, and transforming of daily human life free from the dominations of sex, race, and class. The role of science and technology in the making of daily life is increasingly, inescapably central.

In the face of extreme threat from dangers of nuclear war, and hardly lesser threats to struggles against domination from dozens of directions, many socialists continue to argue that feminists seem coy, seem not to recognize the severity of present crises in their "woman-centered" analysis and politics, to engage in luxury politics. Feminists, on the other hand, continue to feel this left claim presses a seduction and not an honorable suit. Feminism will not be mistress to socialism. Many feminists feel further that marriage is not an honorable estate, in any case, but a proprietary relationship. They can point to efforts of segments of the U.S. male-dominated left to respond to the political threat of the ascendant far right--with its family-centered rhetorics and evident appeal to very large numbers of white working class North Americans--by themselves re-glorifying the traditional family and even appealing to a "revolutionary nuclear family." Feminists, meanwhile, see eroding reproductive rights; growing severe poverty, especially for women of all colors; resurgent sexual violence, including physical attacks on lesbians and gay men; and crippling exclusion of women from most sources of power, most certainly including technical and scientific competence.

But these distinctions between socialists and feminists are too sharp; for one thing, these two points of view often co-exist in the same individual human beings. For another, important parts of the mixed left in the U.S. have increasingly recognized the legitimacy of autonomous women's movements and the strength of the theoretical claims about the ultimate importance of gender domination and related divisions of labor, in generating, or at least in making possible, class domination. In addition, very promising socialist-feminist theory is emerging which incisively critiques sources of trouble in marxist theory unable to perceive women's fundamental role in the making of daily life and which provides the beginnings of exciting political and theoretical synthesis (Hartsock 1983; Sargent 1981). But both white feminists and socialists have been called up short on their culpably ignorant theory and practice around race. In the U.S., both feminist and socialist analyses and movements are missing most of the people who "should" be sympathetic--women and workers, however defined.

Finally, feminist activists themselves frequently feel puzzled and extremely frustrated by the extra-ordinary power of uterine politics to define their movement from the nineteenth century on. Knowing that nuclear weapons and power, science and technology broadly, and class structure generally are feminist issues, nonetheless, feminists write more about and organize most around very sexually defined matters like abortion, pornography, and rape. Some of the reasons are obvious;

reproductive self-responsibility does not exist and is a precondition to much else in non-hierarchical revolutionary transformation, and male dominance continues to be maintained by cultural, physical and sexual terrorism very broadly in and out of the U.S.

But some of the reasons elude us. Why haven't feminists been producing commanding analyses of developments in science and technology, for example, with the same cogency as they do of reproductive rights? Why are these analyses hard to find when women are the major world labor force in the leading modern scientific industries, like electronics? Why are they lacking when about eighty percent of the increase in employment in the U.S. since World War II has been women and teenagers? The traditional male working class doesn't seem to be where much fundamental social transformation is occurring. Why don't we know more about the world historical consequences of contemporary scientific, technological, and economic development strategies within continuing, or sometimes newly imposed, ferocious social relations of worldwide male domination, in both formally capitalist and socialist states? Feminists, especially socialist feminists, should have a great deal to say about, for example, technology transfer within patriarchal social systems. And all socialists, logically, ought to feel a profound need to learn about these things.

Why does feminism seem so linked to sex as a biological matter? Alternatively, why does socialism seem wedded to the "worker" as source of all being and feminism umbilically tied to that other mythically productive being, "woman"? This way of putting the question seems right, especially when neither worker-as-man (or mankind) nor woman-as-mother seems very productive in the old senses these days-- both being about to succumb in myth and in fact to automation. In some non-trivial senses, the laboring-birthing production and reproduction of daily life seems threatened with technological obsolescence-- along with the traditional formulations of socialists and feminists and their family quarrels. Much is challenged by these developments, including our analytical categories of labor and gender.

Productive Nature: A History

Without pretending to resolve all these difficulties, I shall offer some reflections about labor and sex, workers and women, class and gender, from the double viewpoint of a socialist-feminist and an historian of biology. In particular, I offer an argument about the generation of class, race, and sex, and other critical scientific objects of knowledge in the life and human sciences in the last two hundred years, in an effort to explore the profound connections of systems of meaning and systems of effecting meanings--that is, cosmology/myth and technology/science. I conclude with some political reflections about partial achievements and needed steps in socialist-feminist development in relation to science and technology.

The objects constituted by and studied within the life and human sciences have some very interesting common properties during approximately the last two hundred years; they are fruitful objects considered to be ordered by physiological-organismic--or more recently by technological-cybernetic--principles of the functional division of labor. Most importantly, the life and human sciences study generative bodies, bodies that increase and multiply, reproduce, expand, diversify and ramify from internal sources of motion, and bodies ruled by internal logics of control. The functional division of labor ruling the structure of any modern object of knowledge in the biological and social sciences (whether capitalist or socialist) has a teleology of increase and built-in schemae of control of the fruits of natural bodies. These control schemae are intimately interwoven with the changing possible historical forms and technologies of domination of fruitful systems. In short, nature has been thought to be constituted, particularly in modern capitalist societies, as a system of production/reproduction whose chief parts--like woman, race, and class--are ordered by the laws of fruitful labor. In an important sense, nineteenth and twentieth century Western people can only know (rationally, scientifically) objects which are classified into these very specific historical forms; and these forms come laden with both meanings and techniques for enforcing as well as for challenging domination.

Let me illustrate this broad assertion by looking briefly at aspects of the history of life and human sciences, especially parts of biology and social theory. It has been well established that biology and sociology have been functionalist discourses with built-in (and class-interested) theories of power. Marx's own critique of this dimension of social scientific knowledge has been one of the most cogent (Figlio 1978; Harvey 1979; Young 1977). But I would like to return to the late eighteenth and early nineteenth centuries to look at Thomas Robert Malthus, Adam Smith, Andrew Ure, Charles Babbage, Henri Milne-Edwards, Charles Darwin, and Herbert Spencer. Let us look at the laws of population, natural production, and human work emerging from the writings of these people in order to throw some light on the chief object of knowledge in biology up to World War II--the organism. I want to examine the constitution of the organism as a technical and scientific object of knowledge (that is, NOT a mere ideological epiphenomenon of true science) structured deeply by the practices of capitalist patriarchy. If Marx saw the class nature of knowledge in political economy, he did not know how to see the fundamental elements of male domination built into organisms and their properties, including human labor and human biological and social reproduction. He could not see those elements without a materialist feminist standpoint that was not yet historically constituted. Malthus's *Essay on the Principle of Population* (1798) used descriptions of the laws of "natural" productivity of two great sources of increase (agriculture and human populations) in order to arrive at two pregnant assertions. He allowed all kinds of social improvement as long as two social forms were maintained: 1) private ownership of the means of production; and 2) male dominant marriage with male ownership of the productivity of women, especially in children. Malthus represents an early and exceedingly insightful attempt to formulate processes in the natural and social worlds in terms of laws of production, rather than of pre-set harmony. He understood what subsequent theorists have not wanted to see in their race to damn him for his undeniably class-biased science: that is, he understood the conjoint necessity of male domination and capitalism, although male domination's forms would greatly change from the pre-capitalist patriarchal family. Malthus haltingly specified the key elements of labor and sex in the social organization of capitalist patriarchy. He knew what was at stake if his laws should be proven wrong.

Adam Smith, Charles Babbage, and Andrew Ure may be used to represent the formulation of theory about the chief structuring principle of systems of production (including agriculture, human populations, families, women, races, factories): the hierarchical division of labor, whereby the problem of appropriation of the products of increase is faced and solved in theories of organic (social and biological) control systems. Human, plant, and animal bodies, as well as machines and social groups are all organic system parts. Clearly, no theorists of the division of labor from Smith through to contemporary post-Taylorite cybernetic ergonomists ignored the question of system control. And all these theorists tried to formulate a theory of the division of labor (of efficiency and progress in systems of production) that seemed to work entirely from internal (that is, natural and rational) forces. Organismic theories, like the theories of the functionalist division of labor, forbid certain kinds of control. Particularly, they forbid external domination not rooted in the laws of efficient production themselves. Biology (natural economy) and social theory (political economy and sociology) share profoundly the search for understanding (that is, constituting as objects of knowledge) control systems in terms of internally operating principles. Efficiency is a special example of such a principle. Goal-oriented interdependence of system parts to form a modern rational whole (organism, society, or other object of scientific knowledge) is the mode of organization specified. These principles pertain irrespective of issues of the "reduction" of social to biological laws or of the proper relations of social and biological discourses.

The French physiologist, Henri Milne-Edwards, the English naturalist, Charles Darwin, and the English biological and social theorist, Herbert Spencer, may be used to represent the complex of considerations that structured biology in the nineteenth century. Organic efficiency for Milne-Edwards was a function of the physiological division of labor, a principle crucial to both Darwin and Spencer in their understanding of modern natural economy as a system of vast productive power structured and operating without external intervention. The contemporary French microbiologist-geneticist, François Jacob, in his *Logic of Life* (1974), has powerfully argued the absolutely central achievement of nineteenth century biology in formulating its objects (e.g., populations, physiological systems, cells) without needing external principles of harmony or control. Jacob understood that biological objects were working systems. But he, like Marx, could not and did not understand that biological objects emerged as working systems intimately structured by hierarchical sexual principles of efficiency.

The chief aspect of sexual principles structuring organic systems concerned the relations of generativity and control functions. These relations were most clearly seen in the interconnections of reproductive and nervous physiology in the biology of nineteenth and twentieth centuries up to World War II. It is not accidental that biologists of the nineteenth century all across Europe, as well as in the United States and Japan, unearthed a profusion of knowledge about organic reproduction and regeneration, sexual and asexual modes of organic production. The most organically "efficient" systems emerged as mammals-- principally, of course, man, with "his" supreme bodily and social divisions of labor, including the family and divisions of home, market, and workplace, and proper spheres of males and females, as well as of races and classes. The nineteenth and early twentieth centuries abound in the biologies of hierarchical, but strictly internal, interdependencies of reproductive and nervous systems in the production and transformations of organisms. Perhaps the high point of this mode of thinking in biology occurred in the synthesis of physiology, animal behavior, and social theory in the psychobiology of Yale, Chicago, and Harvard Universities in the 1920's and 30's. These are the schools of biology intimately linked to the development of anti-marxist social systems theory before and after World War II in the U.S. But I am ahead of my story.

As scientific objects, sex and labor had race as a co-equal organic partner in the organismic functionalism constituted from the late eighteenth century. Just as class and sex required internal rules of function, so did race. And like sex and labor, the object called race required a physical, even physiological basis: race required a body, and race was given a body in the organic scheme of things that worked by interdependent internal control logic, not by imposed "external" domination. Imperialism and slavery had a known natural touch. Nature constituted in objects of knowledge had a body woven together by principles of control of its fruits. Black slave women in the New World, in their experience of forced reproduction and sexual servitude, experienced most acutely the logic of such systems of control (Aptheker 1982; Davis 1982; Hooks 1981). The history of physical anthropology, psychology, evolutionary theory, and many other branches of the discourses of organic functionalism are replete with constructions of race as an object of modern knowledge (Haller 1971; Chorover 1980; Gould 1981). The history is in too many ways an ugly one, just as is the history of sex and labor as scientific objects. But it is not possible to dismiss the many biologies of racial inferiority as "bad science," as ideology, and salvage the nice biologies that rejected announcements of racial or sexual inferiority. It is not that easy to emerge from the discourses which were part of the social weavings of modern forms of domination. In particular, it is crucial to understand that the scientific understandings of productive control systems, like biology, not only did not rule out principles of domination; they were built in necessarily, or at least logically.

From Biological Organisms to Biotic Components

Before commenting on the social struggles permeating this rather rapid sketch of the history of ideas, let me take this bald argument a step further. I suggest that organic, physiological functionalism and its privileged objects (organisms, races, workers, women) underwent a fundamental transformation during the years between 1930 and 1950, especially during World War II. The social practice of biologists during the war is a large part of this complex story. Biology and other organismic discourses, in an important sense, ceased to exist; they became submerged by the modern communications sciences ruled by principles of cybernetic functionalism. This development greatly enhanced the power of scientific understandings of internally ruled, self-generating control systems (Haraway 1981-82). The objects of knowledge underwent basic transformations; so did the logics of control, and this issue matters a great deal to socialists and feminists in formulating effective political analysis.

The change can be seen everywhere; for example, in the transformation of organismic community theory ecology into the ecology of ecosystems; and, second, in the transformations of the center of biology (and of standards of explanation) from organismic studies of interrelations of mind (nerves) and sex (hormones) to communications systems treatments of coding, copying, and read out function. Genetics, immunology, neuroendocrinology, animal behavior--all show this transformation. Modern biology is about rates of flows across fluid boundaries and control of such rates as problems in information transfer and system productivity. A glance at a modern biology textbook, e.g., *Life on Earth* (Wilson and Eisner 1978), a book· widely used in leading United States biology departments in major universities, will convince the skeptic that organisms are merely interesting and complex technological devices of a very modern kind; that is, communications machines involved in intensely capitalist market competition for optimizing genetic fitness (survival and differential reproduction of least elements of control/generation or code/read-out). A large part of biology has become informatics engineering. Biological objects have been massively miniaturized in the process of these transformations; the least elements of increase and control are not traditional organisms and their hierarchical interdependent systems, as automated copying, replication, and transformations are the key processes of the communications sciences of these biotic components. Much of biology is a very modern communications engineering science. Its objects are automatic command-control systems informed by the genetic and nervous system, immunological system, endocrinal system and other biotic communication technologies.

Cosmologies/Technologies

The preceding representation of recent changes in the theoretical bases of the biological sciences is, of course, too extreme. But rather than qualify the extremism, I should like to probe this representation for some insights concerning the relations of feminist and socialist politics with science and technology. First, it is hard to maintain a strong distinction between science and technology in looking at the historical transformations of biological objects. Biological objects have from the beginning been productive technical systems, whether one refers to populations, organisms, ecosystems, cell organelles, or genomes. Surely, modern machinery (centrifuges, computers, nuclear reactors, etc.) have made modern biology possible. But more than that, biological objects have actually been technological objects, that is, means of effecting meanings in the material world. We should--and did--expect the present developments of recombinant DNA technology and related industrial biologies that so intrigue and threaten our sense of the division between organic and technical. Nature is not a nurturant female, but an internally engineered, highly complex, very productive communication system. That statement operates on the level of myth and on the level of present technical achievement. Biological entities are organs--that is, tools of production. We carve our meanings on our bodies; bioengineering is our tool.

Second, the prized categories of socialists and feminists--labor and sex or gender--and the beings expressing these functional, foundational forces--workers and women (men never possessed gender in the same way) are seen to have a troubling genesis and even more disturbing possible demise. What seemed like stable ontological categories turn out to be historically constituted objects of knowledge in patriarchal social organizations. Historical materialists are not really shocked by that kind of claim; they believe everything is historically constituted on the basis of the ways knowers and doers actually conduct the multifarious aspects of making and remaking themselves in particular times and places. The constructions of materialist historical standpoints that yielded understandings of labor and gender were achieved through complex struggles in world-changing conditions. But the degree to which feminism and socialism are historically humanisms, that is, discourses concerned with the hierarchical production of man as that highest productive-control system, is at least upsetting philosophically. Much of modern humanism is communications engineering capable of powerful simulations of gender and work.

But beyond the indigestion caused by this realization, feminists and socialists can perhaps get some needed insight about some of the sources of our theoretical wooden-ness, our continuing inabilities to form a true and perfect union among ourselves because of our wedding to inadequate and maybe anachronistic categories like workers and women, labor and sex. For example, feminists can become clearer about our fixation on sex and gender in spite of our knowing that the whole world is a feminist issue, not only motherhood and reproductive freedom. Women have been radically historical products; female human beings of all races in these last couple of centuries in the West have not been able to avoid their constitution in sexualized functionalist discourse. Of course, feminists keep re-sexualizing politics and trying to comprehend labor or race within some more sexual category; and feminists see traditional socialists with a wary eye. Feminists after all have not been struggling with sex/gender as merely a system of meanings, but as a highly developed social system for making and enforcing these meanings. Thus feminist analyses of reproduction, of health systems, and even of nuclear engineering keep turning on the cosmologies/technologies of remaking us into women. Similar points can be made for socialist understandings and practices in relation to labor as a system of meanings/technologies for making man, even mankind. Political rhetoric has been almost impossible to formulate without these productive logics. It should also be clear this situation is not all bad. A brief consideration of dialectics and the liberating richness of contradictions in these modern social systems of knowledge/technology, that have yielded workers and women and people of color as their products, reminds us that it is from the standpoints made possible by our places and constitutions in the world that we struggle fruitfully.

Third, the analysis suggested in this chapter might illuminate some aspects of current struggles and debates about class structure as it is emerging in high technology world societies. Here I think attention to the electronics and communications industries is most helpful and most full of important contradictions for socialists and feminists.

On the level of meanings/myths/cosmologies (remembering the distinction between myth and technique is a slippery one (Traweek 1982)), these industries illustrate pictures of power and control logics very different from those known before World War II. Modern regulation works by statistical control of least elements, not by a microcontrol or micro-therapeutics of coherent individual bodies. Modern control is about stress engineering analysis of possibly overloaded systems; modern productive control is about rapid assembly, disassembly, and reassembly of all system components--biotic or otherwise. Females, bodies, and factories are all subject to these logics. Modern control is about the rates of information flows across boundaries; much is permissible within statistically well-policed boundaries, even the belief in and practice of individual autonomy and creativity in work and sex, within bounds. It's all a question of rates and their management. Fiscal managers know rate control is more than a pun; so do embryologists and enzymologists. Stress did not accidentally emerge after World War II as the new historical disease; stress replaced tuberculosis, and this is perfectly reasonable (Hogness 1983).

On the level of technologies and concrete social organizations of daily life (remembering again that technology and meaning are literally two faces of the same coin), we can begin to understand more completely the structure of the international division of labor which depends on the regeneration of women in new ways appropriate to exploitative high technology (Lim 1978; Grossman 1978). Women constitute eighty percent of the production work force in semiconductors, and sixty percent of these are women of color. Yet, most of the secretaries in the industry are white. And communications industries generally are the only areas of professional science and engineering with low or negative unemployment rates for both women and men. Moral 1: women can definitely succeed as electronic cowboys. Moral 2: women had better not be ignorant and professionally marginal in these fields. We--the class of women--need this expertise in women's hands. Moral 3: setting feminist terms for acquiring these skills will be no small historical trick. A feminist friend of mine in Santa Cruz, a Ph.D. communications engineer, cannot now get a needed security clearance to work on civilian aspects of a multinational communications satellite system. The reason is of course not given, but could well be her work in California anti-nuclear politics. Our political allies--and ourselves--can be systematically excluded from acquiring the most advanced scientific-technical skills. Alternative technology and hexing the Pentagon are fatally insufficient feminist politics in struggles with a science-based industrial military system.

The traditional divisions of class and race among women are exploited to make possible world-leading industries absolutely central to male-dominant war-making and modern social systems in general. But at the same time, conditions for building new kinds of conscious, organized connections among women with world-changing consequences are extraordinary and historically new. The electronics and communications industries make real the connections of daily life for women in Sunnyvale, California, and Penang, Indonesia. It is up to all of these women, and socialism and feminism as world movements, to turn these connections into liberating social forces, instead of new ways to exploit women. One thing is sure: women are not a world-wide secondary or marginal work force; they are the key to the world's major modern science-based industries in offices, markets, homes, and factories. All of women's work in the twentieth century is becoming science-based. If socialists continue to think of the traditional male working class as their constituency, at least in the United States, they will miss how work is done, and by whom. If feminists continue to sexualize everything, they will miss how women have been re-assembled in the modern world, and for whom. They will also miss the desexualization of women's "traditional" work, reproduction.

Toward a Socialist-Feminist Politics in Science and Technology

Let me now move away from these grand and extreme claims and look at some more proximate achievements and needs of socialist-feminism (the political position to which we should all be striving, in my view) in relation to science and technology. My own parochialism limits much of this to the United States, and worse, to perspectives of mostly white radicals.

First, let us consider the terrible problem of class and race divisions among women in the U.S. in relation to science and technology. "White" and "minority" women who attended the Purdue Conference are all scientific workers and mostly professionals. Also at this conference, a very clear message emerged: professional opportunities for women in science and technology in the next decade will be in research and development tightly linked to the military sector. Most women in science and technology will continue in the lowest positions; that is, as poorly paid, easily disposed of (individually) "unskilled" labor. (Caution has to be used with the term "unskilled;" it tends to be a synonym for anything women do, especially if they aren't paid much.) Further, clerical jobs will continue to be white dominated, and production jobs more available for women of color. Next, social policy will ensure the steady mass production of nearly illiterate teenagers, especially among people of color, to staff the automated industries in food and other fast growing areas.

Women's lives will be intimately tied, in the details of bodily motion and structure, to the fluid machinery of high technology, but we shall remain vastly ignorant of how we and it all work, and we shall remain vastly powerless in transforming technology, and so we shall remain vastly inept in controlling the technology of creating meanings. That is, we will remain powerless unless we achieve political development much more effective in theory and practice than we now have. And this development must include ways of making sound connections with people who, though outside the United States, are thoroughly built into our lives, usually to our exploitative advantage. How will the Black research computer analyst working for Intel, the first person in her family to get a decent education, be able to form effective liberating connections with the Taiwan teenager in an electronics assembly plant and with the white secretary in Palo Alto? How can we expect resistance to the domination of so much of social life by military technology when daily life increasingly depends on jobs generated by this technology? White feminists have not learned to say much about this, and we won't learn if we are separate. It is also not heartening to note that the U.S. trade unions now trying unsuccessfully to organize in California's "Silicon Valley" rarely involve any women, much less women of color, as organizers and decision makers. Meanwhile, chemical poisoning of women workers is routinely diagnosed as stress. Where are labor's chemical toxicologists? And where are the politically accessible critiques of stress ideologies in modern communications engineering medicine? Why are so many radicals still fixated on male coal miners, auto workers, and steelworkers? And why do feminist professionals feel so unable to talk about more than eroding affirmative action?

We must insist that high technology is for, among other things, the liberation of all women, and therefore usable by women for their self-defined purposes. That demand should be considered in light of the experience of the National Women's Agenda Satellite Project in 1978 to bring together technically competent women to facilitate a national satellite-mediated conference on women's issues, as women defined them. The project did not succeed because male technicians refused to allow such high spatial discussion of abortion and lesbianism (Zimmerman 1979). They wanted space to be pure for male concerns. It would be hard to find a more condensed picture of sexual politics confronting phallic technology posing as neutral. Feminists must find ways to analyze and design technologies that effect the lives we all want without major dominations of race, sex, and class. Those goals will sometimes lead to insisting on small, decentralized, personally scaled technologies. Such technologies are not synonymous with soft, female, and easy. They require disciplined knowledge and skill, but they are not automatically a substitute for larger scale technology.

Finally, feminists must find ways of building broad, stable organizations with socialists that do not subordinate each other, while continuing to struggle for the fruitfulness of our respective insights, even when they contradict each other. In this too sketchy chapter, I have tried to describe some of the symbolic and material barriers to a hoped-for union of marxism and feminism in relation to science and technology. My hope is that in consciousness of our categories of analysis as historical tools which partly determine the kind of bodies we can build, we will better learn a scientific and political craft.

We carve our meanings into our bodies; our bodies, ourselves--and generate questions about communications engineering under stress.

References

Aptheker, B. 1982. *Women's legacy.* Amherst: Univ. of Massachusetts Press.

Chorover, S. L. 1980. *From Genesis to genocide.* Cambridge, Mass.: M.I.T. Press.

Davis, A. 1981. *Women, race and class.* New York: Random House.

Figlio, K. 1978. Chlorosis and chronic disease in nineteenth century Britain: The social constitution of a somatic illness in capitalist society. *Social History* 3:167-97.

Gould, S. J. 1981. *Mismeasure of man.* New York: Norton.

Grossman, R. 1978. Women's place in the integrated circuit. *Southeast Asia Chronicle* (Jan.-Feb., 1979)/*Pacific Research* 9:2-17.

Haller, J. 1971. *Outcasts from evolution.* Chicago: Univ. of Chicago Press.

Haraway, D. J. 1981-82. The high cost of information in post-World War II evolutionary biology. *Philosophical Forum* 13: 244-78.

Hartmann, H. 1979. The unhappy marriage of Marxism and feminism: Towards a more progressive union. *Capital and Class* 8:1-33.

Hartsock, N. 1983. *Money, sex and power.* New York: Longman.

Harvey, D. 1979. Population, resources, and the ideology of science. *Economic Geography* 50:256-77.

Hogness, E. R. 1983. *Why Stress? A Look at the Making of Stress, 1936-56.* Manuscript available from author at 4437 Mill Creek Road, Healdsburg, Calif. 95448.

Hooks, B. 1981. *Ain't I a woman?* Boston: South End Press.

Jacob, F. 1974. *The logic of life.* New York: Pantheon.

Lim, L. 1978. Women workers in multinational corporations: The case of the electronics industry in Malaysia and Singapore. *Michigan*

Occasional Papers 9:60.

Malthus, T. M. 1798. *Essay on the principle of population as it affects the future improvement of society.* London: J. Johnson.

Sargent, L., ed. 1981. *Women and revolution.* Boston: Southend Press.

Traweek, S. 1982. Uptime, downtime, spacetime and power: An ethnogaphy of the particle physics community in Japan and the United States. Ph.D. diss., University of California at Santa Cruz, History of Consciousness Board.

Weinbaum, B. 1978. *The curious courtship of women's liberation and socialism.* Boston: Southend Press.

Wilson, E. O., and T. Eisner. 1978. *Life on Earth.* Sunderland, Mass.: Sinauer.

Young, R. M. 1977. Science *is* social relations. *Radical Science Journal* 5:65-131.

Zimmerman, J. 1979. Women's need for high technology. *Women and technology: Deciding what's appropriate.* 19-23. Missoula, Mont.: Women's Resource Center.

Evolving Views of Women's Professional Roles

Violet B. Haas

From the beginning of recorded history women have made significant contributions to almost every branch of science and culture, despite widely held prejudices that they were intellectually inferior to men. Many have persevered in their intellectual and practical endeavors despite the numerous barriers that have been erected to confine their activities to their kitchens and bedrooms. The achievements of women scientists, philosophers and mathematicians from Sappho to Marie Curie were documented by Mozans in the first book devoted to such a topic (Mozans 1913). But more progress has been made toward achieving equality of opportunity for women in the fields considered by the Purdue Conference in the last decade than in any other ten year time span in American history. This progress can largely be attributed to the success of the Women's Movement and the changes in our cultural value system it is causing. The new feminism is affecting virtually every facet of American life. It is changing the language we speak, our child-rearing practices and our politics. It is affecting our business practices, religion, the law and the mass media. (Yates 1975) During the past decade, women have increased their representation from less than one percent of the practicing engineers to over eleven percent. That this ratio is still increasing is evidenced by the fact that over fifteen percent of the engineering students in our institutions of higher education are women, and their three-year retention rate is now equivalent to that for men. Women now comprise approximately half of all pharmacy students and of all students of veterinary medicine and they comprise about thirty-three percent of all medical students. Still, many problems remain. Although half of the students entering graduate school in biology are women, women receive only about thirty percent of the Ph.D. degrees in this discipline (National Academy of Sciences 1980). Computer Science is an area where women students continue to have retention difficulties even at the undergraduate level. As indicated by Hornig, Briscoe, McAfee and Vetter in their chapters in this volume, women are still not represented in the various disciplines on university faculties in proportions nearly equal to their representation among the holders of the Ph.D. degree, and they are still not rising through the ranks as quickly as their male cohorts in both academia and industry.

The MIT Symposium

The progress toward equality of opportunity can be documented not only by statistics, but also by a comparison of the attitudes toward the achievements of women in the technical fields that are held today with those that were held in the recent past. To this end it is appropriate to make comparisons between the Purdue Conference and other conferences of its type. The 1964 MIT Symposium on Women in the Scientific Professions, (Mattfeld and Van Aken 1964) was held at a time when the proportion of women in these fields was at an all time low in the United States, and when the long dormant Women's Movement was at the beginning of a period of unprecedented activity. Because the planners apparently felt that men were needed to lend legitimacy to the proceedings, the MIT Symposium was both opened and closed by men. In fact, of the seven major speakers, only three were women, and one of these, Dr. Lillian Gilbreth, did not even address the issues of the Symposium. She said she was more concerned about opportunities for *people* than for women. In his opening address, Dr. Bruno Bettleheim espoused all the old prejudices that women professionals have been trying to dispel for generations and probably for centuries. He said that women entering these fields, "in many ways felt more like men than the rest of their sex," and that this was deplorable because, "a woman's most important commitment is to being a woman. Such a commitment should embrace all the activities of her life..." (Bettleheim 1965, 5-6). Today we believe that a woman need not expend time and effort committing herself to being a woman; she is a woman merely by dint of possessing two X chromosomes. Furthermore, since all her thinking is done by a woman, she *must* think like a woman. Bettleheim's words recall to mind a personal experience. In

1951, when I was eight and one half months pregnant with my first child, the Boston area American Association of University Women (AAUW) invited all local AAUW postdoctoral fellows, of whom I was one, to meet the membership. When it was my turn to be introduced, one of the members asked, "How come someone as feminine as you chose a field as masculine as mathematics?" I did not at the time think fast enough to reply, "Obviously, since mathematics is *my* field, it cannot be as masculine as you have been led to believe." A word is in order about the term, "feminine." *Webster's Seventh New Collegiate Dictionary* defines feminine as "characteristic of or appropriate to women... used otherwise than scientifically or statistically [it] has a *contemptuous or patronizing* suggestion" (italics mine).

Bettleheim proposed that working hours for a mother of young children be considerably shortened, and that the location of her employment be close enough to home so that she could be readily available to her children in the event of emergencies. He said, "work and motherhood are not [compatible] unless work and child care are so arranged that neither childhood nor motherhood suffers" (Bettleheim 1965, 15). He seemed totally unconcerned about the relationship between work and fatherhood. Dr. Jesse Bernard advised those women desiring careers in science or engineering to, "decide whether you want to invest a big chunk of your life in your work, or whether you want to reserve a fair chunk for other things... If you want to commit less than a large chunk settle for 'fringe benefit status.' You may not have tenure; you will not exercise a great deal of academic power, but you will be respected, and, best of all, you will feel you are in a rewarding situation" (Bernard 1965, 180). Women in fringe benefit status are uniformly without tenure, are grossly underpaid, receive almost no salary increases from year to year, never know until a few days before classes begin whether they have a job for the semester, are frequently needed only one semester out of each year, get no TA help for large classes and are assigned only those courses the regular faculty dislike. Furthemore, they are held in disrespect and even contempt by the tenured male faculty. Those who opt for this kind of status generally feel cheated after they come to understand the realities of their situations. Today we recognize Bernard's advice as a prescription for professional suicide.

As noted by Hornig, the speakers at the MIT conference were uniformly pessimistic about the level of women's capabilities for contributing to these fields, except for Dr. Alice Rossi, who rescued the symposium with the only rational analysis of the barriers facing those women who choose their life's work in demanding professions. She was prudent in saying that, "part-time employment is this generation's false panacea for avoiding a more basic change in the relations between men and women,... acceptance of the woman's withdrawal [from the work place] for a number of years [is] a pattern that should not be widely or uncritically accepted until we have better answers to the question concerning the effect this withdrawal has upon the contributions we may expect from her" (Rossi 1965, 53). Rossi advocated changing the social climate surrounding young children to encourge more girls to choose math and science-based professions. She called for changing the ways in which parents and teachers deal with children in order to alter the popular view that science is for boys and not for girls. She suggested that girls be encouraged to exhibit more independence, and boys be taught to display greater sensitivity to their environments so as to develop more creativity in each. As the production of research has become increasingly valued and good teaching has become less so in the most prestigious institutions of higher learning, Rossi's admonition to caution in recommending half time academic positions for women is now recognized to make good sense. The publish-or-perish syndrome has become more ingrained in academic life today than it was in 1964, and women do not receive tenure in academia unless their publication rate and quality match those of the most able and prolific men. The performance of scientific research in itself is usually more than a full-time job. It demands long periods of devotion during each day, and it can rarely be done successfully on a half-time basis when other obligations, such as teaching, are required. The body of knowledge in the science-based fields has been increasing so rapidly in the past thirty years that a person who leaves such a profession for a few years finds that her skills are almost hopelessly obsolete when she tries to return. Educated women have become more ambitious since 1964. More of them are opting to work in demanding fields for their share of the rewards that come with achievement. At the Purdue Conference Gonzalez advocated teaching our children, "that self-fulfillment can be obtained through contributing to society at large, and not only through service to our own families" (see her chapter in this volume). Hornig also pointed to this development by noting that career education and support programs during the 1970's have taught women that career progress depends in large measure on career continuity, and this has led to uninterrupted labor force participation by women despite the additional responsibilities of child care.

Dr. Erik Erikson's paper (Erickson, 1965) closed the MIT Symposium, and as Hornig indicated, his talk began with reference to his theory concerning the differences between male and female mental processes. He believed that women were more comfortable dealing with problems in life that unfold within a well-defined "inner space," whereas men were more interested in mastering an external environment. His theory, based on the observations of the play activity of Berkeley, California adolescents, was actually dangerous, for it tended to characterize whole groups of people. In contrast, it is most important that people be treated as individuals for such things as college admissions and employment considerations. There is surely an uncertainty principle involved whenever one tries to design an experiment to determine biologically innate mental processes. Not only are boys and girls differentially treated by the adults in their lives, from almost the moment of birth, but the experimenters also respond differently to the two sexes, possibly causing some of the observed behavior differences themselves.

The NYAS Conference, 1972

Eight years after the MIT Symposium, the New York Academy of Sciences held a conference (Kundsin 1974) which appeared to be a response to the doubt raised by most of the papers at the MIT Symposium concerning the ability to combine a full-time career with motherhood. This second conference was spawned by concern for the scarcity of professional women in our society and had as its objective to explore the subject of women and success. Twelve women professionals representing the fields of chemistry, physics, mathematics, engineering, education, architecture, government, horticulture and medicine talked about their own lives. All these women were successful in male-dominated fields by the usually accepted definitions of success. One was a member of both the National Academy of Sciences and the National Academy of Engineering; several were full professors at major universities; one was a department head at a large university; and all were nationally prominent in their fields. In addition, all were mothers, several of them having as many as four children. The life histories of these women were analyzed for significant similarities by psychologists and sociologists. Economists and educators discussed employment and educational influences on their lives, and one husband spoke about what life was like married to a successful woman. The women all told tales of having experienced discrimination, much of it blatant and gross, and some had undergone serious traumata in their lives because of it.

The NYAS Conference, 1978

In 1978 the New York Academy of Sciences held another such conference, entitled "Expanding the Role of Women in the Sciences" (Briscoe and Pfafflin 1979). Among the thirty-three papers presented there, the most common theme was of discrimination, and there was a feeling of desperation that redress of grievances was virtually impossible. There were personal accounts as well as statistical evidence to show that women working in the scientific disciplines were overrepresented in the low ranks and in the ranks of the involuntarily unemployed, and underrepresented in the high ranks and in decision making positions. There were accounts of personal conflicts caused by the dual roles of mother and scientist. The need for role models and mentors for children and new professionals and the need for women's networks were stressed.

The Purdue Conference, 1981

The Purdue Conference on Women in the Professions: Science, Social Science and Engineering was held exactly three years later. Supplementing the lectures, represented by the chapters in this volume, were a variety of informal workshops in which the conferees participated. The papers consistently confirm conviction in women's ability to make equal contributions to those of the most successful men, and they also sound a clarion call for a reorganization of society in order to make men's and women's participation in all aspects of life more equal. In this sense, they echo Rossi's plea for a socially androgynous conception of sex roles in which men and women are, "equal and similar in intellectual, artistic, political and occupational interests and participation, complementary only in those spheres dictated by physiological differences," (Rossi 1964, 608).

The Workshops

At the workshop on "The re-entry woman," there were repeated accounts by women who were attempting to restart careers after several years of withdrawal for child rearing, only to find that their fields had changed so much as to be almost unrecognizable. Some of these women had already gone through a retraining process. Those who had retrained in a field of pure science in which a Ph.D and the ability to perform research are requirements for employment found the combination of sex and age discrimination almost impossible to bear. Retraining for those science and engineering jobs for which a bachelor's degree is the basic license was easier, in part because of the existence of special fast track retraining programs sponsored by the National Science Foundation. These programs were in operation during the last few years, but by 1983 they are no longer in existence. Their funding has been withdrawn from the NSF budget. A requirement for admission to these programs was usually a bachelor's degree in some science-based field. These programs had very good track records for getting their graduates satisfying jobs regardless of age, and their demise is unfortunate. For a discussion of these programs see Lantz (1980). As noted by Hornig, throughout the 1970's women have been having fewer career interruptions for the purpose of child rearing, and if this trend continues, fewer women will have difficulties associated with restarting their professions.

At the workshops on "Networking" and on "Coping in a male-dominated environment," there were echos of Dresselhaus' thesis that women are in need of support systems and of contact with others with whom they share common problems. It was mentioned that many universities and industries now have either formal or informal women's networks which not only provide encouragement to the women working there but also serve as sources of ready information when information is needed. Formal mentor systems for new employees and for graduate students were advocated.

At the workshop entitled "Up against the clock: the tenure decision and family strategies," it was repeatedly stressed, contrary to Bernard's 1964 recommendation, that full-time commitment is extremely important in a demanding field, and that it is imperative that a beginning faculty member devote a major share of her working hours to research and to the establishment of her professional reputation. Several of the graduate student attendees asked for advice concerning the optimal timing of pregnancies to ensure career success in academia. The response, from Dresselhaus, who has raised four children, was, "Either before or after the assistant professor period, but preferably not during that time." The reason given was that what is expected of an assistant professor is so exceptionally demanding that the additional burden of a pregnancy may ruin a mother's career, given that she assumes the major portion of the child rearing responsibilities. This uncovers a dilemma for women academics. If a woman waits until she has tenure to bear children, she will most likely postpone beginning her family until she is past thirty years of age. But the later in life that a pregnancy occurs, the greater is the risk of birth defects. If the competition for tenure continues to increase, and all indications are that it will, how can we make sure the competition is fair and yet not punish women academics for bearing children early rather than late? Even if all husbands of career-minded women shared with them equally the household chores and child rearing responsibilities, it would not completely solve this problem. For then unfair advantage would accrue to the men whose wives choose to devote their lives to caring for their husbands and children. We probably do not wish to encourage either celibacy or infertility among our talented women. One possible solution to this dilema is the establishment of special fellowships for academic mothers of small children for the purpose of enabling them to perform their research without other faculty duties during, say, alternate years. As society adopts a more androgynous profile, and women no longer carry the major responsibility for child care, these fellowships could be offered to academic parents of either sex whose spouses also hold full-time positions outside the home.

At the workshop entitled, "Double jeopardy: black and female," the relative importance of sexual versus racial prejudice was considered. The consensus among participants was that both forms of prejudice were significant, but each at different times . Racial prejudice felt more onerus in childhood and adolescence, but sexual prejudice seemed more hurtful to women during their professional lives. It was agreed that black women had an advantage in that they never had to decide the question of whether to continue working or to drop out of the work force temporarily while raising their children. Since they always *had* to work, their work was always a career rather than a job. One conclusion was that black women professionals especially need to be assertive, competent, and most important, political, in order to advance in their careers. Participants called for a network of volunteers to serve as role models, by giving lectures in the grade schools and high schools, in order to demonstrate that the opportunities for exciting careers are available, and to encourage young blacks of both sexes to take advantage of them. At this workshop, Dr. Esther Hopkins described a program entitled, "Mathematics and Science for Minority Students," or, "$(MS)^2$," in which talented minority students receive supplementary mathematics and science training on the Andover Academy campus during each summer while they are in high school. The program is tuition free and is supported by industry.

Conclusions

In general, the tone of the Purdue Conference was more optimistic than the tones of the preceding conferences. That many problems still exist was affirmed in no uncertain terms. However, there seemed reason for hope that many problems have reasonable solutions and that with sufficient federal inducements and with sufficient general good will men and women working together could arrive at them. The consensus was that federal intervention has been worthwhile and necessary and should be continued. The conferees held very realistic views of what is expected of professional people working in the scientific disciplines, and they felt that as women, they were anxious to meet the demands and conform to the standards.

Perhaps, at a future conference , arranged to assess similar issues, the participants will be more equally distributed between the sexes and the speakers will have reason to express, even more optimism than was heard in 1981 concerning the status of women in the heretofore male-dominated professions. Ultimately, however, we cannot expect very much improvement in these areas unless work done by women becomes more equitably valued, and unless women earn one dollar on the average for each dollar earned by men.

References

Bernard, J. 1965. The present situation in the academic world of women trained in engineering. In *Women and the scientific professions*, eds. J. A. Mattfeld and C. G. Van Aken, 163-82. Cambridge: MIT Press.

Bettleheim, B. 1965. The commitment required of a woman entering a scientific profession in present day American society. In *Women and the scientific professions*, eds. J. A. Mattfeld and C. G. Van Aken, 3-19. Cambridge: MIT Press.

Briscoe, A. M. and S. M. Pfafflin, eds. 1979. Expanding the role of women in the sciences. New York: New York Academy of Sciences.

Erikson, E. 1965. Concluding remarks in *Women in the scientific professions*, eds. J. A. Mattfeld and C. G. Van Aken, 232-45. Cambridge: MIT Press.

Kundsin, R. B., ed. 1974. *Women and success: The anatomy of achievement.* New York: William Morrow .

Lantz, A. E. 1980. *Reentry programs for female scientists.* New York: Praeger.

Mattfeld, J. A. and C. G. Van Aken, eds. 1965. *Women and the scientific professions.* Cambridge: MIT Press.

Mozans, H. J. 1913. *Woman in Science.* New York and London: D. Appleton and Co. Reprinted in 1974 by the MIT Press, Cambridge.

National Academy of Sciences. 1980. Summary report. 1980 doctorate recipients from U.S. universities. Washington, D.C.: National Research Council.

Rossi, A. S. 1964. Equality between the sexes: An immodest proposal. *Daedalus* 93: 607-52.

——————, 1965. Barriers to the career choice of engineering, medicine, or science among American women. In *Women and the scientific professions*, eds. J. A. Mattfeld and C. G. Van

Aken, 51-127. Cambridge: MIT Press.

Yates, G. G. 1975. *What women want: The ideas of the movement.* Cambridge: Harvard Univ. Press.

Contributors

Anne M. Briscoe, Director, Biochemistry Laboratory, Harlem Hospital Center and Assistant Professor of Medicine, College of Physicians and Surgeons, Columbia University.

Patricia F. Campbell, Assistant Professor of Mathematics Education, University of Maryland, College Park.

Jewel Plummer Cobb, President, California State University, Fullerton.

Mildred S. Dresselhaus, Professor of Electrical Engineering and Director, Center for Materials Science and Engineering, Massachusetts Institute of Technology.

Susan C. Geller, Associate Professor of Mathematics, Texas A&M University.

Nancie L. Gonzalez, Professor of Anthropology, University of Maryland, College Park.

Violet B. Haas, Professor of Electrical Engineering, Purdue University.

Donna J. Haraway, Associate Professor, Board of Studies in the History of Consciousness, University of California, Santa Cruz.

Esther A. H. Hopkins, Patent Attorney, Polaroid Corporation.

Lilli S. Hornig, Executive Director, Higher Education Resource Services, Wellesley College.

Ruth Hubbard, Professor of Biology, Harvard University.

Naomi J. McAfee, Manager, Design Assurance, Westinghouse Electric Corporation.

Carolyn C. Perrucci, Associate Professor of Sociology, Purdue University.

Rachel A. Rosenfeld, Assistant Professor of Sociology and Fellow, Carolina Population Center, University of North Carolina, Chapel Hill.

Martha M. Trescott, Research Associate, College of Engineering, University of Illinois, Champaign-Urbana.

Betty M. Vetter, Executive Director, Scientific Manpower Commission.

Author Index

Abramson, J., 94, 99, 118, 122
Ahern, N., 51, 53, 57
Ahlum, C., 4, 14
Aiken, L. R., 173, 179
Allison, P. D., 89, 122
Alvarez, R., 5, 13
American Association of University
  Professors, 6, 13
American Chemical Society, 149, 159
American Institute of Public Opinion,
  165, 169
American Men of Science, 120, 122
American Psychological Association,
  120, 122
American Society of Mechanical
  Engineers, 196, 202
Aptheker, B., 220,228
Aronoff, J., 2, 13
Astin, H. S., 5, 13, 65, 74, 90, 99, 100,
  106, 109, 111, 120, 122
Auster, C., 182, 190, 202, 191

Bach, R. L., 8, 13
Baxter, S., 28, 29, 40
Bayer, A. E., 5, 13, 90, 109, 111, 122
Becker, J. R., 175, 178, 180
Behymer, C., 111, 113, 122
Benbow, C. P., 177, 178
Berger, M., 99, 127
Berk, R. A., 121, 122
Bernard, J., 25, 28, 32, 40, 44, 57, 95,
  122, 232, 237, 239
Bettelheim, B., 44, 57, 231, 232, 239
Betz, N. E., 173, 174, 178
Bielby, D., 110, 125
Bird, J. A., 91, 92, 124
Blackburn, R., 111, 113, 122
Blau, F. D., 2, 13
Blaxall, M., 38, 42
Blitz, 25, 30, 40

Blum, L., 176, 179
Boulding, E., 26, 36, 40
Braddock, D., 71, 74
Braden, I., 90, 123
Bramsen, M. B., 28, 42
Briscoe, A. M., 151, 159, 235, 239
Brown, D., 91, 100, 122
Bryson, J., 99, 112, 113, 122
Bryson, R., 99, 112, 113, 122
Butler, M., 113, 123
Butz, E., 205, 211

Calderon de la Barca, 26, 40
Caples, W. G., 193, 203
Caplow, T., 92, 100, 123
Carey, E. G., 192, 203
Carter, M. J., 4, 13
Carter, S. B., 4, 13
Cartter, A., 94, 117, 120, 123
Centra, J., 65, 74, 92, 93, 94, 99, 106,
  109, 121, 122, 123
Chaney, E. M., 26, 29, 40
Chaton, J. H., 35, 40
Chizmar, J. F., 5, 14
Chodorow, N., 209, 211
Chorover, S. L., 220, 228
Cicarelli, J. S., 117, 124
Clark, S., 111, 127
Cohen, S. J., 178, 179
Cole, J. R., 2, 16, 63, 65, 74, 89, 90, 91,
  92, 93, 96, 103, 106, 111, 112, 114,
  115, 123, 151, 159
Cole, S., 89, 123
College Placement Council, 74, 164, 169
Conable, C. W., 46, 57
Crane, D., 111, 123
Crano, W. D., 2, 13
Creager, J. A., 100, 123

Davis, A., 12, 13, 220, 228